GENDER

This invaluable volume provides an introduction to the major theories and concepts in Gender Studies. Each of the 37 entries provides a critical definition of the subject, written by an expert in the field, examining its genesis, usage and major contributors. Taking an interdisciplinary and global view of Gender Studies, concepts covered include:

- Agency
- Body
- Class
- Diaspora
- Feminist Politics
- Gender Identity
- Heteronormativity
- Performativity
- Reflexivity
- Subjectivity.

With cross referencing and further reading provided throughout the text, *Gender: The Key Concepts* explores the relationships between different aspects of the field defined as gender studies, and is essential for all students of Gender Studies.

Mary Evans is a Centennial Professor at the London School of Economics, based at the Gender Institute. She has written studies of feminist theory, Jane Austen and Simone de Beauvoir and is currently working on issues related to the continuation of gender inequality.

Carolyn H. Williams has worked in international development and feminism since 1981. She holds a PhD from the Gender Institute, London School of Economics, where she works as a guest teacher, and is currently researching changing forms of intimacy in the context of migration and multiculturalism.

ALSO AVAILABLE FROM ROUTLEDGE

GENDER

The Key Concepts

Edited by
Mary Evans and Carolyn H. Williams

LONDON AND NEW YORK

First published 2013
by Routledge
2 Park Square, Milton Park, Abingdon, Oxon OX14 4RN

Simultaneously published in the USA and Canada
by Routledge
711 Third Avenue, New York, NY 10017

Routledge is an imprint of the Taylor & Francis Group, an informa business

British Library Cataloguing in Publication Data
A catalogue record for this book is available from the British Library

Library of Congress Cataloging in Publication Data
Gender : the key concepts / edited by Mary Evans and Carolyn H. Williams.
p. cm. – (Routledge key guides)
Includes bibliographical references and index.
1. Women's studies. 2. Sex role – Study and teaching. I. Evans, Mary, 1946-II. Williams, Carolyn (Carolyn H.)
HQ1180.G4655 2013
305.4 – dc23 2012017007

ISBN: 978-0-415-66961-0 (hbk)
ISBN: 978-0-415-66962-7 (pbk)
ISBN: 978-0-203-08370-3 (ebk)

Typeset in Bembo
by Taylor & Francis Books

Printed and bound in Great Britain by
TJ International Ltd, Padstow, Cornwall

CONTENTS

LIST OF KEY CONCEPTS

CONTRIBUTORS

Sunila Abeysekera is visiting scholar at the Institute of Social Studies in The Hague. She is Executive Director of INFORM, a leading Sri Lankan human rights non-governmental organization, and since 1992 has worked with the Global Campaign for Women's Human Rights and other global feminist networks.

Rachel Adams is professor of English and American Studies at Columbia University. She is the author of *Sideshow USA: Freaks and the American Cultural Imagination* and *Continental Divides: Remapping the Cultures of North America.*

Suki Ali is Senior Lecturer in Sociology at the London School of Economics. Her research explores processes of racialization, kinship and postcoloniality. Publications include *Mixed-Race, Post-Race: Gender, New Ethnicities and Cultural Practices* and *The Politics of Gender and Education: Critical Perspectives.*

Floya Anthias is Professor of Sociology and Social Justice (Emeritus) at Roehampton University and Visiting Professor of Sociology at City University. Her books include *Rethinking Anti-Racisms: From Theory to Practice* and *Female Migrants in Europe: The Paradoxes of Integration.*

Gwendolyn Beetham is an independent gender scholar living and working in New York. She currently edits *The Academic Feminist* at Feministing.com. Her work appears in *The International Handbook of Gender and Poverty*, *The Women's Movement Today: An Encyclopedia of Third Wave Feminism*, and various journals.

Claire Blencowe is Assistant Professor of Sociology at the University of Warwick. Her publications include *Biopolitical Experience: Foucault, Power & Positive Critique* and she has published various articles in *Theory, Culture and Society.*

Jonathan Dean is Lecturer in Political Theory in the School of Politics and International Studies, University of Leeds. He is author of *Rethinking Contemporary Feminist Politics* and has published on issues relating to gender and politics.

Nikita Dhawan is Director of the Frankfurt Research Center for Postcolonial Studies, Cluster of Excellence 'The Formation of Normative Orders' at Goethe-University. Publications include *Decolonizing Enlightenment: Transnational Justice, Human Rights and Democracy in a Postcolonial World* (forthcoming).

Barbara Einhorn is Emeritus Professor of Gender Studies at the University of Sussex. Her recent publications include *Citizenship in an Enlarging Europe: From Dream to Awakening* and 'Democratization, Nationalism, and Citizenship: The Challenge of Gender' in *Gender Politics in Post-Communist Eurasia.*

Sarah Evans works at The British Library and publishes sociological pieces in her spare time, following her PhD, which she completed in 2008. Her thesis examined the aspirations of a group of young, educationally successful, working-class women. She has published on higher education and social class, and oral history.

Sarah Franklin is a Professor of Sociology at the University of Cambridge. She is the author, co-author, editor and co-editor of 15 books on social and cultural aspects of new reproductive technologies, as well as over 150 articles, chapters and reports.

Stéphanie Genz is Senior Lecturer in Media and Culture at Edge Hill University. She specializes in contemporary gender and cultural theory. Her book publications include *Postfemininities in Popular Culture*; *Postfeminism: Cultural Texts and Theories*; and *Post-feminist Gothic: Critical Interventions in Contemporary Culture.*

Kristyn Gorton is Senior Lecturer in the Department of Theatre, Film and Television at the University of York. She is the author of *Media Audiences: Television, Meaning and Emotion* and *Theorising Desire: From Freud to Feminism to Film.* She has published work on emotion and affect in various journals.

Gabriele Griffin is Professor of Women's Studies at the University of York. Her research centres on women's cultural production. She is editor of the 'Research Methods for the Arts and Humanities' series, and at present working on a project entitled *Not Owning A Story.*

Jeff Hearn holds posts at Linköping University, University of Huddersfield, and Hanken School of Economics in Finland. His books include *Handbook of Studies on Men and Masculinities*, *Sex, Violence and The Body*, *The Limits of Gendered Citizenship*, and *Men and Masculinities around the World*.

Amy Hinterberger is a Research Fellow in the Institute for Science, Innovation and Society, School of Anthropology and Museum Ethnography at the University of Oxford. She received her PhD (2010) in Sociology from LSE's BIOS Centre. She has published work on the sociology of biomedicine and identity.

Ranjana Khanna is Director of Women's Studies and Professor of English Literature and Women's Studies at Duke University. She publishes on Anglo- and Francophone Postcolonial theory and literature, Psychoanalysis, and Feminist Theory. Her current book project is 'Asylum: The Concept and the Practice'.

Elin Lindström holds a MSc in Gender and Social Policy from the London School of Economics.

Emanuela Lombardo is Lecturer at the Faculty of Political Science of Madrid Complutense University (Spain). Her research concerns the analysis of gender equality policies. She co-edited *The Europeanization of Gender Equality Policies* and *The Discursive Politics of Gender Equality*, and has published in various journals.

Clare Lyonette is Senior Research fellow, Institute for Employment Research, Warwick. Her publications include co-editing *Gender Inequalities in the 21st Century*; and a chapter in *Families, Care-giving and Paid Work: Challenging Labour Law in the 21st Century*.

Sumi Madhok is Lecturer in Transnational Gender Studies at the Gender Institute, London School of Economics. Her recent publications include *Rethinking Agency: Gender, Development and Rights in North West India*. She is interested in contemporary and feminist political theory, autonomy, rights and citizenship.

Darrah McCracken is a Visiting Assistant Professor in the Politics Department at Willamette University. Her dissertation was on the world politics of care. She is currently exploring the history of US efforts to limit international humanitarianism and the critique of instrumentality in care ethics and immigration policy.

Maureen McNeil is Professor of Women's Studies and Cultural Studies and Associate Director of CESAGEN (ESRC Centre for Economic and Social Aspects of Genomics), Lancaster University. Her publications include *Feminist Cultural Studies of Science and Technology*.

Lavinia Mitton is Lecturer in Social Policy at the University of Kent. She teaches on welfare states, poverty and social security. She is a co-editor of *Social Policy*, a major social policy textbook. She researches financial exclusion, social security benefit fraud and childcare, housing and employment policy.

Henrietta L. Moore FBA is the William Wyse Professor of Social Anthropology at the University of Cambridge. Her recent books include *Still Life: Hopes, Desires and Satisfactions* and *The Subject of Anthropology: Gender, Symbolism and Psychoanalysis*.

Carolyn Pedwell is Lecturer in Media and Cultural Studies at Newcastle University. She is the author of *Feminism, Culture and Embodied Practice: The Rhetorics of Comparison* and *Affective Relations: The Transnational Politics of Empathy*, and articles in several academic journals.

Maria do Mar Pereira is a Lecturer in Gender Studies and Sociology at the University of Leeds. She has published widely on the epistemic status and the institutionalization of women's and gender studies, feminist pedagogy and issues of language difference and translation in social science research.

Griselda Pollock is Professor of Social and Critical Histories of Art and Director of the Centre for Cultural Analysis, Theory and History, University of Leeds. Her current research includes trauma and sexual difference. Publications include *Encounters in the Virtual Feminist Museum*.

Silvia Posocco is Lecturer, Department of Psychosocial Studies, Birkbeck College, University of London. Her monograph, *Secrecy and Insurgency: Socialities and Knowledge Practices in Guatemala* (Alabama University Press) is forthcoming. She is co-editing a special issue of *International Feminist Journal of Politics*.

Kate Reed is a Senior Lecturer in Medical Sociology at the University of Sheffield. She has published on ethnicity, gender, social theory and the sociology of health and illness. She is the author of *Worlds of Health*, *New Directions in*

Social Theory: Race, Gender and the Canon and *Gender and Genetics: Sociology of the Prenatal.*

Kanchana N. Ruwanpura is Senior Lecturer in Development Geography at the University of Southampton. With an interest in feminism and development, she has published in numerous peer-reviewed journals. She has her PhD from the University of Cambridge, England.

Christina Scharff is a Lecturer at King's College London. Her research interests include gender, sexuality and neoliberalism. Christina is author of *Repudiating Feminism: Young Women in a Neoliberal World* and is co-editor of *New Femininities: Postfeminism, Neoliberalism and Subjectivity.*

Wendy Sigle-Rushton is Reader in Gender and Family Studies at the Gender Institute and associate in the Centre for Analysis of Social Exclusion, both at the LSE. She works on family formation and dissolution, fertility trends, and child health and development. Recent projects include family policy in Sweden and Norway.

Alessandra Tanesini is Professor of Philosophy at Cardiff University. She is the author of *An Introduction to Feminist Epistemologies*; *Wittgenstein: A Feminist Interpretation*; *Philosophy of Language A–Z*; and articles in feminist philosophy, the philosophy of mind and language, epistemology and on Nietzsche.

Joan C. Tronto is Professor in the Political Science Department at the University of Minnesota. In addition to publishing many articles, she is the author of *Moral Boundaries: A Political Argument for an Ethic of Care*, which has been translated and published in Italian, French and Greek.

Sadie Wearing is Lecturer in Gender, Media and Culture at the London School of Economics. She has published on issues of postfeminism, ageing and culture and she is currently working on a book on feminist theory and representations of ageing. She is co-author of *Gender and Media* (forthcoming).

Jeffrey Weeks is Emeritus Professor of Sociology at London South Bank University. Author of over twenty books, chiefly on sexuality and intimate life, recent publications include *The World We Have Won*; *Sexualities*; *The Languages of Sexuality*; and a new edition of *Sex, Politics and Society.*

Kalpana Wilson is a Visiting Fellow at the LSE Gender Institute and teaches Development Studies at Birkbeck. Her publications include co-editing *'Race', Racism and Development: Interrogating History, Discourse and Practice*, and *Gender, Agency and Coercion.*

INTRODUCTION

The recognition of gender as one of the major forms of social difference has now been accepted throughout much of the world. As such that recognition has come to play a formative part in the policies and practices of various institutional contexts, not the least of which is the academy, where gender now forms an integral part of many aspects of the curriculum. Although the nature of the links between the academic study of gender and the world outside the classroom have sometimes been a subject of debate and dissent it is now possible to record a widespread consensus that gender has as important a part as class and race in the making and definition of individual and collective circumstances. The past forty years have seen the growth of a specialist area of academic work, that of gender studies, and with it the emergence of an increasingly developed and constantly evolving and wide-ranging intellectual vocabulary.

It is that vocabulary that constitutes the content of this volume in the Routledge Key Concepts series. As with any specialist area Gender Studies (and its very close relation Women's Studies) has acquired a number of terms and concepts that are used to indicate particular debates and ideas. But our purpose in this collection is not just to offer definitions of words and concepts, although that is certainly part of the entries contained here. This is not, we wish to suggest, a dictionary, even though this comment should in no way be taken to imply that such a text is unimportant. What we have asked our authors to do is both to explain the meaning of a concept in the context of gender studies and then, in the limited parameters offered by a word length of 2,500 words, to consider the implications of that concept in the making of debate and discussion in gender studies. We have asked our authors to pursue the idea of what can be done with a certain concept in the sense of exploring and enlarging our understanding of the meaning of gender and gender difference. We were very fortunate in being able to call upon a group of exceptionally distinguished academics to write the various entries and all of them have more than fulfilled our expectations of that dual task of both clarification and elucidation.

Readers, and we hope users, of this volume will see that the entries are arranged in alphabetical order. Each entry follows the required word length and each entry gives not just details of the references related to the text but also a number of suggestions for further reading. This part of each entry was a particularly important part of our purpose in composing this volume, namely that thinking about gender should not begin and end with the recognition of gender as a major form of social difference (even though this very recognition has been, and continues to be, a matter of contest) but that the implications of gender difference are still only partially and often imperfectly understood. Thus this volume is as much about work to be done as work done: gender studies has fulfilled every promise in establishing a place for itself in intellectual and academic life but such is the endlessly biologically reproduced blank canvas of gender that new forms of its social manifestation are constantly emerging and as such require attention, just as constantly changing social and cultural representations of gender are producing new forms of embodiment.

It is also appropriate to note here that we hope that this volume will assist in what is seen as the unnecessarily opaque language that sometimes surrounds the study of gender. All specialist academic subjects acquire a specialist language, in which some subjects are closer to complete incomprehension by non-specialists than others. There is no reason why questions about the social and symbolic meaning of gender should follow this pattern but there are certain circumstances in which a specialist term is a useful shorthand term to denote a complex debate. However, those occasions should be few and one further purpose of this collection is to encourage readers to acquire access to important terms that might otherwise limit engagement with questions about gender. The absolute democracy of the need of every individual to define, in whatever way, their gender suggests that it is only appropriate that the debates and the terminology of this process should be democratically available.

There is one further reason for the production of this work. It is that – as much of the content indicates – the question of gender and questions about gender are universal. In the past fifty years there has been a very considerable extension of debate and discussion about gender, a good deal of it within Anglo-American contexts. Yet, that academic specificity does not indicate the boundaries of concerns about gender. Thus, we hope that in making the conceptual terminology about gender more available we are also enlarging the possibilities and the locations of debates.

Our last task should be to thank all those who have contributed to this volume for the way in which they have recognized that complex ideas are not necessarily inaccessible ideas. It has been a great pleasure to compile this volume and a very important part of that pleasure has been the constant reminder of the depth, the range and the excitement of the study of gender. We assume that readers will turn to this guide for particular information about particular concepts. But we also suggest that the volume can be read as a narrative (albeit a narrative organized somewhat unconventionally in alphabetical order) that attests to the vitality of the study of gender. So our thanks go to all our contributors and to those who have helped us with various stages of the editorial process. We are grateful to Rebecca Shillabeer of Routledge for inviting us to undertake the project and for being a constant source of encouragement and efficient assistance. We thank Hazel Johnstone for her invaluable editorial work on the final version of the manuscript and last, but not least, our thanks to Ralph Kinnear for compiling the Index.

Mary Evans and Carolyn Williams
Gender Institute, March 2012

GENDER

The Key Concepts

AFFECT

Kristyn Gorton

In its basic definition, the term affect means to move emotionally and generally this refers to a physical response from the body, a blush or tear, for instance. Some argue that emotion refers to a sociological expression of feelings whereas affect is more firmly rooted in biology and in our physical response to feelings; others attempt to differentiate on the basis that emotion requires a subject while affect does not;[1] and some ignore these distinctions altogether. Elspeth Probyn suggests that: 'A basic distinction is that emotion refers to cultural and social expression, whereas affects are of a biological and physiological nature' (2005: 11). The term has attracted significant attention in recent years within academia, particularly within cultural studies, feminist theory and film and television studies, as a way of explaining public feelings and affective relationships.

The term itself is defined in a variety of ways, which adds to some confusion around the meaning of the concept. For instance, in her work on the 'cultural politics of emotion', Sara Ahmed argues that: 'Affect is what sticks, or what sustains or preserves the connection between ideas, values, and objects' (Ahmed 2010: 30). Here affect is a sort of glue that binds and connects 'ideas, values, and objects'. Ben Highmore offers a more physiological interpretation, writing that: 'Affect gives you away: the telltale heart; my clammy hands; the note of anger in your voice; the sparkle of glee in their eyes' (Highmore 2010: 118). Here affect is more of a bodily response that is visible and palpable. In her work on 'ordinary affects', Kathleen Stewart puts forward another way of thinking about affects and argues that: 'Affects are not so much forms of signification, or units of knowledge, as they are expressions of ideas or problems performed as a kind of involuntary and powerful learning and participation' (Stewart 2007: 40). Here affect is conceived more abstractly as a kind of expressive learning and participation. These definitions illustrate the various ways in which affect is used within cultural and critical theory and demonstrate the slipperiness of the term and its usage within academic study. Michael Hardt uses the verb 'straddles' to describe the in-between nature of affect: 'affects straddle these two divides: between the mind and the body, and between actions and passions' (2007: xi). In their introduction to *The Affect Theory Reader*, Melissa Gregg and Gregory J. Seigworth also make reference to affect's messy in-between-ness arguing that: 'There is no single unwavering line that might unfurl toward or around affect and its singularities, let alone its theories (…)' (2010: 5).

The 'affective turn' can be traced to a return to the body (or 'a demand for the concrete', Highmore 2010: 119). The two dominant locations for this return are in feminist theory and in philosophical renderings of the body via Spinoza and Deleuze. Silvan Tomkins, a radical American psychologist, is often seen as one of the primary originators of the concept of affect within the humanities. Tomkins argues that: 'Reason without affect would be impotent, affect without reason would be blind. The combination of affect and reason guarantees man's high degree of freedom' (1995: 37). Here affect works in combination with reason instead of straddling reason and passion. Tomkins theorizes affect in relation to Freud's theories of 'drives' and offers an alternative way of understanding human motivations and passions. He designates affects as a primary motivational system and considers shame, interest, surprise, joy, anger, fear, distress, and disgust as the basic set of affects (Sedgwick and Frank 1995: 5). His work has had a significant influence on feminist theorists such as Eve Kosofsky Sedgwick (*Touching Feeling: Affect, Pedagogy, Performativity*, 2003).

In feminist theory, a focus on the body and on the emotional lives and labours of women has led to a vast corpus of work on emotion and affect.[2] In the 1980s, feminist theorists such as Lila Abu-Lughod (1986), Arlie Russell Hochschild (1983), bell hooks (1989), Alison Jaggar (1989), Audre Lorde (1984) and Catherine Lutz (1988) took interest in women's emotional lives and labours.[3] While these earlier influences are still resonant, it is only over the past decade that we have witnessed what Woodward et al. (1996), Berlant (1997) and Nicholson (1999) have referred to as an 'affective turn'. The body still plays a central role in these examinations, however they extend into interest in language (Denise Riley's *Impersonal Passion* (2005)); shame (Elspeth Probyn's *Blush: Faces of Shame*); and the proximity we have towards others, which extends into discussions on race (see Ahmed 2004, Probyn 2005). Sara Ahmed's work in *The Cultural Politics of Emotion*, for instance, focuses on how 'emotions work to shape the "surfaces" of individual and collective bodies' (2004: 1). Whereas Teresa Brennan takes a more physiological approach, beginning her exploration of affect with the following question: 'Is there anyone who has not, at least once, walked into a room and "felt the atmosphere"?' (2004: 1) She argues that an increase in the perceived 'catchiness' of emotions 'makes the Western individual especially more concerned with securing a private fortress, personal boundaries, against the unsolicited emotional intrusions of the other' (*The Transmission of Affect*, 2004: 15).

In her work on affect in cultural theory, Clare Hemmings argues that: 'In contrast to Tomkins, who breaks down affect into a topography of myriad, distinct parts, Deleuze understands affect as describing the passage from one state to another, as an *intensity* characterized by an increase or decrease in power' (2005a: 552, author's italics). Deleuzian interpretations of affect, which stem from his reading of Spinoza, also dominate work on affect. Spinoza uses the terms 'Affectio' and 'affectus' to differentiate between the way in which: 'Affects can be either active or passive (…) The more the mind has inadequate ideas, the more it is liable to the passions; the more it has adequate ideas, the more it is active' (Lloyd 1996: 73). Deleuze picks up on Spinoza's theorization of affect in *Spinoza: Practical Philosophy* (1988), which has led to interpretations of affect, such as Brian Massumi's *Parables of the Virtual: Movement, Affect, Sensation*. Massumi argues that: '… the problem with the dominant models in cultural and literary theory is not that they are too abstract to grasp the concreteness of the real. The problem is that they are not *abstract enough* to grasp the real incorporeality of the concrete' (2002: 5, author's italics). Massumi's, along with others', reconceptualization of the body has led to interest in 'new media' and 'biomedia' (Clough 2007; Hansen 2006; Parisi 2004).

While the concept of affect is taken up primarily within critical and cultural theory, it is important to note that it is also being considered outside the humanities. In *Descartes' Error: Emotion, Reason and the Human Brain* (1994), for instance, Antonio Damasio challenges Descartes' proclamation 'I think; therefore I am' through modern neuroscience. His trilogy of research into emotions and affect has attracted a great deal of attention within neuroscience and the humanities.

Although Tomkins and Spinoza (or Deleuze on Spinoza) are perhaps the most referenced in terms of studying affect; some theorists draw on Freud, William James' work on emotion, J. L. Austin's interpretation of speech acts, Aristotle's *Rhetoric*, and eighteenth-century notions of sensibility (for instance, David Hume and Adam Smith) in their understanding of affect. The concept of affect has also been linked by numerous theorists to work by Raymond Williams. Kathleen Stewart (2007), for instance, defines 'ordinary affects', as 'public feelings that begin and end in broad circulation, but they're also stuff that seemingly intimate lives are made of' (2007: 2). Her use of affect in this context shares similarities with Williams' 'structures of feeling'. Williams' interest in the 'ordinary' and the everyday, has led to work, such as that by Lawrence Grossberg, which re-thinks the significance of peoples' affective relationships. Grossberg identifies Williams' 'structure of feeling' and Hoggart's 'what it feels like' as the moment he 'met' affect (2010: 310). His work on fandom illustrates a move within cultural theory towards using the concept of affect to explain fan culture. He argues that it '[i]s in their affective lives that fans constantly struggle to care about something, and to find the energy to survive, to find the passion necessary to imagine and enact their own projects and possibilities' (1992: 59). He uses the term 'mattering maps': to explain the different ways in which people invest their energies and passions towards particular texts (1992: 57–58). Viewers often have various programmes they have invested their energy in but also different levels of engagement: they might be casual fans of one programme but dedicated fans of another. Matt Hills argues that: 'Without the emotional attachments and passions of fans, fan cultures would not exist, but fans and academics often take these attachments for granted or do not place them centre-stage in their explorations of fandom' (2002: 90). The concept of affect, and the renewed interest in it, has led to a resurgence within the study of fan cultures whereby affect and emotion have now become centre-stage in examinations of fan cultures and of ordinary viewers' relationship with television texts (see Kavka 2008; Gorton 2009; Hills 2010). More recent work contemplates the affective relationship people have with social networking sites and other online media.[4]

The use of the term 'affect' has generated a lot of momentum and has been considered a 'trendy' concept despite the fact that work on affect has been going on since (at least) the seventeenth century. Academic research on the concept of affect has led to a greater understanding of the role of emotions within cultural study and has helped to identify the close, emotional engagements viewers have with the screen – whether film, television or computer.

Further Reading: Ahmed 2004; Brennan 2004; Gregg and Seigworth 2010; Probyn 2005; Riley 2005.

Notes

1 Sianne Ngai draws attention to the definition of emotion and affect offered by Brian Massumi and Lawrence Grossberg. Grossberg (1992), for instance, writes: 'Unlike emotions, affective states are neither structured narratively nor organised in response to our interpretations of

situations' (cited in Ngai 2005: 24–25). See also Berlant and Warner 2000.

2 See Gorton (2007: 333–48).

3 Probyn suggests that Alison Jaggar's article, 'Love and knowledge: emotion in feminist epistemology' (1992 [1989]), was one of the first to consider what emotion might mean for feminism (Probyn 2005: 8).

4 See Garde-Hansen and Gorton, *Emotion Online: Theorizing Affective Relationships on the Internet*, forthcoming Palgrave; Melissa Gregg (2010) 'On Friday night drinks: workplace affects in the age of the cubicle,' in Melissa Gregg and Gregory J. Seigworth (eds), *The Affect Theory Reader*, Durham: Duke University Press, 250–68; Arvid Kappas and Nicole C. Krämer (eds) (2011) *Face to Face Communication on the Internet: Emotions in a Web of Culture*, Cambridge: Cambridge University Press.

AGENCY

Amy Hinterberger

Agency often refers to human action or the capacity and ability to act. Within feminist theory the question of women's agency in the context of patriarchy, domination, oppression and inequality has been long-standing and continues to generate debate. In contemporary feminist and gender studies the concept of agency has emerged in relation to theories of subjectivity (or the subject) and power. The construction of subjectivity through certain historical, social and cultural systems of knowledge has led to an approach that emphasizes the variable and complex aspects of human subjectivity. Agency can be seen as the ability of the subject to resist, negotiate and transform certain forms of power that work on the subject both internally and externally.

The use of the term agency is heterogeneous both within and outside of feminist and gender studies including areas of anthropology, economics and sociology. Broadly then the concept of agency provides an avenue to explore both theoretically and empirically how people think and act within the social conditions in which they find themselves. There is significant debate over the extent to which people are seen to be thinking or acting independently from the constraints placed on them by social systems.

Early feminist work on agency challenged the exclusion of women as social actors or legitimate objects of study. These challenges came from a variety of disciplines. In psychology, Carol Gilligan (1982) disputed assumptions about dominant models of moral agency and capability. Through her critique of pornography Catharine MacKinnon (1987) argued that social structures not only pose external obstacles for the life choices of women but that they also internally distort women's desires and sense of self. Cross-cultural perspectives from anthropology demonstrated that Western assumptions of gender identity were not universal thus challenging any presumed coherence of gender (Strathern 1988).

Agency is drawn on to understand the constraints under which women live their lives particularly in relation to gendered bodily practices. Practices such as cosmetic surgery, sex work, diet and exercise, wearing high heels, veiling and female genital cutting are often discussed in feminist theorizations of agency. In contrast to feminist approaches that emphasize the manner in which the formation of the female self is a construct of masculine desire, some feminist analysis is dedicated to conceptualizing agency in contexts where agency has traditionally been presumed to be absent. For example, Kathy Davis (1995) has investigated women's agency in cosmetic surgery both to explore the workings of power in certain social and political structures and to suggest the recognition of female agency in decisions about cosmetic surgery.

A significant amount of work in feminist theory deals with addressing binary divisions that characterize accounts of agency, where for instance, one is represented as either having agency or not. These binary *representations* of agency can work through categories such as: free will/false consciousness, choice/coercion and agency/structure. Feminist theorists have critically questioned any straightforward use of binary representations to describe and understand the lives of subjects living in gendered worlds. For example, Elizabeth Grosz (1994) argues that the *body* and mind are not separate and thus the relations between the inside and outside of the subject need to be rethought. In this regard, agency is more than just a synonym for action. Agency is a relationship, often between subjects, which is embedded in social relations, practices and structures.

Agency and the subject

Those working in feminist and gender studies have drawn attention to the ways in which the concept of agency is rooted in Enlightenment understandings of the individual. Enlightenment thinkers constructed the individual as a free agent whose actions and thoughts were based on rational choices. The idea of this kind of individual continues to shape accounts of freedom and progress where agency is understood as the ability of human beings to influence and change their circumstances. In this approach agency is possessed by individuals who are autonomous from the diverse spatial or temporal locations that they inhabit.

The feminist critique of the rational autonomous individual has had far-reaching consequences for ideas about human action as well as the capacity of subjects to respond or resist particular social arrangements and structures. Judith Butler (1997) has developed an influential account of agency where agency can no longer be seen as belonging to a person or subject that exists prior to social life and the operations of power. Drawing on the work of Michel Foucault (1926–84) among others, Butler identifies what she calls the bind, or paradox of agency. Butler points out that if we understand power as forming subjects and individuals then this means that power also sustains our agency and existence. The paradox of agency is this: subjection (or the process of becoming a subject) is fundamentally dependent on discourses that we have never chosen, but these discourses also sustain and initiate our agency. Subordination to particular discourses is thus part of what it means to become a subject. But this also means that subordination is a condition for agency. In Butler's account agency can no longer be put in opposition to subordination as they are formed with and through one another. As a result, Butler concludes, 'ambivalence is at the heart of agency' (1997b: 18). Agency works in conjunction with and is formed through the very things we often see as limiting agency, the operations of power.

The position that ambivalence or inter-determinacy underpins agency raises the question of who or what is acting when 'we' act. From this perspective agency is not transparent and actions are not done under the full control of the subject. Feminist appropriations of psychoanalysis for instance have sought to explore how psychic and emotional life forms the subject that is divided and decentred. Henrietta Moore (2007) has pointed to how social structures and cultural values become internalized to produce a dynamic unconscious. Moore explores the motivations for individual investment in certain subject positions as well, arguing that accounts of agency require a space for the role of fantasy and desire with regard to compliance and resistance (2007: 36).

Other approaches to agency have resisted an approach to the subject, which deconstructs the notion of core identities for fear that this approach may jeopardize the concept of agency for women.

Here the importance of the emancipatory ideals of the women's movement where women require a degree of political agency in order to achieve their goals is emphasized (Benhabib 1995). From this perspective the deconstruction of the category 'woman' is seen to be politically risky. For example, Lois McNay (1993) has argued that if agency is thought of primarily in feminist studies as a discursive abstraction, particularly through an emphasis on inter-determinacy, this risks ignoring agency as a capacity of embodied subjects.

Resistance and representation

Taking into account gendered experiences across different times and places has required attending to the theoretical dimensions of the concept of agency in order to account for increasing global interconnections between people, places and things. The question of who has agency, or who is the subject of agency is significant for feminist and gender studies as it intersects with studies in postcolonialism and transnational feminism.

In her now-classic essay, 'Under Western Eyes', Chandra Mohanty (1984) argues that feminist approaches to agency are fundamentally rooted in colonial attitudes and understandings. In particular she critiques what she calls 'Western feminist representations of Third World women' as devoid of agency and passive victims of their circumstances (1984: 207). Western feminism she contends has adopted a homogenous notion of the oppression of women where Third World women are represented as uneducated, tradition-bound and victimized, and First World women are represented as having freedom and control over their bodies and sexuality.

There is continued debate over how feminists draw on and represent what might be called cultural practices in discussions of agency, coercion and autonomy. One concern is that Western feminism continues to discursively colonize the material and historical heterogeneities of the lives of non-Western women by representing them as either 'prisoners of patriarchy' or 'dupes of patriarchy'. Transnational feminists have thus sought to develop approaches to agency that neither patronize nor exoticize. Drawing on the case of women from the conservative Sufi Pirzada community in Old Delhi who live in relative purdah (seclusion) within the home and are excepted to veil when they are in public, Uma Narayan (2002) argues that women are neither 'prisoners of patriarchy', nor 'dupes of patriarchy'. Narayan rejects an emphasis on group or cultural rights and advocates a position that recognizes the autonomy of women who choose to participate in practices that may appear repressive to Western feminists. Narayan suggests that there is active agency involved in women's compliance with patriarchal structures even when the stakes involved in noncompliance may be very high.

Saba Mahmood (2005) has offered a particularly influential account of agency through her ethnographic research of the piety movement in Egypt. Mahmood argues that the meaning of agency be kept open by allowing it to emerge from semantic and institutional networks. One consequence of this is that agency should be delinked from the goals of progressive politics. Mahmood is critical of some feminist approaches to agency that focus on operations of power that either re-signify or subvert norms. In order to challenge this dualism of resignification and subversion, Mahmood draws on examples where social norms are inhabited in a variety of ways. For example, she argues that the women in the piety movement do not regard emulating authorized models of behaviour as an external social imposition that constrains individual freedom. Rather these women treated socially authorized forms of performance as potentialities, a diverse ground through which the self can be realized (2005: 31). The approach offered by Mahmood thus challenges the paradigmatic example of agency as resistance to power in feminist theory. For Mahmood, to conform to social norms does not necessarily indicate a lack of agency (see also Moore 2011: 187–96).

There is an increasing emphasis on portraying women as agents, or actors as opposed to victims, particularly in different cultural and geopolitical contexts. The increasing focus on women's agency in various spatial and temporal settings has contributed towards developing deeper and more diverse understanding of agency. Clare Hemmings (2011) notes that these newer articulations of women's agency have challenged feminist presumptions about who needs saving, from what, and by whom. However she also argues that while agency offers hope of tracing different histories of a range of possible feminist subjects it often continues to leave a Western feminist subject position largely intact (2011: 212). There is also the concern that women's agency may be overemphasized in particular contexts and this risks leaving coercive conditions under-examined in feminist studies. For example, in addressing the relationship between culture and gender, Anne Phillips has argued that it is important to acknowledge that 'everyone has agency, even though some clearly have more options that others' (2011: 11).

Do only humans have agency?

Some feminist theorists have argued for a more expansive idea of agency that takes into account not only other human beings, but also non-human objects or entities which mediate, shape and inform our understandings of ourselves and others. This approach to agency emphasizes that not all actors are bounded by the human body. In her landmark essay *A Cyborg Manifesto,* Donna Haraway asks 'why should our bodies end at the skin or include at best other beings encapsulated by skin' (1991a: 178). Haraway's argument here turns on the assertion that there are many non-humans with whom we are woven together. Coming to terms with the agency of 'objects', not just subjects, means recognizing that actors come in many different forms.

If social life includes interaction with non-humans, then as Myra Hird and Celia Roberts (2011) have asked under the provocative idiom of non-human feminisms 'who has or does agency'? This question challenges the notion that agency belongs to those who have ownership over the self. It is also rooted in a long-standing feminist critique of the ontological separation between nature and culture. Karen Barad (2007) has offered a theory of agency that draws on the materialization of non-human bodies. Barad is interested in not just how the contours or surfaces of bodies come to matter, through for example particular social identities, but also how things like cells and atoms make up the body. Her approach, which she calls 'agential realism', offers an explanation of how discursive practices are related to material phenomena (2007: 132). This approach to agency questions processes of materialization that mark a distinction between what does and does not count as human. This approach reflects a movement in feminist and gender studies that formulates the human and the nonhuman not as two separate spheres but rather emphasizes political entanglements with objects, the inorganic, the biological and the artificial.

Conclusion

Feminist projects of producing and affirming agency have been diverse. Feminist critiques have pointed to the ways in which agency is historically produced thus demonstrating that the universal concept of the free and rational autonomous individual is false. From a feminist perspective understanding agency requires taking into account multiple subject positions including, but not exclusive to gender, sexuality, class, religion and race. Representations and debates over who has and does not have agency continue to be a central characteristic of feminist discussions particularly in transnational approaches that seek to dislodge the dominance of the Western feminist subject position.

Agency is directly linked to the political projects at the heart of feminism. One of the most powerful critiques offered by feminist theorists is that undermining the notion of core identities, or a coherent inner self does not necessarily preclude the kind of subjectivity required for agency. However, contentions over the operation of power and multiple subjectivities continue to mark debates on agency. Within these debates feminist authors have sought to establish agency where it has traditionally been presumed to be absent as well as to keep agency at the forefront in order to establish common political ground. For feminist and gender studies the manner in which agency is framed at the level of knowledge is central for the kinds of political projects envisioned by feminism. In this way agency will remain a significant, albeit contested concept within feminist theory.

Further Reading: Chodorow 1999; Foucault 1977; Hill Collins 1999; Spivak 1988.

THE BODY

Kate Reed

The body is a living biological entity, a collection of sleeping, eating, breathing parts. These parts are also routinely marked by gender, social class, race, ethnicity, generation, disability, sexuality and so on (Woodward 2008: 76). Bodies and body parts are therefore both biological and social constructs that become classified in particular ways and with particular effects. The aim of this section on the body is to give a brief overview of current and past debates on the body with particular focus on gender. The section will start by outlining a recent history of the concept of 'the body'. It will also chart the uneasy relationship between the body and feminism – paying particular attention to the problems posed by binary conceptualizations of the body. It will move on to give examples of some of the recent developments in the area: for example, the focus on 'embodiment', the impact of technology on theories of the body, and finally the increasing interest in the male body. The section will conclude by highlighting the continued importance of work on the body for gender studies.

Over the past twenty years 'the body' has become a major area of academic interest. Bodies have also been central to activists' campaigns particularly those relating to identity politics (Woodward 2008). Within the humanities and social sciences an explosion of publications on the body occurred from the 1980s onwards (Shilling 2007). During this time, the potential of the body was articulated along with the understanding that it is impossible to talk about a 'fixed' and 'natural' body. In contemporary society we are encouraged to look after our bodies, through diet and exercise. The emphasis on individual responsibility has become part of the regulatory strategy of the neo-liberal state; good citizens look after themselves and their bodies (Woodward 2008: 77). This emphasis on the body as a malleable entity susceptible to change and alteration has led some social theorists such as Chris Shilling to develop the idea of 'the body as a project' in contemporary society (Shilling 1993). We are expected to take control of our bodies and our lives, suggesting bodies can be changed by active agency (Woodward 2008). This interest in the body is often presented as a new fad, another ephemeral feature of consumer culture (Shilling 2007). However, although perhaps not central to the work of early social theorists whose key concerns related to the structures and processes of industrial society, the body was not absent in the work of the classics. Marx for example was the best-known critic of the effects of capitalism on our human 'bodily' being (Shilling 2007: 5). Furthermore, as Evans (2002) argues, it is also misleading to suggest that interest in the potentially malleable properties of the body is a novel phenomenon. For example, as she argues the ancient art of medicine has never taken for granted the realities of pain or disease, but has always sought where possible to offer relief and alteration through medical intervention (Evans 2002). The body therefore, as a biological, social and cultural entity with potential for modification has long captured our interest across the humanities, medical and social sciences.

Despite this interest, the body has often proved problematic for feminist theorists working within the area of gender and women's studies. During the women's health movements of the 1970s, women's bodies took centre stage in debates over issues such as abortion and women's reproductive rights (e.g. Corea 1985). As Kathy Davis (2007b) has argued, however, beginning with debates on equality versus difference, the female body has tended to prove problematic for feminist theory. During the 1970s some feminists located women's disadvantage in the public sphere in their capacity to bear children. This perspective held the biological body responsible for women's subordinate position in society. Transcendence of the body was identified therefore by authors such as Shulamith Firestone (1970) as providing the solution to women's oppression. Other feminists however, such as Sandra Schwartz Tangri (1976), identified women's bodies and reproductive abilities as a source of female power. Women's ability to 'give life' was viewed in this context as a distinct advantage over men. According to Davis (2007b), the inability to deal with this set of dualisms effectively (equality versus difference and transcendence versus celebration) led second wave feminists to deconstruct the association of women with the biological body (Bordo 1987). It also contributed to the separation of biological sex from socially and culturally constructed concepts of gender. Feminists such as Ann Oakley (1972) cited the blurring of these two concepts as contributing to women's disadvantage. These concepts were then separated with sex becoming associated with biology and physiology of the body and gender with social and cultural meanings attached to being female or male (Richardson 2008). As the socially constructed concept of gender became the preference of much feminist analysis, interest in biological sex and the body became marginalized.

The separation of sex and gender led to a hiatus in terms of feminist theories on the body. As Davis (2007b: 53) argues, for a long period there was a fear in feminist thinking that any mention of the body would open doors to biological determinism. The body became more central to feminist theory with the advent of postmodernism and the discovery and application of the work of philosopher Michel Foucault. Foucault's (1977) work highlighted the ways in which bodies are constituted and re-created and it has informed many feminist analyses (for example, Bordo 1993, Butler 1990, McNay 1992). The body according to Foucault is not a naturally different entity whose biological make-up permanently determines or limits human potential (Shilling 1993). It is a cultural text, a surface upon which culture can be written, a site for understanding the workings of modern power (Davis 2007b). Viewed through this perspective, the female body was no longer linked explicitly to biology, or viewed as the seat of authentic experience; the body was identified instead as a cultural construct in need of deconstruction (Davis 2007b: 54). Foucault (1977) saw individuals as instruments of power and the body as a site where dissent is articulated. This approach offered many feminists the possibility of resistance and transformation to women's bodily practices. It unveiled the ways in which women's bodily practices complied with dominant cultural discourses (for example diet, exercise, surgery in the quest for the perfect female body). Others felt this approach sat uneasily with women's agency, failing to support collective forms of feminist action (Bordo 1993, Davis 2007b). In many respects therefore, the Foucauldian approach to the body was useful in moving debates away from essentialist approaches to the body. However, it still proved problematic for feminist theory in its quest to challenge and transform broader patterns of gender inequality.

In recent years feminists and others have attempted to develop new approaches to the study of the body, in order to transcend the often dualist and conflicting relationship between the natural biological body and the socially constructed body. One such approach has focused not on the 'body' per se but on the issue of embodiment. Embodiment in this context refers to the lived experience of our bodies in the world along with our emotional relations with other embodied beings or agents (Gabe et al. 2004). This perspective takes a constitutive approach to the body. It views the body as both a product of society but also sees the body as contributing to the production of society and social relations of which it is part (Gabe et al. 2004). The roots of this approach can be traced back to the rise of phenomenology in the twentieth century, particularly to the work of Merleau-Ponty (1962) who sought to overcome the mind/body split in Western philosophy (Gabe et al. 2004). The notion of embodiment has become popular again in the twenty-first century. For example it has been central to recent studies on the experience of health and illness in contemporary society, particularly around issues of the body and pain (Gabe et al. 2004, Morgan 2002). Some have also argued that it has surpassed theories of the body in many areas of gender and women's studies. Using the idea of embodiment, the body is viewed as being part of who we are, linked explicitly to an understanding of the self (Woodward 2008). Through focusing on the idea of embodiment the role of the material body in shaping experience is acknowledged along with the embodiment of difference across class, race, disability, generation and gender (Woodward 2008: 82). Embodiment therefore appears to transcend the problem of dualistic thinking which has proved so problematic for feminist theorizing in the past.

Another unique approach to the study of the body has developed around the emergence and proliferation of new technologies. The development of novel technology has according to Shilling (2007: 8) contributed to a growing uncertainty about the reality of the body and has thrown into doubt the idea that there is anything 'natural' about human embodiment. Technological progress in such areas as transplant surgery, *in vitro* fertilization and stem cell research have enhanced the degree to which bodies can be controlled. They have also contributed to a deconstruction of the boundaries between science, technology and bodies (Shilling 2007: 8). This has led authors such as Donna Haraway (1985) to reconceptualize humans as cyborgs. According to Haraway the body does not exist in isolation but is mixed up with other things, with technology or technoscience. In Haraway's argument the boundaries between the body and technology are socially inscribed, indistinct and arbitrary (Balsamo 1999: 149). Biotechnology and technoscience challenge our understanding of the body, and transform bodies by overcoming their limitations – for example enabling previously infertile women to conceive and give birth to healthy babies. They also challenge the dualism through which nature and culture and mind and body are constructed (Woodward 2008: 88). The ability to challenge existing dualistic thinking has led to the popularity of this approach within feminist thought, particularly for feminists working on gender, technology and the body. For example, feminists have applied the ideas of cyborg thinking to routine obstetric ultrasound during pregnancy, the production of the fetal image demonstrating the ultimate coupling of human and machine (Mitchell and Georgies 1997: 374).

One final area to be considered in this context is writing on men's bodies. Women's bodies have tended to be the focus of gender and women's studies, largely because of the role the body has played in women's subordination (Sheldon 2002). According to Sally Sheldon men's bodies in contrast have often been viewed as the standard, the norm against which women are compared. While work on the female body has often been contrasted to the male norm, this norm has until recently remained unchallenged. With the advent and rise of work on men and masculinity, the social and cultural construction of men's bodies has begun to be explored in more detail in work on gender and the body (Bordo 1999). Men have traditionally been understood as more rational, autonomous and less controlled by their bodies than women. This type of thinking has been challenged by work for example on men's bodies and reproduction (Sheldon 2002) and extreme sport (Robinson 2008). Recent work has also explored the ways in which the male body is also subject to classification according to issues of race, disability, sexuality and so on (Stuart 2005). The previously hidden and uncontested male body therefore has become increasingly important to debates on gender and the body.

Given the brevity of this entry only a small sample of work on gender and the body has been explored. Other areas worthy of note include work on the 'disabled body' (Thomas 2002), and the 'transgendered body' (Newman 2000). Despite these limitations, this section has aimed to highlight the important yet complex nature of research and writing on gender and the body. As emphasized throughout, work on the body and gender has often been conflicted, particularly regarding feminist debates over the role of the material versus the socially constructed body. Furthermore, while some have argued that our current preoccupation with 'the body' is just an academic 'fad', others have clearly shown that this is far from the case (Shilling 2007). The body continues to be an important theoretical and substantive concern across the humanities and social sciences. For gender studies, it still remains an important aspect of theorizing and transforming inequality. As medical and other technologies involving bodily interventions and enhancements continue to rise, the importance of the concept of the body in gender studies is set to remain for some time yet.

Further Reading: Davis 1997; Evans and Lee 2002; Fraser and Greco 2004; Price and Shildrick 1999.

CARE

Darrah McCracken and Joan C. Tronto

Most care work in the world has been done by women, so it is no surprise there are lively debates in gender studies about its meaning and significance. These debates in fact span several disciplines, engaging scholars in the social sciences, political theory, and philosophy in contestation about what it means and why it matters. The word 'care' has many usages in the English language; it can refer to both dispositions and to practices and can be synonymous with such different terms as 'love' and 'burden'. Perhaps the broadest account of care was offered by Fisher and Tronto: 'a species activity that includes everything we do to maintain, continue, and repair our "world" so that we can live in it as well as possible' (1990: 40). This conceptualization includes care for the self as well as care for others, and care for animals, objects and the environment. A number of scholars have found it to be too broad and have sought to restrict its meaning. Many narrower conceptualizations exclude care for the self and focus just on care for others; some focus even further on the significance of care for the most dependent and vulnerable, rather than on care for everybody, at every life stage. Still other decisions about scope involve whether to think of care as having to do with basic needs or with grander individual and collective aspirations, whether to consider paid or unpaid care, and whether to distinguish care that is 'nurturant' from care that is 'non-nurturant' (Duffy 2011). To some extent, how a particular scholar resolves these conceptual issues will depend on considerations related to the academic and political setting of the work. Broader definitions lend themselves to viewing care as an expansive part of human life. Narrower definitions might be more appropriate if one is thinking of care primarily as work or as a concern for social policy.

The evolution of thinking about care helps to illustrate how conceptual decisions are made in the context of broader scholarly and political concerns. It should be noted that while it is tempting to see the conceptualization of care as a recent Western intellectual project, an idea of care is evident in diverse languages, religions, and traditions, some of them ancient. Confucianism, for example, includes something like care in the concept of *Jen* (Li 1994). To give another example, the term *ubuntu* in some Southern African languages expresses an understanding of humanity realized in relationships rather than in individual virtues and behaviours. Still, when American academics began systematically to treat care in the early 1980s, it was in the context of heightened concern about women and their social and political roles and perspectives. Working within the discipline of moral psychology, Carol Gilligan's *In a Different Voice* (1982) offered a critique of Kohlberg's account of moral reasoning in which normal development proceeded through stages to reach a level of 'justice', the stage at which reasoning was oriented to abstract social rules and individual rights. Through her research, Gilligan discovered a 'different voice' for moral reasoning. It was characterized by three elements: first, an emphasis on moral qualities and responsibilities emerging from relationships rather than on rules and rights; second, a greater concern with concrete and particular moral settings rather than with formal and abstract logics; and third, a concern with an activity of care rather than with fixing principles. Gilligan and her associates found that in present societies an 'ethic of care' was more likely to be voiced by women and by people of colour. While Gilligan realized the different voice she identified was fundamentally one of 'theme, not gender', most readers assumed the 'different voice' was distinctively feminine. At any rate, Gilligan's concern with an ethic of care gave rise to a long-standing care–justice debate, in which mainstream philosophers argued care should be seen as merely supplemental and personal, compared with the more broadly applicable theory of justice offered by Kohlberg's account of morality.

In the meantime, other thinkers were more decisively linking care with women. Sara Ruddick argued in her book, *Maternal Thinking* (1995), that the task of raising a child was a moral activity traditionally undertaken by mothers that often entailed balancing competing and complicated values. Drawing upon Wittgenstein, Ruddick emphasized care was a practice, thereby overlapping in some ways with Gilligan's account of the nature of an ethic of care. In *Caring* (2003), Nel Noddings, a philosopher of education, drew upon the work of Martin Heidegger to argue against any overly abstract, universalizing account of morality in favour of an ethical perspective focused on the specific dyadic relationships in which caring is provided and received. Her discussion presented teachers and mothers as paradigmatic caregivers. In the late 1980s, Patricia Hill Collins emphasized that the 'ethic of care' (which some of Gilligan's associates seemed to identify with women) was also present within African American communities that drew upon attempts to reconcile 'individual expressiveness' with connections 'in which truth emerges through care' (1990: 264). The marked focus on practices of care predominantly done by women, along with the hostility to what was taken as a 'masculinist' conception of universal reason, often led people to characterize care as part of the 'cultural feminist' moment, that is, an approach that celebrated something innately feminine as worthy of value.

By the mid-1980s, though, arguments had also begun to emerge rejecting any essentialist and feminine quality to care. Feminists began to look critically at the separation of public from private activities that has shaped, in different forms, the Western tradition, and to notice the association of more private, caring virtues with women. Feminists contended care was a universal feature of human life that oppressive institutions of social organization had assigned little value and had identified with women and others (Tronto 1987). Olena Hankivsky (2004) labelled this a change in 'generations' in care theories. While the first generation had largely focused on private and feminine expressions of care, in the second generation, care came to have more public and broader relevance. Care began to be understood as a key for interpreting forms of political and moral life as well as a rubric for evaluating those systems and imagining better alternatives (Tronto 1993). Theorists wrestled with the historical and contemporary relevance of care to democratic citizenship. Critiques of the models of citizenship that rested upon the male breadwinner and the female housekeeper changed the ways in which scholars characterized welfare states (Fraser 1997). And scholars highlighted the promise of care for orienting democratic judgements and practices of citizenship (Sevenhuijsen 1998). An awareness of differences in how individuals and groups value and provide caring, such as differences among cultural and racial groups, also emerged as a vital part of the scholarship on care.

At present, the care–justice debate has receded in importance. Theorists of justice have largely conceded that abstract ideal theories need to be supplemented by non-ideal theories that attend to caring in concrete situations. In this vein, theorists of care have raised a variety of additional questions about how caring is organized and delivered today. For example, scholars have inquired into the nature of needs and how needs are best interpreted (Fraser 1997) and whose needs count. They have also questioned distributions of caregiving work within the household such that usually women caregivers disproportionately bear additional burdens of caring while 'ideal workers', usually men, rely upon the invisible work of care within the household to meet their physical needs (Williams 2000). Scholars have thought about the nature of power in these practices of care. They have considered relations of power in care for 'vulnerable' people such as children, disabled people, elderly people, and the infirm. They have also considered whether and in what circumstances giving care makes one powerful or vulnerable oneself, or both at once. For example, Eva Kittay (2001) has proposed that caregivers' special vulnerability, given their large burdens towards their charges, be compensated.

Recent work has also taken care out of the narrow contexts of North America and Europe and has begun to more fully appreciate the variety of ways care is organized cross-culturally and cross-nationally. Scholars in social policy, social work, and economics have begun to explore the connection between care and social and political institutions in different countries. Political scientists, among others, have called attention to serious problems governments have faced in delivering healthcare and other social services given the pressure to adopt austerity measures, sometimes due to conditions on International Monetary Fund and World Bank loans.

Scholars have begun to consider care as something that occurs not only within states but between them. Feminist writers are beginning to recognize providing care is very much a global phenomenon as care workers, including nurses, nannies and domestic workers, increasingly move across national borders and meet needs (Ehrenreich and Hochschild 2002). Helma Lutz (2011) has observed that this complex 'bottom-up transnationalism' (p. 24) remains embedded in traditional, gendered understandings of domestic work but brings to the forefront the need for intersectional analysis. She concludes that 'ethnic justification models are resorted to in order to legitimize asymmetrical power relations' (p. 110). Martin Manalanasan (2006) has shed light on the heteronormative tendencies of this literature, pointing out scholars generally presume that women migrants are heterosexual married mothers, and also that men and single women will seldom if ever be migrant care workers. Such presumptions and exclusions have meant, for example, that the literature on gender and migration has not adequately appreciated the range of possibilities for desire and pleasure to be a motivation for migration, nor has it adequately considered how discrimination on the basis of sexuality shapes the motivation for and experience of migration. To 'queer' this literature, Manalansan argues, would mean not only considering these specific issues, but also, more generally, attending to how dominant norms related to sexuality are made to seem natural and universal through their constant reproduction in social institutions and practices. Like Lutz, he sees intersectional analysis to be vital to this work.

Much thinking about care and international relations has involved the elaboration of ethical considerations that arise when we take relationships of care seriously. Fiona Robinson (1999) pioneered the view that care needs to be more thoroughly integrated into international relations theory. Specifically, she has presented a care perspective as an alternative to existing ethical perspectives on international relations like communitarianism and cosmopolitanism. Others like Virginia Held (2006) and Daniel Engster (2007) have considered national and international forces, processes, and relationships in theoretical accounts of the politics and ethics of care. More recently, scholars have turned their attention to care under colonialism and the prevalence of care in postcolonial discourses (Raghuram 2009; Choy 2003). Finally, as neoliberal economic ideas come to inform the policies of states around the globe, scholars of care have observed how new languages of 'personalization' and 'accountability' seem to be about care, but turn out to be ways to limit the state's obligations to care for citizens (Barnes 2011).

Whether or not it is explicit, concepts of care inform virtually all theories of social life, and notions about who should do care work for whom underpin social and political organization everywhere. As a basic feature of human life, one whose practices and concerns have been highly gendered throughout history, care will continue to play a central role in how to think about gender.

Further Reading: Engster 2007; Held 2006; Kittay 1999; Robinson 2011; Tronto 1993.

CLASS

Sarah Evans

Introduction

The concept of social class is central to understanding how social inequalities are structured and experienced within the context of the economic structure of a given society. In contemporary sociology, social class is defined primarily in terms of the economic relationship between people occupying different positions within the occupational structure, as well as by the living conditions that these differences determine. This way of theorizing social class is influenced by the work of Karl Marx and Max Weber. Social class is a key concept through which to examine gender inequalities in the distribution of resources and access to knowledge and power in the social world. An understanding of social class provides the theoretical basis for exploring and answering questions about issues such as employment and opportunities, educational advantage and disadvantage, social mobility, social justice and discrimination.

During the twentieth century, the intricacies of class difference have been explored to achieve greater understanding of how social class is lived and experienced; the politics and culture of class difference and, how classed inequalities are connected to the inequalities of gender, race and sexuality. This chapter aims to introduce some of the key writers and notions in developing our understanding of class, tracing the connections between work on class and gender.

Historical background

Two social theorists in particular were central to the development of social and economic understandings of how a capitalist system produces social classes: Karl Marx (often writing with Friedrich Engels) and Max Weber. Both Marx and Weber reflected on capitalist industrialism during the nineteenth century to analyze the impact of economic change on the relationships between different economic and social groupings.

Marx's work examined the relationship between individuals and the ownership of capital and the means of production, to describe two major classes: the *proletariat* and the *capitalist* class. The capitalist class were the owners of the means of production, while the proletariat did not own property or capital, and relied upon the sale of their labour to the capitalist class in order to survive. Marx theorized that the persistent exploitation of the proletariat by the capitalist class would lead to increased 'class consciousness' amongst the proletariat, leading to the potential for organization by the proletariat as a class 'for itself'. This class, once organized to revolutionary capacity, could remove the ownership of capital and the means of production from the capitalist class for redistribution. *The Communist Manifesto,* first published in England (1848) by Marx and Engels, describes class conflict between the proletariat and capitalist class.

It was in the work of Marx's colleague, Engels, that the social position of women under industrial capitalism began to be examined. In *The Origin of the Family, Private Property and the State* (first published in 1884) Engels wrote about the relationship between women's subjugation and patriarchy. His work describes the subordination of women in the home and the role of women's domestic labour in upholding the patriarchal ownership of capital and property. It was during the second wave feminist movement in mid-to-late twentieth century Europe and North America that writers including Sheila Rowbotham, Juliet Mitchell, Nancy Fraser and Ann Oakley examined these issues in detail.

The work of Max Weber also focused on economic differences between groups, but as well as this considered the impact of skills and education, as well as occupations which had more ambiguous relationships to capital and property than those described by Marx and Engels. For example, Weber considered not just the relationship between the owners and producers of capital, but inserted the position of the intellectual, the small business owner and the managerial class into his schema. In doing so, Weber developed his notion of how social status can affect the 'life chances' of individuals. This has been very influential in class analysis in twentieth and twenty-first century Western societies, paradigmatically explored in the work of Goldthorpe, described below.

Class analysis

During the twentieth century in post-war Britain, considerable work was carried out to examine the distinctions between different economic and occupational groups and to devise schemes that would accurately reflect the occupational positions of different classes with respect to one another. The work of John Goldthorpe and his colleagues at the Social Mobility Group at Oxford University during the 1970s was central to the development of a schema for class analysis in mainland Britain.

Goldthorpe led large-scale quantitative data collection and analysis that would lead to his construction of a class schema based on the social value and economic relations of 12 occupational categories. The schema assumed a 'male breadwinner model', examining men's social class in relation to their paid work. Women's social class was derived from that of their husband or father. This assumption sparked a lively debate in class analysis. Indeed, Goldthorpe's model was criticized by those who sought a schema for class analysis that would recognize the economic activity of women (for example, Wright 1989). Furthermore, it was argued by a number of academics (such as Heath and Britten 1984) that the additional assumption that families are unitary in terms of class position is open to question. Goldthorpe later revised the model to one which locates a family's class position with reference to the occupational position of the main earner.

His work has been of considerable importance in understanding the relationship between class position and occupation in Britain, as well as in the understanding and analysis of intra- and intergenerational social mobility.[1] Yet it also demonstrates the significant difficulties of constructing a model for class analysis that is generalizable, given the numerous variables, which may be taken into account.

In the United Kingdom, the National Statistics Socio-economic Classification (NS-SEC) has been used as the official schema for class analysis for official surveys and statistics since 2001.[2] The NS-SEC also uses occupation as the basis for classification but includes revisions that aim to cover the whole of the adult population.

Lived experiences of class

While class analysis has helped provide the tools for improving our understanding of the structural relationship between people occupying different class positions, it offers little insight into the *lived experiences* of individuals occupying these different positions. For example, what do people occupying similar positions in the occupational structure have in common in terms of their everyday existence? Does 'class consciousness' exist and if so, what form does it take? How do differences in material conditions impact on how different groups experience the social world? Do men and women experience the same class position differently, and if so, how and why?

The work of feminist theorists and writers, the discipline of cultural studies, and sociological work which draws on anthropological, literary, philosophical and psychoanalytic approaches, have all contributed important work that addresses these questions. The Centre for Contemporary Cultural Studies at Birmingham (founded in 1964) provided the intellectual space for those interested in developing a cultural approach to understanding class and led to work such as Paul Willis' (1977) book on working-class 'lads', which has been influential in sociological accounts of young working-class men. During the past thirty years in particular, feminist writers such as Beverley Skeggs, Carolyn Steedman, Miriam Glucksmann (also writing under the name of Ruth Cavendish) and many others have explored in depth the lived experiences of working-class women in twentieth-century Britain. As a group, women's experiences in the home and in paid employment have been largely neglected from historical and sociological accounts, and working-class women's lives even more so. Indeed, Carolyn Steedman's (2009) book on female domestic workers of the eighteenth to early twentieth centuries shows that despite the huge numbers of working-class women employed in domestic service across this period, their lives and work were almost entirely ignored by social historians. In countries outside the UK, but also within the West, other feminist writers (for example, in discussions of the United States by Nancy Folbre (1994) and by Tracey Warren for countries across mainland Europe) have pointed to the problems of 'ungendered' accounts of class and the various qualifications that need to be made about the use of the term.

It is important to note the contributions to elucidating lived experiences of class that have been made by novelists, dramatists and filmmakers. Indeed, these accounts have often provided inspiration for sociological and cultural analysis, particularly with connection to social assumptions about morality, aspiration and class 'cultures'. Examples include nineteenth-century novelists such as George Eliot,

Charles Dickens, Henry James and Elizabeth Gaskell and twentieth-century filmmakers and dramatists such as Alan Sillitoe, Caryl Churchill, Ken Loach, Andrea Arnold and Willy Russell.

The reproduction of class

The French social theorist and anthropologist, Pierre Bourdieu, is now recognized as having developed conceptual tools that have helped explicate both the lived experience of class and the social and cultural process which cause class position to be reproduced across generations. His work was first translated into English in 1973 with the paper 'Cultural Reproduction and Social Reproduction' which appeared in R. Brown (ed.) *Knowledge, Education and Cultural Change* (Jenkins 1992: 182), but his impact on British sociology was not realized until much later. It has been over the past fifteen to twenty years that Bourdieu's work on the reproduction of class has become central to the sociological study of class.

Bourdieu's work draws upon a range of theories, traditions and approaches, and is influenced (for example) by the work of Marx and Weber as well as by philosophers such as Maurice Merleau-Ponty and Martin Heidegger. The concepts of *habitus*, *cultural capital* and *field* are central to Bourdieu's thesis and the widespread use of these concepts in the sociology of class warrants their brief introduction.

The *habitus*, as Bourdieu describes it, 'ensures the active presence of past experiences, which, deposited in each organism in the form of schemes of perception, thought and action, tend to guarantee the "correctness" of practices and their constancy over time more reliably than all formal rules and explicit norms' (Bourdieu 1990: 54). The habitus is therefore one's class history and the cultural memory of this in its embodied form, accounting for embodied class differences such as social confidence within particular fields (see below) and physical deportment.

The *field* is a site of social action which has its own 'rules' that are determined by the group of social actors who hold power within that field. An example of a field is the elite university. It is a site of social action with its own 'rules of the game' which are obvious to those with the corresponding class habitus, but far less so to those from different class backgrounds. Thus, in this example, habitus and field interact to determine which groups are able to interact with, and benefit most, from the elite university.

Bourdieu argues that middle-class parents transfer class advantage to their children through equipping them with *cultural capital.*

Cultural capital is knowledge of the culture and values of the dominant class that facilitate advantageous interactions within particular fields. For example, Bourdieu wrote about how the cultural competence (such as knowledge of 'high culture') that many middle-class parents transfer to their children, ensures success in schools and in education more generally; fields which value these particularly middle-class competencies.

Contemporary feminist theorists have significantly reworked Bourdieu's work. Academics such as Beverley Skeggs, Terry Lovell, Lisa Adkins, Valerie Hey, Diane Reay and Steph Lawler have adopted Bourdieu's central notions to examine the processes by which different bodies and groups *attain value* in the social world, in ways which can be enabling as well as limiting (Skeggs 2005: 46). The issue of embodiment, explored by Bourdieu, has been further developed by these writers to understand how the social value attributed to classed, gendered and racialized bodies affects how people are able to move through the social world.

Intersecting identities

The way in which our social class intersects with other aspects of our identity is an increasingly important area of study with two key strands. The first strand takes a macro approach to explicate relationships between class and (primarily) race and gender, within the context of globalization and global capitalism. For example, the economic exploitation of women, men and children within developing countries by Western nations overseas (as well as by the economic elite within their own country), necessitates an examination of how exploitation operates across both national boundaries and ethnic difference. Class, gender and race are therefore often examined in relation to one another to understand how different forms of inequality are produced both within nations, as well as across nation states. Recent work by Sylvia Walby (2009) is particularly insightful in exploring the tensions and interconnections between class, race and gender within the context of globalization.

The second strand of this work focuses on untangling how these inequalities are constituted, connected and experienced in everyday life, within particular nations and locales. This second strand explores the subjective experience of intersecting identities such as class, race, gender, sexuality, age and disability. For example, feminists and sociologists have examined the experiences of minority ethnic and working-class women within social spaces that have been historically dominated by white middle-class men. This work has uncovered how *difference* (also considered to be inferiority) is often read into the bodies of minority ethnic and working-class women. It has also exposed how a minority ethnicity and 'working-class-ness' are sometimes conflated by those in dominant positions, which can have a very real impact on experiences and opportunities within employment and education (see, for example, Puwar 2004). Recent work on intersecting identities has, for instance, explored issues such as the lived experiences of inequality and processes of resistance by working-class lesbian women (Taylor 2007).

Further Reading: Devine 2008; Lutz, Vivar and Supik 2011; Nussbaum 2000; Reay and Ball 2005; Scott, Crompton and Lyonette 2010.

Notes

1 Intra-generational mobility refers to the change of class position across the lifetime of an individual. Inter-generational mobility refers to changes in class position between parents and children.
2 http://www.ons.gov.uk/about-statistics/classifications/current/ns-sec/index.html. Accessed June 2011.

CITIZENSHIP

Barbara Einhorn

History and contestations

The Western concept of citizenship originated in fifth century BC Athens. Aristotle defined citizenship as active participation within the *polis*. Neither slaves nor women could aspire to citizenship status, being defined as legally equivalent to children.

The exclusion of women remained largely unchallenged until the late eighteenth century when the French Revolution in theory conferred universal, egalitarian citizenship status on all members of the nation-state. In practice, distinctions of class and gender were always decisive. Most theorists continued to debar women from citizenship on the basis of the notorious mind–body dichotomy in which reason is associated exclusively with active masculinity, and (ungovernable) emotion seen as the attribute of weak femininity. Even when Mary Wollstonecraft challenged this binary, making a powerful plea for women's education, she did not argue for equality of access to the public worlds of work and politics. During the period of industrialization and Empire in the nineteenth century, social mores across class lines were dominated by expectations that men's involvement in the public spaces of factory and politics should be complemented by a pure domestic space tended by the 'angel of the hearth'. This distinction between public and private worlds has to differing degrees characterized most societies and cultures throughout history. An example is the doctrine of 'outside' and 'inside' spaces in Confucianism that long dominated East Asia and is enjoying a resurgence in the twenty-first century.

It took the activism of first wave feminists to achieve formal voting rights, granted first to women in New Zealand in 1893, and in Britain in 1918. After World War II, T. H. Marshall extended the definition of citizenship beyond suffrage to include a bundle of social as well as civil and political rights. Even his socially progressive theories, however, remained problematic, focusing on class to the exclusion of issues of gender.

Feminist citizenship theory

Since the 1980s citizenship has been at the heart of feminist concerns. Scholars have stressed that a gender lens is essential, not only to understand how and why citizenship has been historically exclusionary, but also as a tool for greater social justice. As Karl Marx had recognized in the nineteenth century, the level of gender equality is a marker of the extent to which democracy has realized its ideals of social justice.

During the 1980s and early 1990s, feminist political theorists engaged critically with earlier (mainly male) theorists of citizenship, unveiling the universal citizen as invariably and exclusively male. Ursula Vogel contended that 'it is not merely that citizenship is gender-specific but that the very formulations of this concept in past and present have been *predicated* upon gender division'.

This was a revelation: ostensibly universal citizenship was in fact an exclusive club with rules that ensured its members could only be men. Feminist scholars considered how best women could attain membership. Should access be based on gender-neutral approaches stressing equality, or on gender-specific terms stressing women's special needs, which arise from their reproductive role? This led to the so-called equality versus difference debate. The women's peace camps protesting nuclear weapons at Greenham Common during the 1980s helped instigate this debate (Roseneil 1995, 2000). Media portrayals of women as somehow 'naturally' predisposed – because of their role in bringing life into the world – to oppose the destruction of life through military means overlooked some women's clamorous support for nationalist causes and conflicts such as World War I. Feminist activists rejected these representations as essentialist, based on a biology-driven approach that paradoxically reproduced the mind-body dualism that in earlier eras had been used to exclude women from eligibility for citizenship status. Lesbian feminists too felt that representations of femininity as primarily defined by maternity excluded them, privileging a heterosexist view of the family and society.

Another critique came from women of colour and women from the South who attacked Western feminists for speaking in their name, and for failing to locate the struggles of women worldwide within their specific locations. This legitimate critique of Western-centric theory emphasized the differences *between* women, focusing on diversity and the heterogeneity of women's experience, but lent itself over time to a problematic focus on 'identity politics' (itself a precursor of the postmodern turn) which rendered it impossible to generalize about the term 'woman' let alone construct joint political struggles in the quest for gender equality and social justice. Such solidarity, Chandra Talpade Mohanty argued in 2003, is especially crucial in the face of the growing power of gender-blind global capital.

Important contributions during the 1990s attempted to overcome the apparent impasse of the equality versus difference debate. Anne Phillips argued for the 'importance of the specifically political', arguing that 'the value of citizenship lies in the way it restates the importance of political activity'. Theorists like Ruth Lister asserted that citizenship was not merely a status but a process necessitating active involvement (Lister 1997, 2007). This notion of 'active citizenship' saw civil society activism as crucial to the achievement of democratic political change. Catherine Hoskyns noted in her analysis of the European Union that EU gender directives, to which for example Central and Eastern European countries had to conform to become members of the European Union, themselves resulted from grassroots feminist pressure from below.

The concept of 'transversal politics' developed by Nira Yuval-Davis addressed diversity by embracing a coalition politics that would acknowledge and respect differences of origin, location or political position but unite women in the quest for gender-equal citizenship.

Nancy Fraser addressed the gulf between what has become known as the 'cultural turn' which stresses 'recognition' of particular identities or locations, and a politics of 'redistribution' driven by the quest for social justice, arguing that both are necessary ingredients for a citizenship which integrates the cultural politics of difference with the social politics of equality. Others too endeavoured to balance the desire for gender equality with the need to recognize discriminations based on other markers of difference such as ethnicity, class, disability or sexuality. The concept of inter-sectionality, first formulated by Kimberlé Crenshaw, attempts to address the globally relevant issue of linked multiple discriminations that must be acknowledged in inclusive citizenship. A more recent attempt to broaden the remit of citizenship theory is represented by the notion of 'intimate citizenship' encompassing the politics of sexualities and intimate social relations.

Some institutional approaches to gender equitable citizenship

August Bebel wrote in his classic work *Woman and Socialism* (1879) that 'there can be no emancipation of humanity without the social independence and equality of the sexes'. Marxists like Friedrich Engels saw economic independence as the necessary precondition for this. After World War II, the state socialist countries of Central and Eastern Europe and the Soviet Union translated this into a top-down policy, which hoped to achieve gender-equal citizenship rights by integrating women into the labour market. Legislation for equal pay and social supports such as publicly available and affordable childcare facilities would buttress this approach. This privileging of the economic sphere contrasts with Western European approaches which prioritized civil and political rights. In Western countries, measures to facilitate gender-equal citizenship were achieved not by top-down government directives, but by bottom-up feminist demands. Both approaches remained incomplete. The state socialist neglect of civil and political rights and failure to harmonize the privileged sphere of (economic) production with that of reproduction, ensured that equality remained a chimera; in capitalist market economies, neglect of social and economic rights and an unwillingness to legislate for – for example – quotas for equal political representation resulted in minimal levels of female representation until recently in state legislatures, boardrooms, university professorships and all senior executive positions.

Both post-World War II regime types therefore failed to resolve the tensions created by gender inequalities within and between both private and public spheres. This ensured that women's access to the public spheres of economics and politics remained constrained, thus limiting their social and political citizenship status. Carole Pateman elaborates on the public–private divide as a hindrance to gender-equal citizenship, following Jean Bethke Elshtain's earlier expose of this fundamental contradiction in the work of classical liberal political theorists like John Stuart Mill (Elshtain 1981).

Official rhetoric portrayed the post-1989 transformations as a shift from totalitarian to democratic rule, thus prioritizing the role of the civil and political rights that had been lacking under communist regimes. In practice the shift prioritized the economic transition from centrally planned to market economy, hence the economic over the political. Herein lies a historic irony, which presents a problem from the perspective of equal citizenship. The neo-liberal paradigm constructs the citizen as economic actor in the marketplace, rather than as political subject – paradoxically reproducing the economistic focus of the ancient-regimes. Neo-liberal attacks on 'big government' in the West as in the East meant cancellation of public or state-subsidized childcare facilities in the name of self-reliance and individual entrepreneurship. This in turn renders the marketplace an uneven playing field, which women enter with a considerable handicap. Attempts to 'teach' democracy to the citizens of formerly totalitarian polities at the time of the transformations were ironic, coming as they did from countries such as the UK and the US, which in 1990 had extremely low levels of female political representation.[1] Given this poor record, official US rhetoric attempting to justify the Afghanistan and Iraq 'wars on terror' in the name of women's human rights or citizenship status would appear to border on the cynical or opportunistic.

Why citizenship?

What does the concept of citizenship add to considerations of gender equality that is not covered by the discourses and practices of human rights, civil society activism, agency or empowerment? Despite its problematic association with a universalist, ostensibly gender-neutral political theory that privileges the male political subject, citizenship theory offers greater potential – both theoretically and politically – for transcending nationalist, ethnic, class and religious divides in the quest for gender equitable and socially just societies. The language of empowerment tends to be paternalistic and individualist in its approach, especially in development discourses. It is also driven by neo-liberal economistic approaches that ultimately devolve responsibility to women themselves, rather than locating gender equality as an essential political goal.

Human rights discourse (like the language of generalized anti-discrimination legislation designed to deal with increasingly diverse societies) appears attractive in establishing transnational standards, yet it rests on a juridical approach, which is deeply problematic. It echoes the neoliberal paradigm in stressing individual rather than social responsibility, de-linking citizenship rights from state jurisdiction and making courts of justice such as the European Court of Justice or the European Human Rights Court the relevant arbiter. This juridical approach establishes citizenship not as a positive right claimable from the nation-state (or even a supra-national instance like the EU), but as a negative right claimable individually, and retrospectively, after the human rights in question have already been violated. Thus it embodies retributive rather than redistributive justice, negating social, national or supra-national state responsibility for the care and welfare of citizens.

Citizenship theory and the practice of active citizenship also enable the overcoming of the economic turn in which the citizen features as economic producer or consumer, rather than autonomous political subject. By identifying the state as addressee for political and social citizenship claims, citizenship discourse enables the establishment of linkages between the political, the economic and the social, between state, market and household-level social relations (Richardson 2005). Thus citizenship discourse links the political with the personal, the economic with intimate aspects of citizenship such as familial gender regimes, child and elder care, disabilities, sexualities and gender-based violence.

Several political theorists have suggested during the 2000s that the power of the nation-state has declined in the face of the dual processes of economic globalization – spurring large-scale migration and labour mobility – and the establishment of supra-national political bodies such as the European Union. The terms 'post-national', 'European', and even 'cosmopolitan' citizenship have gained currency. However, the example of migrants, refugees and asylum seekers makes clear that it is the national state rather than any human rights body or court of justice that at present retains the power to determine inclusion and exclusion. The nation-state remains the source of locally claimable anti-discrimination legislation, the provider of social welfare regimes, and the monitor of labour market conditions such as issues of equal pay for work of equal value. Nor have all EU gender equality norms been adopted by every nation, so that in the EU context, struggles to achieve gender equitable citizenship are, perforce, located within individual member states. The nation-state is more accessible and accountable to citizens than any supra-national courts, labour-regulating bodies like the ILO or polities like the European Parliament. So notions of trans-national forms of citizenship remain for the moment somewhat utopian.

In contrast to neoliberal rhetoric, which vilifies the state in favour of individual endeavour or voluntary social initiatives, the state still has a crucial role to play in implementing the conditions for gender equitable citizenship. As this requires a level playing field in the marketplace, childcare facilities are one necessary precondition. It is clear that in this case, as in many others, the private sector does not and will not fill the gap left by publicly available, state-subsidized social supports. Citizenship can remain an empty paper right unless both women and men have equal capacity to exercise their rights in the public spheres of the market and the polity. Amartya Sen's notion of 'capabilities' – developed by Martha Nussbaum – addresses this issue. The language of entitlements, degraded by conservative associations with 'welfare dependence' and lack of self-reliance, needs to be rehabilitated to restore the balance of rights and responsibilities inherent in the concept of citizenship. This is a necessary step towards achieving gender equality, which is in turn – along with other equalities with which gender intersects – a measure of the level of democracy and social justice in any given society.

Further Reading: Crenshaw 1991; EJWS (*European Journal of Women's Studies*) 2009; Anon (*International Feminist Journal of Politics*) 2009; Lombardo and Verloo 2009; Pateman 1989; Phillips 1992; Mohanty 1984; Fraser 1995; Fraser and Honneth 2003; Yuval-Davis 1997, 2008.

Note

1 In 1990, women held only 6.3% of parliamentary seats in the UK, a figure exceeded in the first democratic elections held that year in Czechoslovakia (11%), Poland (13.5%) and even Hungary (7.2%). By 30 June 2011, female political representation in the UK had reached 22%, matched by the Czech Republic, with Bulgaria at 21% and Poland and Estonia at 19%, while it was still only 16.7% in the US, just ahead of Albania (16.4%) and Azerbaijan (16%). Only Hungary lagged conspicuously at 9% (Source: http://www.ipu.org/wmn-e/classif.htm).

CULTURAL DIFFERENCE

Floya Anthias

In this contribution, I will explore the rather 'fuzzy' but commonly used notion of cultural difference. I will do this with reference, first to 'difference' and then to culture and ethnicity. I will then look at the related notion of cultural diversity, using examples from the current diversity agenda in the UK which is concerned with the governmentality of difference, and looking at gendered issues around body covering and honour-based crimes which raise issues about culturalization and stigmatized difference.

Difference

The concern with difference is reflected at a range of levels and addresses a range of social phenomena. 'Difference' is a term that is used in a variety of ways in different literature and political discourses. Difference and identity are related concepts and live together. Identity relates to sameness, which is a necessary corollary to difference. To be able to identify one means identifying the other. Both involve a sorting exercise and are discursive constructions. Stuart Hall (1996b) has argued that we need to understand identity constructions 'as produced in specific historical and institutional sites … they emerge within the play of specific modalities of power' (p. 4).

Difference is never neutral, boundaries are rarely just innocent markers, and typologies are rarely like flowers, interesting for the enthusiast or for the pleasure of our senses. Difference points to certain aspects of our world, constructing them as such, making them socially meaningful. Meanings are themselves products of a range of socio-political forces; locating difference therefore is a necessary step for understanding the various terms of reference of cultural difference. What type is being signalled, where are the boundaries placed between the same and the different, how is this evaluated and who is marking the difference and why? – all are questions to be raised. How is such marking received by those who are marked as different, and what strategies do they employ in return, either to negotiate, or to struggle/resist such markings and – most importantly – the social practices that accompany them? Brah (1996) also raises the issue of the ways in which the marking of difference is experienced, seeing experience as 'the site of subject formation' and as 'a process of signification which is the very condition for the constitution of what we call "reality"' (p. 116).

Marking difference involves a political project of governmentality and therefore this is the first principle of the notion of cultural difference. So the boundaries between man and woman, black or white, English and minority, are already imbued by forms of hierarchy and social placing, in and of themselves; difference marks distinction and does it usually in a hierarchical way. The boundaries of difference of various kinds do not enter a posteriori into the realm of the hierarchy produced by the class system, found within the system of production or the market place: they already have been part of its very fabric. The notion of difference uses varied benchmarks for drawing boundaries between self and other. The categories of difference and identity are never merely relational and neutral, therefore. They serve as nodes for practices and discourses of inferiorization and inequality. Within such analysis difference is seen not as representing an empirical reality but as a social construction with discursive and material elements and as depicting relations *between* groups rather than being *about* group difference as such.

Difference is not static or politically neutral and may be claimed as part of a strategy of domination or contestation (as in the growth of ethnicization as a response to the dehumanization of racialization). Difference and identity are located in terms of attributions and claims to resources of different types and to political projects by those in power and those who contend with power. There has been a great deal of discussion of the ways in which the social construction of difference is related to resource and recognition inequalities and hierarchies (e.g. Fraser 1997, Anthias 1998). A relational and locational depiction of difference and its uses is therefore required.

The use of difference for minorities does not mean that it doesn't also pertain to other boundaries, particularly those of gender and of sexuality. However with gender and sexuality the adjective cultural is usually absent. Derrida (1982) is concerned with the ways difference (as 'difference') establishes a space between objects giving rise to hierarchy and binary categories. In the case of sexuality, for example, the rules of heteronormativity establish the difference as that which lies on the deviant homosexual, gay or lesbian side of the sexuality binary. In the case of gender it is woman that embodies difference. The role of power relations, which are not only discursive but also structural, is important here, in the ways in which difference depicts the 'other' inferiorized side. If we look at the case of gender, what this means is that the gender difference is not an unproblematic given result of either sex difference or of socialization practices that establish particular internalizations of social relations and produce gendered subjects. Rather, gender difference involves articulations that are overdetermined by their locational and relational positions within the sphere of boundary making as an exercise relating to power and in relation to performativity (see Butler 1990). However, this operates within structural arrangements including those of capital and the state, which produce and reproduce as well as change social hierarchies (Anthias 1998, Walby 2007).

Cultural difference and 'ethnic' minorities

Cultural difference and cultural identity are related notions, both linked to modalities of power (Hall 1996b). Cultural difference can refer to a range of boundaries in social life that are treated as cultural: this can include and has included in the past concerns with lifestyles, with cultural practices by different groupings (which include those of gender and class as well as ethnicity). The term 'culture' also appears in different ways in relation to what it signals (for example as content or product, as ways of being and doing or as a world view; see Anthias 2001). In addition there are notions of culture as emergent (see Bourdieu 1990 on 'habitus' who links it with agency), culture as a set of typifications or recipes (in Schutz 1932), culture as 'performative' (Butler 1990). Given the range of different meanings that can be attached to the notion of 'culture', the object of reference in cultural difference is far from clear and indeed is opportunistic.

The notion of cultural difference in relation to gender is inflected by the ways in which gender constructions and discourses mark the boundaries of the social and particularly of the nation (see Anthias and Yuval Davis 1992). Although men and women haven't usually been seen within academic debates as 'culturally' different, gender theorists have pointed to the ways in which society constructs them differently, in terms of notions of passivity, dexterousness, multi-tasking, caring and a range of other supposed attributes which women have in contrast to men. These are social constructions that have marked effects on ideas and practices by men and women, and of course, about men and women in society.

The contemporary focus on cultural difference is very much concerned with the governmentality of dangerous difference, usually linked to migration and securitization discourses and practices (where gender is also involved as I explain later on). It is also part of a turn to the cultural in social science and the growth of recognition politics.

Within the framework of cultural difference, there is a signposting of the centrality of culture (defined in a particular way) as embodied in the values and practices of minority ethnic subjects who have been transnational travellers and settlers in the reception society, and their accommodation. It is therefore useful to take ethnicity as an example of how difference appears in terms of culture. Ethnic difference is often elided with cultural difference and there is an assumption that what marks 'ethnic' minorities is a difference in cultural traditions and values providing a distinctive cultural repertoire for the actors involved, usually imagined as arising from distinct territorial or nation-state units within which a notion of a shared culture is established. Frederick Barth was one of the first critics of such an approach with his view that the cultural contents of group or ethnic boundaries were less important to ethnic group making, which he saw as a boundary-making exercise. He held the view that 'the cultural differences of primary significance for ethnicity are those that people use to mark the distinction, the boundary' (1969: 12). It was the way in which cultural difference was used and deployed that was crucial to the ethnic boundary rather than cultural difference itself, which had little meaning outside this particularly given the heterogeneities of cultural understanding and practices within ethnic categorizations.

Cultural difference is best understood in terms of attributions and 'claims' made by groups (e.g. the claim to be a nation rather than an ethnic group), which is tied to context and political strategy as well as particular imaginings of boundaries and their chief symbolic carriers (as found for example in the racist imagination).

Cultural difference, cultural diversity and gender

Cultural difference generally lives alongside its sister notion cultural diversity, although it is important to try and distinguish between these two. Difference usually denotes boundaries that are seen as creating a social problem whereas diversity is a concept which is generally given positive connotations – with the proviso that recent debates around multiculturalism and migration have been organized around the problems posed by living in a society that is too diverse and that contains 'bad' difference.

Cultural diversity has appeared strongly in recent EU and national legislation, although the forms it takes have arguably changed with the demise of multiculturalism as a state project. One facet of the changes to the face of diversity is the growth of diversity management, which, compared to the earlier multiculturalist diversity paradigm that was concerned with ethnic or race difference, increases the range of markers of difference and includes those of gender, sexuality, faith and disability. Here, there is a concern with mainstreaming as opposed to merely supporting cultures to co-exist.

Within a highly charged and political diversity (and integration) discourse, we have seen an emphasis on gender and the female body in particular as central elements depicting undesirable others, as well as signalling the unwillingness of migrants to integrate. Debates on the veil and on so-called honour-based violence (including forced marriages) are often framed within a gender equality discourse, which aims to protect minoritized women.

In Europe there have been different intensities and strengths of response to the body covering of women (such as the use of the hijab and the chador). Although there is no prohibition in the UK, there has been a great deal of debate on the veil (see Meer et al. 2010) and particularly on the burka, seeing it as a manifestation of the unwillingness of Muslims to integrate and as a security threat.

There is also a strong concern with so-called honour-based violence, which articulates the need to protect women who are seen as victims from their ethnic or Muslim culture in particular. These tend to divest it of its gendered aspects, viewing such crimes as the result of cultural values rather than practices of gender-based violence more widely (e.g. see Begikhani et al. 2010). The problematization of difference and diversity is especially clear here, where there exists a thorough culturalization of the social issues involved and they are depicted as only related to the 'other'. To critique such culturalization is not to deny problems of such gendered crimes or issues they raise about gender equality, however.

This also indicates how gender is often at the heart of culturalist constructions of collectivities (Anthias and Yuval Davis 1992). Indeed the culturalization of violence against women means that individual cases are seen as representing collective patterns and leads to demonization of the whole culture, fuelling Islamophobia in particular.[1] Often arguments about the oppression of women within multicultural societies (e.g. see Okin 1999) are used to critique migration, Islam or the incorporation of minority ethnic groups in society; they are judged to be non-assimilable because they are regarded as unwilling to conform to the supposed universalist principles of Western democracies. Such culturalizations, drawing often on stereotypical versions of religious faith or 'ways of life' of the 'other' are prominent not only within debates on honour-based crimes, but also debates on forced marriages and genital mutilation.

I would like to end with a quote by Gloria Anzaldúa the writer of *Borderlands*, who tells us that difference is not just something between us but also within us:

> The struggle is inner: Chicano, indio, American Indian, mojado, mexicano, immigrant Latino, Anglo in power, working class Anglo, Black, Asian – our psyches resemble the bordertowns and are populated by the same people.
>
> (1999: 109)

Further Reading: Anthias 2002; Eriksen 2006; Maynard 1994; Moore 1994; Phillips 2010.

Note

1 According to a recent report (Begikhani et al.), over 500 women are killed, mainly in Asia and the Middle East but also Europe. This is likely to be an underestimate as many women are abducted or disappear.

CYBERSPACE

Maureen McNeil

The term cyberspace has its origins in science fiction: it was coined by William Gibson in his cyberpunk novel, *Neuromancer* ([1984] 1995). Gibson contended that the term registered the 'consensual hallucination' that there is 'some kind of actual space behind the screen [of a computer], someplace you can't see but you know is there' (McCaffery 1990, cited in Wolmark 1999: 3). The word itself registers the lineage of computing: its link with cybernetics (the science of information regulation and systems theory, Hayles 1999). The conceit of the term involves the attribution of location to the flow of digital data through networks of computers and to the resulting computer-mediated communication.

Gibson's coinage predated the establishment of the internet and the advent of the web. Nevertheless, this metaphor (Wolmark 1999) has subsequently been used widely to designate both the realm of and the possibilities for the operations of electronic communications networks, particularly the internet, and the computer-mediated communications they enable. As a relatively new domain without physical location, cyberspace or the cybersphere (which is a sometimes used as its synonym) has been regarded as a site for social experimentation and the focus of speculation – particularly about whether it is distinctive from, or continuous with, other spheres of human social activity, most notably in the modes of relationality it enables.

With regard to gender, the notion of cyberspace denotes a highly complex and much contested terrain. As will be outlined below, it has figured prominently in two of the most important social and political movements of the late twentieth and early twenty-first centuries: feminism and queer activism. It also designates the realm of an evolving array of practices, which are implicated in, and themselves generative of, gender relations. Moreover, as digital technology expands and diversifies (as they have since the last decades of the twentieth century), cyberspace practices and affordances have become increasingly pervasive in and consequential for everyday life. Hence, in many respects, cyberspace is at the centre of gender and sexual life and politics of the twenty-first century.

The related term cyberfeminism is the collective label that has been given to a set of visionary responses, consolidated into manifesto appraisals of the prospects for gender transformation in and through engagement with cyberspace. Donna Haraway's landmark 'Cyborg Manifesto' (1991 [1985]) is frequently cited as the first and most influential cyberfeminist text. Haraway invoked the figure of the cyborg (human-machine hybrid), rather than cyberspace, as the iconic image relevant to the technological conditions facing women in the late twentieth century, offering her overview of recent developments in both biotechnology and information/communications technologies. While Haraway offered a generally optimistic feminist appraisal of the prospects for cyberfeminism, she was by no means sanguine about how women were located in the 'digital circuits' of contemporary information and communications technologies (ICTs).

In contrast, Sadie Plant (1998) conjured a vision of 'cybernetic feminism' offering one of the most celebrated and unequivocally optimistic appraisals of the prospects for women in the emerging digital culture of the late twentieth century. Plant referenced Freud's views on women's activities, used Irigaray's theory of phallic culture and power (deemed the culture of 'one'), invoked Charles Babbage's collaborator, Ada Lovelace, as a heroine, likened computing to the feminine craft of weaving, and played with digital binaries (*Zeros and Ones*) to proclaim computing as a female sphere. Cyberspace was identified by Plant as a feminine domain: a place of freedom, associated with the prospect of disrupting patriarchal culture and achieving female liberation.

Towards the end of the twentieth century feminist manifestos about the prospects for cyberspace gave way to diffused appraisals of what was happening on the ground in and through digital networking. Discussion focused on cybercultures and the ways in which digital communication was being used in feminist campaigns, women's networking, and forms resistance to gender norms and conventions (Harcourt 1999). Probing the body politics of cyberspace – as a unique realm characterized by not requiring co-presence – also became a feminist concern.

Queer theory and activism and the cybersphere linked to the internet came into public life, predominantly in North America, almost simultaneously. Cyberspace was heralded as a particularly promising queer domain, propitious in its capacity to engender and sustain sexual diversity, and unsettle sexual identities and labels, as well as being a promising realm for queer communities, activism and practices. The convergence of cyberculture and queer was cast as energizing and transformative by queer commentators/activists including Allucquere Rosanne Stone (1995) and Sue Ellen Case (1999). The distillation embodied in the term 'cyberqueer' signalled assumptions about this affinity – they were regarded as synergetic (rather than 'natural') 'bed-fellows'. Nevertheless, the high level of investment in this coupling and the resulting optimism about cyberspace as a site of queer enactments and transgression caused at least one researcher to step back a bit. Nina Wakeford reflected that: 'Perhaps the closeness of fit is a bit too convincing?' (Wakeford 1997a: 412). Despite her questioning of this connection, Wakeford did herself extend and encourage such linkings, by offering her own typology of cyber/queer intersections in computer-mediated communication (Wakeford 1997a).

From the late twentieth century proprietorial claims about cyberspace as queer space gave way to growing awareness of the complexity and diversity of queering practices in and around the realm of digital communications (see O'Riordan and Phillips 2007). In addition, as increased attention was given to harassment, 'flaming' (escalating hostile exchanges), cyberstalking and other forms of cyber violence (Kuntsman 2007) it became difficult to be sanguine about cyberspace as inherently safe queer space. Although recently there has been considerably less complacency about cyberspace as necessarily queer space and increasing awareness of the 'control and constraint' and forms of surveillance within the sphere (O'Riordan and Phillips 2007: 3), queer theory continues to be deployed fruitfully in the study of evolving queer practices online (see esp. O'Riordan and Phillips 2007).

As the foregoing account suggests, cyberspace was a pivotal concept as feminists and queer activists in the Western world and in some other parts of the globe came to grips with what was widely perceived as the digital revolution of the late twentieth and early twenty-first century. Assessments about the prospects for transforming gender and sexual relations in the digital age were often broad-brushed. In this sense, the term was not just a technological metaphor but it became something of a metonym for the possibilities and challenges movements orientated towards gender and sexual change faced in the wake of digitalization.

The manifestos and macro perspectives on cyberspace have given way to more localized evaluations and research on sex and gender and ICTs. References to cyberspace in these contexts tend to be much more circumscribed and specific. Although the term continues to be employed, the foregrounding of practices, rather than location, involves a conceptual shift and signals increased interest in the micro-processes of gendering and sexualization. This may be connected to the pervasive infiltration of digitalization into everyday life but it is also consonant with increasing emphasis on the performativity of gender (Butler 1990). The next section explores three crucial forms of digital activity – computer games, pornography and social networking on the net – in which gender and sexuality issues are to the fore to discern how such micro deployments of the concept of cyberspace have worked.

Games have been amongst the most popular activities associated with cyberspace. In the early phases of digital technology games were orientated towards the mainly male hackers who were the initial shapers of the field. Young male enthusiasts ('nerds') predominated in early digital gaming as both designers and users and they continue to figure prominently both as producers and consumers in the contemporary computer gaming scene. Early computer games were overwhelmingly structured as masculinist adventures, playing out variations on the 'Dungeons and Dragons' theme. Shooting and killing became the staple activities of cyberspace game playing and military-like operations were popular, referencing the origins of the internet itself in US defence operations. Hence, gaming in cyberspace emerged, and to some extent remains, coded as a boys' world.

As computer gaming expanded and the computer-aided capacities in animation improved there was a growing proliferation of female protagonists in cyberspace – that were rendered as three-dimensional figures – avatars. These were often stereotypical figures, displaying hyper-feminine traits, leading one commentator to describe computer game design in the late twentieth century as 'prone to rigid styles of representation based on men's fantasies' (Flanagan 2002: 425).

Flanagan traced the gendering of cyberspace around such figures, most notably the iconic avatar Lara Croft, the hero of *Tomb Raider*. She contends that the gendering instantiated by these kinds of digital products and interactions with them are best understood through attending to: the representation of these figures, the styles of play and the relationship of the user to the media experience (Flanagan 2002: 425). She is particularly interested in how 'the body of the virtual game character is distanced' and in 'the performance of the gender of the virtual body and the relationship between this secondary performance and that of the gender of the knower' (Flanagan 2002: 439).

Flanagan called for an end to the 'non-consensual fantasy engine' (Flanagan 2002: 449) which she sees animating and populating cyberspace with negative representations of women and offering intensely gendered modes of interaction in the popular electronic media she studied. Others have been somewhat more optimistic in their appraisals of the prospects for de-gendering of the enactments of gaming cyberspace – citing women's entry into the industry (Cassell and Jenkins 2010) and girls' experimentation and transgressive appropriations (Mazzarella 2010) in this domain. Furthermore, like other ICT sectors, gaming is continually evolving and it remains to be seen how these changes may impact on its gender profile. Ongoing explorations of the gendering of gaming cyberspace representations and practices will have to consider matters such as women's (particularly young women's) increasing presence in this scene and the digital gaming industry's efforts to respond to this and to extend its markets by diversifying its products. Indeed, recently a game designed to get participants to 'care', rather than capture, defeat, shoot or kill has appeared on the market.

The rather generalized term 'social networking' is now the label for the currently most popular form of encounters in and through cyberspace. Social networking sites sustain diverse forms of communication. They are computer platforms which draw on, combine and transform a variety of older vehicles for expression and communication including (just to mention a few): diaries, social notices, photograph albums, through a range of digital activities – emailing, messaging, website creation, blogging, uploading and downloading music and videos. *Facebook,* which began in 1994, has been a phenomenally successful financial venture, and is now globally the most widely used social networking site, but there are a number of other related outlets (for example, *Bebo*, *Friendster*, *MySpace,* etc.).

Such sites enable and encourage new forms of sociality at a distance and they offer distinctive tools for identity construction and projection. Gender issues loom large in this growing digital domain. The most obvious feature of digital social networking is its success in attracting women in enormous numbers – primarily as consumers. In addition, young women are considered to be particularly vulnerable users of social networking sites and highly-publicized cases of 'grooming' (especially older men cultivating relationships with young women) have raised questions about intimacy, sexualization and surveillance in cyberspace.

It is impossible to consider gender and cyberspace without addressing the issue of pornography. Pornography has been characterized as 'in its myriad digital manifestations the killer app of the World Wide Web' (Morais 1999, in Bell et al. 2004: 151). Indeed, the web is now the main engine for the circulation of pornographic material. The ease of access and privacy of consumption which digital communication provides has ensured the proliferation of pornographic websites and the growth of the pornographic industry. Nevertheless, surveillance of some forms of pornographic consumption has increased and there have also been some high-profile prosecutions – particularly associated with the use of paedophilic sites.

Pornography is a complex and fraught issue of gender and sexual politics, as feminists discovered in the 1970s to 1990s. Cyberspace has proved to be a nourishing environment for both the pornographic industry and pornographic consumption, which feminist and other social commentators have yet to fully assess. Since women continue to be the primary object of pornography and much of this is misogynistic, cyberspace pornography is intensely gendered. Nevertheless, it has been important to register diversity and to take account of the pleasure women may derive from pornographic experiences in cyberspace, not least because women's access to and participation in pornography have extended and diversified with digitalization. Feminist commentators have also noted that it is the objectification of children, rather than women, in cyberspace pornography that has garnered most public concern (Adam 2002; Cicitira 2004).

It is difficult to distinguish between genuine issues and moral panics in considering gender and cyberspace. As a new, continuously changing realm it has elicited much attention as a site of promise and danger. The risks that have garnered most attention generally pertain to sexuality and gender relations. As noted above, the vulnerability of children and young women in cyberspace has been accentuated. Fears about 'grooming' and the consumption of paedophilic pornography have fuelled controversy and panic in recent years.

Cyberspace is a slippery concept: eliding fiction and technoscientific developments, operating as metaphor and metonym, and analyzable from macro and micro perspectives. Moreover, the frantic pace of digital hardware and software innovation and continually changing patterns of ICT use render cyberspace a shifting focus for gender analysis. For example, some practices that previously captured the attention of gender researchers now seem mundane and old-fashioned (see, for example, Wakeford 1997b on 'surfing' the net). Likewise, the proliferation of devices which render cyberspace a more ubiquitous realm of daily life and related practices – including the move to hand-held devices including the iPhone and the tablet – may have specific consequences for gender relations, the gendering and sexualizing of subjectivities. More generally, in a world in which economic inequality is profoundly gendered, the intensification of the commercialization of this sphere, one key moment of which was the emergence of the commercial vehicle of the world-wide web in 1994, means that cyberspace must be regarded as a dynamic arena.

Invoking economic inequality is a reminder that questions about access cannot be ignored when notions of cyberspace and gender are linked. Just as the phrase 'ubiquitous computing' masks inequalities in use of this technology, notions of global digital networks and the label 'world-wide web' obscure uneven patterns of internet and broadband provision and access. Cyberspace is thus not a freely available domain and it is by no means open to all. Gender is not the only determining factor here but it does loom large. This is crucial since women continue to be underrepresented at the top end of achievement in ICT education, training and career structures. This means that, while women are increasingly consumers of cyberspace and have been, for some time in various parts of the world, involved in the manufacture of the components for digital technology, they are still generally not its designers and shapers (Terry and Calvert 1997: 8).

Further Reading: Bell 2004; Boellstorff 2008; Flanagan 2002; McNeil 2007; O'Riordan and Phillips 2007; Terry and Calvert 1997; Wolmark 1999.

DIASPORA

Nikita Dhawan

Definition and history of the concept

The etymology of the word 'diaspora' can be traced back to the Greek verb *diasperien*, consisting of *sperien* (to scatter) and the preposition *dia* (across). Around 300 BCE Jews of Alexandria first used the term to signify their scattering away from the homeland into *galut*, or collective exile (Braziel and Mannur 2003: 1). The Jewish diaspora is considered the paradigmatic example of traditional diaspora.

The academic field of diaspora studies was established in the late twentieth century, with a more expanded meaning of diaspora to refer to any people or ethnic population coercively expelled or forcefully displaced from their traditional homelands. Subsequently the term has been extended to include old and new dispersions, for instance, of people of African, Indian, Chinese and Latin American origin (Cohen 1997).

Diasporas are deterritorialized imagined communities constructed as sharing a collective past and common destiny. Displacement can be physical, emotional and psychological leading to alienation, marginalization and exploitation. Marked by a common historical experience of catastrophic violence and struggle for survival, diasporas are identified by their efforts to maintain traditional identities and retain contact with communities in the homeland and elsewhere (Tölölyan 2007: 649). They are embodiments of cultural, political and economic performances that exist through exchange of goods, capital and ideas (Werbner 2002).

The label 'diaspora' is employed to signify diverse groups like political and war refugees, victims of ecological and financial crisis, ethnic and racial minorities, asylum seekers, labour migrants, queer communities, domestic service and care workers, executives of multinational corporations, and transnational sex workers (Tölölyan 2007: 648). The semantic, legal and affective nuances of the term are widely contested, even as its difference to concepts such as expatriate, refugee, resident alien, migrant has not been clearly demarcated. Disagreement over divergent uses of key concepts, such as diaspora and dispersion, transnational, global and local, mobility and rootedness has led scholars to bemoan the loss of rigour in the employment of the term (649). This is not merely about 'terminological fussiness' (649), rather the hope is to facilitate a better understanding of the indeterminate processes of diasporization. It is argued that migration and mobility by itself does not translate into the emergence and persistence of diaspora, which is not to be understood simply as a group of people living outside their homeland. If based only on assumptions of racial descent, there is the danger of biologism in the definition of diaspora. Paul Gilroy (1993), for instance, warns against the homogenization and 'ethnic absolutism' involved in linking all African diasporic individuals worldwide as sharing a common ancestry and heritage.

In the face of the proliferation of the use of the term to encompass differing phenomena, it is necessary to have an operable definition of diaspora, so that it is analytically useful and not ahistorical or celebratory (Tölölyan 2007: 649). One of the defining characteristics of diaspora is the effort to preserve a collective identity through culinary, musical, religio-festive, and linguistic practices and rituals. Moreover, diasporas are informed by nostalgia for reunion and return to the homeland, even as memories of the homeland are marked by ambivalence and contradictions. Their relationship to the homeland takes material, literary and symbolic forms through travel, communication, remittances, cultural exchange, and political lobbying. Furthermore, the differing experiences of settlement are equally crucial in the emergence of diasporas. Even as diasporic communities seek citizenship without assimilation within host countries, they also experience exclusion, persecution and violence, which once again influence their formation. The delicate balance of inclusion without assimilation in the host society is maintained through the demand for strict adherence to tradition and loyalty to homeland (650).

How the concept is used: colonialism and globalization

One of the most innovative aspects in recent scholarship on diaspora is the effort to unpack the deep historical link between colonialism and the flow of people, ideas, commodities and capital with the aim to explore how the scale and nature of these movements changed through colonial travel, trade and war (Braziel and Mannur 2003: 2).

Colonial trajectories of globality can be traced within contemporary diasporic formations. It was this historical condition that led to the displacement of millions of people across the world under different forms of compulsion, transforming traditional understandings of community, belonging and mobility. Resisting explaining migration between the metropolitan centres and colonial peripheries in straightforward terms, postcolonial analysis involves a nuanced mapping of 'roots' and 'routes' (Gilroy 1993) to unpack the complex link between diaspora and colonialism. Colonialism compelled people to move as settlers, traders, missionaries, transported convicts, slaves, and indentured labourers. Consequently the culture produced by diaspora cannot but reflect the diverse experiences of displacement, settlement and return. Post/Colonial diasporas are multilocal and polycentric, developing their own distinctive creolized or hybridized cultures that both preserve and transform 'originary' cultures even as they modify and are modified through contact with indigenous cultures. Diasporic cultures necessarily question essentialist models of 'pure' cultures and theories of nativism, which suggest that decolonization can be effected by a recovery of pre-colonial cultures and a return to the homeland (Gilroy 1993).

The problematics of space and territory is central to the study of diasporas. As transnational social formations, diasporas challenge the sanctity and boundedness of the nation-state and draw attention to dimensions of transnational existence (Ong 1999). Inscribed within the idea of diaspora is the notion of border. These are not just physical territories policing those constituted as outsiders and aliens, rather borders are simultaneously social, cultural, imaginary and psychic constructs, demarcating who belongs and who does not. Yet another closely linked notion is of transnationality and 'diasporic consciousness' (Chow 1993). Diasporans have come to be celebrated as embodiments of multiple belongings, hybridity, and cosmopolitanism. This is contrasted with the sedentary and the immobile, which is associated with parochial forms of nationalism. However the celebration of privileged mobility of diasporic elites needs to be more carefully examined. In spite of the hype of unlimited opportunities of mobility, diasporans – especially women – often find themselves in vulnerable social and economic positions (Ong 1999). The highly exploitable and precarious status of diasporic women can be very well illustrated with the example of the border towns in Mexico. The expansion of the *maquiladoras*, which are duty-free zones for manufacturing assembly line products for export, has attracted domestic mass migration of young women from the rural areas. The Chicana feminist Gloria Anzaldúa charts the 'topography of displacement' along the Mexican–U.S. American border, which she calls the 1950 mile-long 'open wound, where the Third World grates against the first and bleeds' (Anzaldúa 2007: 25). She traces the emergence of the *mestiza* consciousness in these 'borderlands', which at once challenges and subverts the collaborative bond between native patriarchy, imperialist feminism, indigenous nationalism and colonial-racism and capitalism, even as it ruptures monolithic notions of community, language and belonging.

Feminist analysis of gender and nation (Yuval-Davis 1997; Brah 1996) challenge discourses of organic wholeness and 'naturalness' of community. Unpacking the socially constructed nature of collectivities, they highlight how norms, boundaries and structures are deeply contested in the formations of belonging and otherness, of 'us' and 'them'. Even as diasporas exist between nation-states and in-between cultures, inhabiting plural spaces socially, politically, culturally and economically, paradoxically, nationalism often flourishes in the diaspora. Pnina Webner (2002: 120) unpacks how diasporas are deeply implicated both ideologically and materially in nationalist projects as an effort to overcome loss and breakdown of ties with the homeland. She gives examples of emancipatory diasporic politics pursued by Jewish peace groups, who have critiqued expansionary anti-Palestinian moves by right-wing Israeli governments. On the other hand is the nativistic diasporic politics, which engages in 'long-distance' nationalism. A case in point is the ideological and financial support provided by the Indian diaspora to Hindu nationalist movements. Advancement in global media and communication technologies has greatly contributed to the ability of diasporas to participate and intervene in the politics of the homeland. In particular, feminist and queer theorists have made significant contributions in this context to unpack the hetero-sexist nationalism emerging within diasporic formations (Gopinath 2005). In the name of protecting one's women and maintaining one's culture, identity and community from assimilation, masculinization and retraditionalization within diasporic communities have significant impact on gender relations, both in the diaspora as well as the homeland (Ong 1999).

Significance and impact of the concept on gender studies

Even after decades of feminist research, gendered diasporization remains inadequately theorized to the extent that gender is understood within a framework of traditional sex roles. Gender is a key organizing principle of cultural, political and economic relations structuring every aspect of social interaction. Thus the focus should not be merely at making women in diaspora visible, but to show that patterns, causes, experiences and social impacts of diasporization are gendered. Some of the major issues that need addressing in this context are how gender organizes processes of diaspora formation and settlement and how diasporization alters gender relations.

With the increasing feminization and informalization of the labour force, there is a predominance of diasporic women, specifically in the care sector, domestic service and sex industry. The gender norms underlying the current international division of labour subject diasporic women to a racializing discourse that naturalizes them as uniquely suited to domestic and affective labour (Hochschild 1983). This necessitates the revisioning of traditional models of economy, namely, an understanding of how the intersection of gender, race, class, sexuality and religion shapes the status of diasporic women in the labour market as well as how paid labour alters gender relations in the diaspora (Luibhéid 2004: 231). Despite the important role of diasporic women, their agency has not been adequately acknowledged, and they are still considered to be economically and socially dependent on their male relatives and community leaders. To challenge the victim discourse and highlight the complex space of diasporic women's agency, attention must be paid to the diverse ways in which they negotiate their roles and the strategies they deploy to cope with exploitative circumstances. After all, diasporic women have to at once negotiate with structures such as the state, family and community. Moreover, the economic ramifications of diaspora equally shape gender relations both in the homeland and host society. For example, Filipino diasporic women have emerged as important economic actors through their remittances. Thus on the one hand, transnational mobility provides opportunities for empowerment and prosperity, even as it can be exploitative and unfair. Diasporic women are increasingly influential within political and cultural organizations both in their homeland and host society, even as they carve out new forms of socialities and negotiate the gender roles.

Queer diasporas

While gender has been stereotypically rendered as female in most research, sexuality has invariably equated with heterosexual reproduction and family life (Manalansan 2006: 224). Recent scholarship on queer diasporas contests the heteronormative definitions of citizenship and nation. Sexuality, specifically as it is understood in queer studies, not only expands the understanding of diaspora, but also challenges diaspora studies' implicit heteronormativity and disrupts the presumption that all diasporans are heterosexual (Luibhéid 2004). Focus on queer diasporic subjectivity enables a critique of heteronormative ideas that are inadvertently stabilized even by critical theorists in the field of gender and diaspora (Gopinath 2005: 11). The aim here is not only to bring sexuality more to the fore in diaspora studies, but also to highlight the role of diaspora in queer studies. Some key questions are: What role does sexuality play in diasporization? How are diasporic spaces differentiated by sexuality? How does sexuality interact with other factors such as race, class and religion to construct and heterogenize diasporic communities? How do transnational movements enable or hinder queer practices and subjectivities (Luibhéid 2004)? Another issue is the relation between queer diasporas and labour, namely, how paid employment offers opportunities to renegotiate one's status, for example, in the context of remittances or on one's ability to live as queer.

The queer diasporic body becomes the site where the racialized, ethnicized, and gendered disciplinary measures come together. Many diasporic women and sexual minorities find themselves caught between the gendered racism of host societies and hetero-sexism of their communities. Sexuality is a key site where concerns about family, community, culture, and assimilation are vigorously contested. Diasporic communities often challenge dominant cultural racism by policing the bodies and sexualities of its members, who are marked as repositories of ethnic identity, cultural embodiments of collectivities and their boundaries, and carriers of collective 'honour' (Yuval-Davis 1997). On the other hand, the construction of diasporic women as well as queer diasporas as victims in need of protection from their culture and community legitimizes state intervention and regulation of minority communities in the name of tolerance, freedom and equality.

The claim that the status of women and sexual minorities improves with diasporization can be traced to colonialist and racist assumptions that immigrant women and queers flee repressive contexts with exposure to modern and enlightened European culture and values translating into liberation and equality (Luibhéid 2004: 232). This narrative silences the discrimination experienced by female and queer diasporics in the West, who endure exclusion and violence from both their own communities as well as from mainstream heterosexual as well as gay society. Future scholarship needs to explore how queer diasporas transform ideas of family, nation, belonging and community by contesting the twin processes of masculinization and heterosexualization of the diaspora.

To conclude, diasporas are both provincial and cosmopolitan with a constant negotiation between these tendencies (Werbner 2002: 120). Diasporic groups are characterized by diversity, multiple consciousness and internal dissent. Subsumed under the term is a multiplicity of identities, experiences, histories, traditions, cultures, lifestyles and 'modalities of existence' (Brah 1996).

Further Reading: Grewal and Kaplan 1994; Patton and Sánches-Eppler 2000; Sharpe 2001.

DISABILITY

Rachel Adams

The United Nations Convention on the Rights of Persons with Disabilities defines disability as 'an evolving concept' that 'results from the interaction between persons with impairments and attitudinal and environmental barriers that hinders their full and effective participation in society on an equal basis with others' (UN Convention 2006). This definition highlights the interconnection of body, performance and environment in shaping the meaning of disability, and it acknowledges that these factors contribute to persistent discrimination against people with disabilities. Defined in this way, disability starts to look a lot like gender, a concept that also refers to the relation of bodies to acts and environment and that is the basis for inequities among a sizeable minority of the human population. Yet the relationship between the two terms is more than just an analogy. Gender and disability are inextricably related social, political, and historical phenomena, each working to define and illuminate the other.

The body is central to understandings of both gender and disability. Feminist critics have established the importance of decoupling sex – defined as the raw material of the body, from gender – the stylized repetition of acts by which the sexed body becomes identifiable as male or female (Rubin 1975). Although sex and gender typically correspond, sex need not be determinative of gender, as is evident in the examples of transgender and intersexuality.

Disability studies makes a similar distinction between impairment – defined as an acquired or innate bodily condition, and disability – the social and environmental factors that exclude people with physical and intellectual impairments from full participation in the social world. By this account, the body is differentiated from, although informed by, acts and environment. This is an important distinction because it shifts the problem of disability away from the impaired body and onto the limitations imposed by physical and cultural barriers. For example, a person in a wheelchair is disabled not by being unable to walk, but by the broken elevator that prevents her from accessing the upper floors of a building. People with autism are disabled by overstimulating or unfamiliar surroundings, while a deaf person is disabled in a context where verbal speech is the only mode of communication.

One way that people with impairments are disabled is by being seen as imperfectly gendered. In the eyes of able-bodied culture, disabled women are stigmatized as asexual, incompetent, and unattractive. Their right to parent is called into question, as if disability necessarily disqualified them from bearing and mothering children (Thomson 2002). Where disabled female bodies are seen as sexless and unmaternal, male bodies are feminized by disability. The passivity, vulnerability, and weakness associated with disability effectively neuter the male body, stripping it of the qualities of an idealized heterosexual masculinity. While there are obvious disadvantages to being degendered in these ways, some people with disabilities claim an empowering freedom from the traditional constraints of masculinity or femininity (Thomson 2002). Over the past two decades, the movement for disability rights has given rise to a prolific expressive culture that seeks to establish or reclaim the gender of the disabled body through literature and the arts (Crutchfield and Epstein 2000, Kuppers 2003, Thomson 2009, Siebers 2010).

Disabled bodies also confound the assumed correspondence between gender and sexuality. Disabled bodies are unconventionally gendered bodies. In an ableist society, people with disabilities are often seen as asexual. They are portrayed as both undesirable and lacking the same needs and desires as able-bodied adults. People with intellectual disabilities and those who require assistance of a caregiver have long been denied the right to sexual intimacy. At the same time, the sex lives of people with disabilities can also serve as a resource for complicating heterosexual norms (Siebers 2009). They may need the help of a third party, endure chronic pain, use prosthetic devices, or find pleasure in nonstandard positions or activities. But, given the complexities of human sexuality, it would be wrong to suggest that these departures from the norm apply only to people with disabilities. Rather than making a clear distinction between disabled and able-bodied sexuality, it is more accurate to say that disability offers a particularly vivid example of the diversity of all human sexuality. In this respect, there are obvious affinities between disability and queerness (McRuer 2006, Tremain 2005).

The disabled body is a hybrid body, one that is open to and shaped by its interactions with the world. Wheelchairs, prosthetic limbs, cochlear implants, and alternative communication devices form an interface between body and environment. Feminist theory has long been interested in the porous and shifting nature of embodiment. Scholars of gender studies have found evidence for the malleability of the human body in transsexuality, cosmetic surgery, and the health and fitness industry. Monsters, grotesques and cyborgs have been held up as feminist icons because of their shape-shifting abilities, their challenge to binary oppositions, and capacity to break down entrenched hierarchies (Haraway 1990; Braidotti 1994; Russo 1994). Although disabled bodies often inspire such figures, their material referents tend to be overlooked in feminist affirmations of their transgressive potential. The disabled body may be slower, more discomfiting, and less sexy than the imagined bodies of monsters and aliens, but it can tell us something important about the realities of undisciplined, hybrid forms of embodiment in a culture that presumes the body to be closed, singular and complete (Thomson 2002). Making disability an integral part of feminist understanding can help to invest theory with historical and sociological depth.

Disability also draws attention to the temporality of embodiment. The term 'temporarily able-bodied' refers to the fact that anyone who lives long enough will eventually become disabled. Disabilities that involve chronic pain and illness ebb and flow, meaning that the same person may experience different degrees of impairment at any given time. And because the majority of disabilities are not congenital but acquired, most people will experience life as both disabled and able-bodied. Theories of gender have been less attentive to the temporal dimensions of embodiment than has disability studies. The insights offered by the disabled body might provide a way of thinking diachronically about gender, attempting to understand how ideas about masculinity and femininity change over time, as well as the shifting experience of embodiment that comes with age.

Identity is another crucial point of intersection between disability and gender. Within the movement for disability rights, as in the women's movement, identity has been an extremely important, if vexed, basis for coalition. Second wave feminism began with the problematic assumption that 'woman' was a fixed and unitary category. Almost immediately, issues of race, class and sexual identity surfaced to trouble the idea that the struggle against gender oppression could be organized around a singular Woman. These fissures made it harder to define shared concerns and challenges, but they have also been tremendously productive of dialogue, debate and theorization. The concept of 'intersectionality' has been essential for understanding how multiple axes of difference work together to produce systemic social inequality (Crenshaw 1989). Identity has been no less significant to the movement for disability rights. However, disability differs from such relatively permanent forms of identity as race and gender in that one can become disabled at any time. A person cannot go to bed a woman and wake up a man, but she can cross the border from able bodied to disabled in an instant. Unlike 'woman', 'disabled' wasn't an identity until the disability rights movement brought it into being (in this, it is more akin to composite ethnic identities like 'Chicano/a' and 'Asian American'). Disabilities were compartmentalized into cases according to symptoms and types of impairment, each figured as discrete and particular unto itself. Such radical individuation has made it hard to imagine coalitions among such seemingly dissimilar groups as people in wheelchairs, those with chronic illness, the deaf, and people with intellectual disabilities (Siebers 2008). Claiming these disparate experiences as 'disability' enabled the formation of a coalition to demand the same kinds of political recognition that had been granted to women, GLBT people and people of colour. However, since the passage of the landmark 1990 Americans with Disabilities Act (and its British equivalent, the 1995 Disability Discrimination Act), the challenges of finding common ground among such divergent constituencies persist. Some argue that it is important to try, as disabled identity constitutes a source of strength and theoretical wisdom (Siebers 2010). Others argue that disability, by its very nature, confounds the notion of a stable, coherent identity and as such, should serve as the grounds to overturn all identitarian discourse (Davis 2002). Yet these positions are not irreconcilable. From the women's movement, disability studies might take an understanding of the strategic uses of identity, a necessary fiction that also serves as a powerful organizing tool and a source of knowledge.

The rationale for a conjoined consideration of disability and gender is not simply theoretical. Together, they illuminate important problems of social justice arising from such issues as selective abortion and caregiving. Reproductive freedom has been a cornerstone of the modern feminist movement because it is seen as the key to gender parity. Women cannot be equal citizens, advocates argue, without the ability to decide if and when to conceive. Many of those who otherwise oppose abortion believe that women should have the right to terminate a pregnancy in which the fetus is severely disabled. However, proponents of disability rights argue that the practice of 'selective abortion' denigrates not just the disabled fetus but all people with disabilities, by suggesting that their lives are not worth living (Saxton 1998; Hubbard 1990). At the same time, many in the disability community are strongly committed to women's reproductive freedom. Sensitivity towards *both* disability and gender is required to find a viable position that acknowledges the rights of pregnant women, as well as the potential personhood of the disabled fetus (Asch and Geller 1996).

The status of care and caregiving is another important matter of social justice illuminated by a joint consideration of gender and disability. In Western culture, care is gendered female and caregiving is accordingly marginalized and devalued. The majority of caregivers are women, whose work is often unpaid and unrecognized. Not only do women care for their own children and ageing parents, but they also dominate 'helping professions' such as nursing, teaching, social work and psychology. Care is essential to the rights of people with disabilities. However, the movement for disability rights has sometimes downplayed the issue of dependence, focusing instead on the importance of autonomy and self-determination. Placing a premium on independence as the prerequisite to citizenship and full personhood excludes many people with disabilities, such as those who require assistance for daily life activities and those who are incapable of self-representation. It also overlooks the caregiver, almost always a woman, whose labour, paid or unpaid, is unrecognized and inadequately compensated. Attention to gender places new emphasis on the political and social significance of care and caregiving. Taking caregiving seriously might also remind us of the ways we are dependent, recognizing interdependence rather than autonomy as an aspect of all social life (Kittay 1998).

Analogies between gender and disability can be traced back at least as far as Aristotle, who wrote of women as 'monstrosities' and 'mutilated males' (Thomson 2002). Such allusions are more than just figures of speech. Femininity has often been treated as a disability, a reason to bar women from full participation in society (Young 2005). So too, disability strips or reconfigures the relationship between body and gender, depriving men and women access to the idealized qualities of masculinity and femininity. Recognizing the long, entwined and reciprocal relationship of disability to gender can only enrich and broaden our understanding of both terms.

Further Reading: Davis 2010; Hall 2011; Thomson 1997.

FEMININITIES

Christina Scharff

Femininity can be understood as a culturally constructed ensemble of attributes, behaviours and subject positions generally associated with women. Over the last century, scholars have conceptualized femininity variously and from different disciplinary perspectives. Many influential conceptualizations of femininity have stressed its staged nature, arguing that femininity is something that is not *natural* but that is *done*, i.e. is socially constructed and continuously produced. For example, early psychoanalytic conceptions described 'womanliness' as a 'masquerade' (Riviere 1929). The French philosopher Simone de Beauvoir (1949) famously wrote that 'one is not born, but rather becomes, a woman'. And the ethnomethodologists Candace West and Don Zimmerman (1987) described gender as 'something that one does, and does recurrently, in interaction with others'. One central perspective, which continues to inform much contemporary research, is Judith Butler's performativity theory. Butler regards gender as the outcome of repeated performative acts, which create the illusion that femininity (and masculinity) is natural. Crucially, the performative character of femininity does not refer to wilful enactments of femininity. Performances of femininity are not planned or consciously put on, but are done continuously and, through that, bring femininity into existence. As can be seen from the title of this entry, it is now common to refer to femininity in the plural. The plural expresses at least three features of contemporary thinking about femininities: the socially constructed nature of femininities, the way they intersect with and are in part constituted by class, sexuality and race, as well as femininities' historical and cultural variability.

Femininities are multiple which means that a mapping of the field is necessarily incomplete. This entry focuses on femininities in contemporary Western societies and the Anglo-American context in particular. Here, research on femininities has been particularly vibrant in the emerging field of girls' studies, focusing mainly on the experiences of younger women. Key conceptual tools that are used to study contemporary femininities are the concepts of postfeminism and neoliberalism (see below). In light of prevalent discourses about women's alleged freedom in the West, and their patriarchal oppression in 'other' communities, femininities have also been studied through a critical postcolonial lens which critiques portrayals of Western sexual politics as more progressive. This entry attempts to highlight key issues in the conceptualization and study of femininities. The first section discusses the broader socio-cultural context where women's increased opportunities are celebrated and structural inequalities disarticulated. Instead of subscribing to such a celebratory account, the second section contours how femininities continue to be circumscribed and focuses on some of the ways in which they intersect with sexuality, race and class. The final section observes that contemporary power dynamics in relation to femininities seem to be increasingly lived out at the level of subjectivity, i.e. at the level of who counts, and does not count, as acceptably feminine.

Stories of female success

Femininities are lived out in a context that is characterized by both intense social change – with regard to employment, education and the private sphere – but also gender inequalities, and other forms of inequality, that are still deeply embedded in the socio-economic order. For example, women have been the driving force behind employment in the European Union in recent years; and yet, there remains a gender pay gap of around 17½ per cent (European Commission at www.ec.europa.eu). Although the terrain of femininities is marked by both opportunities and inequalities, discourses of gender equality and female success prevail. Shifts in late modernity, such as the feminization of employment, are perceived as unshackling women from the patriarchal past. Young women in particular are thought to have taken advantage of the feminization of labour with its emphasis on the flexible, presentable and capable *female* worker. The shift in the economy from that of production to consumption further privileges the feminine through the long-standing association between women and consumption (Gonick 2006). Now out of the domestic sphere and in work, financially independent and able to consume, young women are imagined to be able to 'have it all'.

The discourse of young women's success and improved opportunities resonates with a postfeminist and neoliberal context that makes it difficult to think and articulate inequalities. In a postfeminist era, feminism is said to have achieved its goals and, consequently, is forcefully repudiated (McRobbie 2009). Inequalities, such as the pay gap, become difficult to articulate. In addition, neoliberal expectations of individual responsibility call upon young women to manage their lives independently. Instead of supporting a collective politics, such as feminism, young women are called upon to deal with opportunities and challenges self-responsibly. This individualized positioning of young women is disturbingly well captured in the slogan of the Nike sponsored project 'the girl effect – the unique potential of 600 million adolescent girls to end poverty for themselves and the world' (www.girleffect.org). As Marnina Gonick (2006) noted several years ago, young women have come to represent one of the stakes on which the future depends.

The postfeminist and neoliberal story of female success is articulated in a context that frames Western societies as progressive, whilst depicting 'other', often Muslim countries and communities, as patriarchal and backward. As has been shown by a wide range of critical feminist research, discourses of sexual liberation shape orientalist narratives of Western modernity as opposed to traditional discourses. Sexual freedom is linked to secular, rational, liberal subjectivity. Muslim femininities, for example, are regarded as being determined by culture, while secular femininities are constructed as autonomous, precisely because of their alleged ability to step in and out of culture. Neoliberal and postfeminist discourses construct 'Western' femininities as liberated and free. The intelligibility of this construction involves processes of othering, whereby some non-Western communities are constructed as fundamentally different from 'the West'. These binary oppositions fail to capture differences both within the West and those communities depicted as 'other'. Religion and culture are portrayed as the sole factors shaping femininities, leaving no room to account for the ways in which sexuality, race and class intersect with gender in particular contexts.

Intersections with sexuality, race and class

While sexual liberation features prominently in discourses of Western superiority, femininities continue to be shaped by heterosexual norms. Heterosexuality is frequently imagined to be an indispensible element of 'proper' femininity. Although the links between sex, gender and sexuality are not fixed and can be taken up differently, heterosexual conventions structure the doing of femininities. For example, feminism and femininity are frequently perceived as mutually exclusive. Feminism is commonly associated with man-hating women, with lesbians and with women who are and look 'unfeminine'. Women may reject feminism because they do not want to be associated with man-hatred, lesbianism and an absence of femininity. While femininities are lived out differently in relation to feminism, negotiations of feminism provide insight into the workings of heteronormativity, and how it shapes femininities.

Femininities are not circumscribed by sexuality alone, but also by race and class. Beverley Skeggs (1997) has argued that dominant notions of what constitutes respectable femininity tend to be grounded on, and evoke, images of white, middle-class women. This shows that not everyone is positioned equally in relation to notions of respectable femininity. A critical analysis of femininities must therefore attempt to identify the inclusions and exclusions produced by prevalent conceptions of who counts as feminine. For example, research on race and beauty has highlighted the influence of whiteness as a yardstick for beauty, privileging white/light skin, straight hair and what are seen to be European facial features. Non-white women have been found to be excluded from representations of beauty, or included to the extent that they approximated the appearance of whiteness, or could be framed as exotic beauties. While beauty standards are contested, change over time and are becoming more inclusive (Craig 2007), they remain unattainable for many. And yet, beauty matters particularly in an era where femininity seems to be increasingly understood as a bodily property. In a Western and postfeminist context, femininity tends to be no longer associated with psychological characteristics and behaviours (such as being nurturing or caring and having homemaking or mothering skills). Instead, femininity is increasingly understood as a bodily characteristic and is associated with having a young, able-bodied, and 'sexy' body (Gill 2007). Exclusionary and unattainable beauty standards, in conjunction with an understanding of femininity as a bodily characteristic, point to the boundaries around desirable and respectable feminine appearance.

Sexuality, race and class affect the ways in which femininities are lived out. However, as explained above, the conjunctures of postfeminism and neoliberalism suggest that successful femininity is attainable for all. Feminism, so the logic goes, has achieved its goals in contemporary Western societies. If women find themselves in disadvantaged positions, it is their fault. Structural inequalities become individualized and women are called upon to manage opportunities and challenges self-responsibly. While structure and culture are over-determined in discourses about non-Western gender regimes, social structures seem to disappear almost entirely from narratives of Western, female success. As Valerie Walkerdine (2003) has however argued, the neoliberal emphasis on self-transformation and fashioning of the self is bourgeois; the neoliberal, autonomous subject is middle-class. Success and self-realization are not equally available to everyone. On the contrary, failure is inbuilt in the neoliberal imperative to become somebody, revealing the illusionary character of notions that 'everybody can do it'.

Normative femininities and subjectivity

While material and structural inequalities continue to shape the gender order, it appears that power dynamics in relation to femininities are increasingly negotiated at the level of subjectivity. Reflecting the individualizing tendencies of postfeminism, and the ways in which power works in and through the subject under neoliberalism, some of the exclusions related to femininities seem to play out in terms of intelligible (normative, acceptable) and abjected (outside the normative realm, unacceptable) subjectivities. The figures of the imperilled Muslim woman, the feminist that transgresses heterosexual boundaries, the woman who does not have the right appearance, or the woman who lets herself go and does not try hard enough to live up to the demands of neoliberal subjectivity, mark some of the boundaries of the terrain of normative femininities. These boundaries are contested – for example in the resurgence of feminist politics in several countries. However, conceptualizations of the terrain of femininities increasingly attend to the ways in which power operates on and through the making of subjectivities. These subtle workings of power call into question discourses of Western women's emancipation; not simply in terms of highlighting old and new inequalities, but also in terms of demonstrating that the very promise of freedom and autonomy may produce its own exclusions and constraints.

Indeed, analyses of femininities will ask questions about the psychic life of femininities. How do women deal with the ambivalences produced by cultural environments where new modes of regulation exist alongside discourses of female success, and where the convergences of postfeminism, neoliberalism and processes of othering foreclose a critical engagement with regulatory norms? Crucially, power constellations are also challenged and subverted. Feminist researchers have emphasized and shown that women are not cultural dupes, but that they exert agency, even if they do so under conditions that are not of their own making. Contemporary feminist research thus explores how intersecting power dynamics play out in the terrain of femininities but also focuses on the ways in which power relations are subverted. Currently, there is a vibrant field of research on femininities that crosses various disciplines, such as sociology, critical psychology, gender studies and cultural studies. While this entry has focused on young women in contemporary Western societies, feminist researchers study femininities in various geographical sites, exploring a broad number of topics ranging from analyses of celebrity magazines and makeover shows to examinations of the experiences of older women, female migrants, and (new) forms of feminist activism (Gill and Scharff 2011). Most research conceptualizes femininities as socially constructed and spatially and temporally contingent, and attempts to explore their intersections with sexuality, race and class.

Further Reading: Aapola et al. 2005; de Beauvoir 1949; Nayak and Kehily 2008; Riviere 1929; West and Zimmerman 1987.

THE FEMINIZATION OF POVERTY

Lavinia Mitton

The 'feminization of poverty' refers to the argument that women increasingly form a disproportionate percentage of the world's poor and that their risk of poverty is increasing. The term was first coined in the 1970s in US debates about single mothers and welfare and was linked to questions about the vulnerability of female-headed households (see Pearce 1978). Pearce highlighted the irony that although women's employment had increased dramatically and legislation had enhanced opportunities for women in education and the labour force, their likelihood of living in poverty was increasing relative to men. Pearce argued that the feminization of poverty was occurring for two reasons: first, that women could not earn enough to be self-sufficient because of occupational segregation and low wages and second, that both the private and public transfer system for supporting children were seriously flawed, in that in the private system the funds were too meagre and in the public system the enforcement too limited.

Labour market conditions are some of the reasons why women in general have higher poverty risks than men. Women more often interrupt their employment. Employers can be less willing to invest in training for women because they expect to have smaller benefits. As a result, in some countries, women participate less in work related training, work in jobs with lower status, and, except at the start of their working lives, have shorter work experience. Further, single women more often take care of children than single men. Since the upbringing of children is demanding, single women with children are more likely not to work, or to work part time. Even if they work full time, they will tend to work in jobs that pay less well than the jobs of men and of women without children. For poor women earning income can compound heavy burdens of domestic work and thereby undermine well being. Whether single men and women without a job will be poor depends to a large extent on the social security arrangements in their country.

Demographic differences between single men and women can also be a cause of gender differences in poverty. The result of the difference in life expectancy between men and women is that elderly people are predominantly female and many are without partners. Gender differences in poverty are likely to be larger among older singles than among younger singles for two reasons: first, because of cumulative disadvantage during their life course (e.g. the effect on earnings of having had a career break) and second, because the current cohort of older women have not been able to profit from increasing opportunities in education and the labour market as much as younger women have.

Strategies for minimizing gender differences in poverty rates

The feminization of poverty has been observed in many industrialized countries, although countries differ considerably in the extent to which their labour markets and welfare states create or equalize poverty between women and men (Christopher et al. 2002). Casper, McLanahan and Garfinkel's (1994) cross-national comparison revealed that there is a choice of strategies for minimizing gender differences in poverty rates. For example, in Sweden, the key to having a low gender gap in poverty rates was employment: Swedish women and men had very similar rates of labour force participation. Thus, Sweden shows that economic equality by gender can be achieved by equalizing employment patterns for men and women. A second strategy is to take steps to encourage men and women to marry and stay married. Casper et al. (1994) also argued that a low gender gap in poverty rates can be achieved in countries with a generous welfare system where policies do not encourage women to enter the labour force, but instead protect unmarried women by providing a relatively high income floor beneath which no citizen is allowed to fall.

When looking at the cause of female : male poverty ratios it has been shown that how much poverty is feminized is not closely associated with the extent of overall poverty in society and is a distinct social problem (Brady and Kall 2008). As Bianchi (1999) concludes, the divergence between the trend in the absolute poverty levels of women and the trend in their poverty rates relative to men therefore requires some caution about measures as well as the interpretations we attach to the notion of the 'feminization of poverty'.

Characterizations of the 'feminization of poverty'

The term 'feminization of poverty' entered development vocabulary in the mid-1990s. Since then it has been much discussed in both academic and policy circles. Of particular concern has been the observation that the feminization of poverty would appear to refute the idea that economic development and growth are generally accompanied by a trend towards the lessening of patriarchal gender relations and advancement in the status of women. Despite its currency, there is ongoing debate about what the feminization of poverty means. Common characterizations of the 'feminization of poverty' listed by Chant (2007: 1) are that women experience a higher incidence, depth and severity of poverty than men; that for women poverty is more likely to be persistent and difficult to escape and that there are significant associations between the 'feminization of household headship' and inter-generational poverty. Perhaps most important is that women's disproportionate burden of poverty is rising relative to men's. Nevertheless, there are various problems with the 'feminization of poverty' thesis, both conceptually and empirically, and therefore in terms of implications for policy. One of the problems is that the 'feminization of poverty' is often used in a vague and unsubstantiated manner and, if income inequality is stressed, it does not necessarily highlight aspects of poverty that are most relevant to poor women. Chant (2008) argues that there are few theoretical or practical reasons to continue using the term as it is currently construed and deployed, that is, with a focus on women's monetary poverty and an over-emphasis on female-headed households.

Over-emphasis on income

One can ask: what is the meaning of poverty? Various authors, including Fukuda-Parr (1999), have stressed that the feminization of poverty is 'not just about lack of income'. Poverty can mean more than a lack of what is necessary for material well being: it can be defined as the denial of the opportunities and choices most basic to human life. Income, along with longevity, can be less rigorous in assessing women's relative deprivation than other criteria such as access to land and credit, powerlessness, legal and inheritance rights, vulnerability to violence, overwork, and (self)-respect and dignity. A person without adequate income may not be excluded from decision-making or participating in the life of a community, and may enjoy good health. It is therefore relevant that in societies throughout the world women face restrictions on their choices and opportunities that men do not. These factors can be more relevant for a gendered understanding of poverty than income poverty alone. In consequence there is a problem with using income as a key indicator of gender gaps in poverty on account of the fact that it fails to capture dimensions of poverty that can be most meaningful to women (Chant 2009).

Intra-household resource allocation

Not only has measurement often been cast in a narrow framework of poverty that focuses on incomes alone, but also on the household as a unit, a focus that leads to ignoring intra-household disparities (Fukuda-Parr 1999). Since information on incomes, consumption and assets are usually only available at the household level they are difficult to convert into individual equivalents without problematic assumptions about equality of distribution, or about the different needs and preferences of individual household members. Feminist research has shown that inequitable resource allocation can often lead to 'secondary' poverty – poverty that arises not through low income but by the uneven distribution of that income among women and children in male-headed households. Therefore, for many women the capacity to command and allocate resources may be considerably more important than the income of their households.

Emphasis on female-headed households

Female household heads have been used as a proxy for 'women' in poverty research (e.g. Goldberg 2010). Putting stress on the links between female headship and poverty suggests that when women are without men their situation is worse. Yet women may positively choose household headship as a means by which they are able to enhance the well being of their children or exert more control over their own lives. Without a male head, households may be able to distribute household tasks and resources more equitably.

The feminization of responsibility and obligation

We must also take into account gender differences in inputs to household livelihoods to a greater degree, as well as their outcomes for women's lives. Chant (2008) argues for re-orienting the 'feminization of poverty' in a manner that more appropriately reflects trends in gendered disadvantage among the poor and which highlights the growing responsibilities and obligations women bear in household survival. Gender differences in time and labour inputs are of significance to a 'feminization of poverty'. For example, in some economies where men are finding it harder to be the primary breadwinner they are not significantly increasing their participation in domestic work either. Further, care in budgeting for expenditure often falls to women, with the responsibility for household survival burdening women disproportionately with no corresponding increase in rights and rewards. Women often prioritize expenditure on the family and sacrifice personal spending on themselves. Yet women's efforts to cope with poverty do not necessarily give them much power in negotiating with men. This may be reinforced by cultural notions of what behaviour is deemed 'feminine' and the homogenization of women as a single group. Yet, to take one national example, there are distinct origins and patterns in the United States of women's poverty across racial and ethnic lines (Elmelecha and Lu 2004). Women's risk of poverty is also crosscut by other factors such as stage in the life course, household circumstances, education, and employment, which can place women at particular risk of vulnerability and privation, all of which can make it difficult to generalize about the situation of women.

Empirical evidence

There is also debate about whether such a trend can be confirmed empirically. Beyond the apparent paradox posed by the disjuncture between women's rising capabilities and opportunities, and assertions about their worsening poverty relative to men in some countries, another problem attached to monetary emphasis in the 'feminization of poverty' is that while it may be the easiest dimension of deprivation to quantify, relevant data are extremely scarce (Chant 2008). It has been argued that 'poverty has a woman's face – of 1.3 billion people in poverty 70 per cent are women' (UNDP 1995: 4). But as Rodenberg notes: '... there is too little gender-specific data to substantiate the oft-quoted figure of 70 per cent. Nor are there sufficient data to prove that there is a trend toward a "feminization of poverty"' (Rodenberg 2004: 1). Irrespective of whether we consider households or individuals, another major problem in sustaining the 'feminization of poverty' thesis as a trend is the dearth of sex-disaggregated panel data that permit longitudinal comparisons.

Conclusion

Given the diversity among women it is important to have a gender-aware approach to poverty and not to simplify problems, as generalizations that describe women as 'poor' risk obscuring women's potential and strength. The narrowing of gender concerns into an income poverty agenda can reduce the scope for working for gender equality generally, and can thereby become a hindrance to the identification of adequate interventions.

Nevertheless, the concept of the 'feminization of poverty' has proved persuasive enough to gain the attention of policymakers and practitioners. It has been recognized in 'gender budgeting', in which the differential impact of change in government tax and transfer systems by gender is analyzed. According to Wennerholm (2002: 10–11) its conceptualization as a term has called for women to be recognized more in the development process and led to advocacy on behalf of poor women. In the process this has helped to raise the status of women's concerns in national and international discourses on poverty and social development (Chant 2008). An increasing amount of resources has been directed to women in the interests of their economic advancement through education, vocational training, micro-credit and other forms of gender specific assistance. The term 'feminization of poverty' may be poorly elaborated or substantiated but it is nonetheless a succinct and hard-hitting slogan, effective as a way of underlining the point that poverty is a 'gendered experience' (Chant 2008: 171).

Further Reading: Chant 2007; Daly and Rake 2003; Goldberg 2010.

FEMINISM AND PSYCHOANALYSIS

Ranjana Khanna

Gender is a term that has only recently made its way into the psychoanalytic lexicon, and the related vocabulary of psychoanalysis has been the source of contestation whether in battles concerning scientific technicalities, accuracy, authenticity, or the spirit of translation, and jargon and the prosaic. None of this is surprising given the international reach and interdisciplinary purchase of psychoanalysis as a field of clinical practice and critical thought. Gender has not historically been in the vocabulary of psychoanalysis partly because the term exists in its specificity and in distinction from sex in only one of the four dominant psychoanalytic languages – English. By contrast *Geschlecht* in German, *genre* in French, *género* in Spanish all designate type, kind, genre, sex, and all have grammars in which nouns carry gender not necessarily associated with male or female bodies, particularly of course in relation to the neuter. Contemporary theories of gender (for example Butler 1990) nonetheless are indebted to psychoanalysis for its theorization of sexual difference, which begs the question of the specificities concerning the use of the term *gender* for which translation is impossible.

At its inception, psychoanalysis, largely through the figure of Freud, considered diverse ways in which matters of sexual difference and its psychical manifestation played out, and these are the precursors to what we understand as the notion of gender in psychoanalytic thought today. The famous phrase 'anatomy is destiny' that Freud borrowed and adapted from Napoleon's 'geography is destiny' highlights usefully how debates around psychoanalysis and gender have occurred in distinct languages – is gender a matter of body (anatomy/sex) or context (geography/gender)? Are these to be thought in opposition? And does psychoanalysis favour one over the other, or does it try to understand both alongside the epiphenomenal (psychical manifestation of the biological and the contextual). Freud wrote of primary and secondary characteristics; associations of masculine activity and feminine passivity though these were not necessarily tied to biological certainties of male and female; and sociological issues that distributed power and priority in diverse ways in different cultures and periods in history (1905: footnote added in 1915: 220).

In the early days of psychoanalysis, there were fewer struggles over a question of relative biologism in Freud's work than argument over androcentrism, highlighting in a sense that sexuality and sexuation – a non-biological and non-identificatory process of gendering – took place in psychic life rather than in either biological or social life. Karen Horney, Ernest Jones, Helene Deutsch and Melanie Klein in the 1920s and 1930s, for example, all took issue with the Freudian register in which pre-Oedipal infants seemed to have masculine desire, partly because the clitoris was associated with the penis in the phallic phase that followed the oral and the anal phases of infant development. Because sexual difference manifests itself only through the oedipal phase in Freud, the clitoris and penis as sources of pleasure are both diminutive versions of the phallus, and this phallic phase, as it were, becomes an important ground that traverses in to the desiring distinctions, which occur in the period in which the child moves from the desire to kill the father and sleep with the mother, through to sexual identification (not identity) characteristics or 'masculine and feminine attitude' an object choice that he frames within the context of normative heterosexuality. An identification model was thus built around the idea of castration. But beyond identification, an implicit idea of sexuation emerged that is a theory of gender (though counter to a theory of gender that understands it in terms of cultural or social construction): the unconscious relation to the phallus, and therefore the existence of a relation to a phallic economy that affects all subjects whether male or female.

Freud understood the Oedipal phase to distinguish boys from girls who did not greatly differ before that moment. Between approximately three to six years, children negotiate their own role while contemplating the relationship between their parents. More often than not, this leads to sexual jealousy, erotic longing, and is accompanied by envy for the penis and castration anxiety when the children recognize the difference of their genitalia from that of the other. Freud analyzes the path through the Oedipus complex into normative heterosexuality as being more difficult for girls than for boys. Girls have to undergo a change in the sex of the love object – from mother to father, and then onto another male, whereas boys simply transfer their affection from the mother to another woman. The girl's transfer of affection from female to male is ascribed by Freud to penis envy. On recognizing that she has no penis, she apparently seeks one from her father, which results in the reproductive desire to have a child. Both the male and female child and adult become Subjects who manifest unconscious desires, rather than conscious beings who direct the world or who exist at its centre, ideas that trouble any easy relation between psychic and legislative life, feminist politics organized around consent, or the distinction between fantasy and consciousness so central to some modes of feminist thought about issues such as consent.

Doubt was raised as to whether girls ever gave up their attachment to their mothers (Deutsch 1944), whether the model was fatalistic and whether there was a corresponding envy for and denial of the vagina (Horney 1967: 147–61), whether something like penis envy could have the status of a primary symptom through which girls were propelled into femininity (Jones 1927 [1948]), and whether the penis was as significant as the withdrawal of the breast by the mother, or womb envy (Klein 1928 [1988]: 186–98). One could take issue with the biologism of Horney, the moralism of Deutsch, the investment in the originary feminine mother of Klein, as Juliet Mitchell did (1974), but they were important in their ongoing investment in psychoanalysis as a tool for understanding the unconscious processes of sexuation, even if their criticism of Freud would be taken up by those who were less sympathetic to his work, such as Kate Millet (1970), Germaine Greer (1970), and others. Joan Rivière (1929) who was a significant precursor of the gender theory espoused by Judith Butler, and who translated much of Freud's writing into English, theorized sexual difference in terms of masquerade rather than in relation to anatomy or indeed a notion of depth. For Rivière, femininity was a mask of social performance, but it was unclear if there was anything beneath it. Many later feminists, including Simone de Beauvoir in *The Second Sex* (1949) and Betty Friedan in *The Feminine Mystique* (1963) raised similar questions, and these became increasingly important for feminist cultural criticism and theory.

Simone de Beauvoir claimed that psychoanalysis was biologically determinist, and she is often credited with the beginning of 'gender' theory when she wrote that 'one is not born, but rather becomes a woman' (de Beauvoir 1949: 267). De Beauvoir criticized psychoanalysis's androcentrism, frustrated by the way in which psychoanalysis foreclosed the possibility of its rejection by seeing this as misunderstanding the work it performs, and by its doctrinaire attitude if you accept any part of it. If the penis is to be envied, she claimed, it would be because of the value attributed to it, and this would have to be explained and explored. She suggested the penis could as easily be the object of disgust. Socially constituted sovereign power, like that attributed to the father, needed, in de Beauvoir's view, to be explained in terms of social and material forces rather than biology or indeed sexuality. While she did not reject psychoanalysis in its entirety, she criticized most of what characterized it: the concept of sexual difference, the unconscious, and transference – or the presenting of symptoms to authority figures.

Betty Friedan was not unsympathetic to psychoanalysis, but felt it was outdated. Concepts such as penis envy, she thought, may have been more relevant to turn-of-the-century Vienna than for American women in the 1960s, and findings Freud assumed to be biological were now proved to be social. She took issue with his treatment of his family, and also his mother's overbearing devotion. For the most part, she was frustrated by doctrinaire approaches to psychoanalysis, which she thought had a detrimental impact on women, and perpetuated a feminine mystique (1963: 166–94).

Object relations theory, which began with the work of Melanie Klein, offered an alternative to the focus on the penis and the phallus (1928 [1988]). Klein emphasized the importance of the pre-verbal maternal bond with the infant in the first year of life and the way the infant makes strong bonds with objects. The prototypical object is the breast, which is good or bad depending on whether it feeds the child or is withheld from it. Klein understood a process of gendering through a theorization of melancholia as a known loss of polysexuality in the advent of a kind of compulsory heterosexuality, something that Judith Butler will address later in her theories of disidentification, gendering and sexuality.

Jacques Lacan offered an interpretation of the concept of penis envy that was shaped by the linguistic theories of Ferdinand de Saussure. Lacan questioned the idea that sexual difference was shaped by the absence or presence of the penis, and wrote instead of the relation to the phallus. For Lacan, the phallus was a signifier of desire, the symbolic form of the penis. The phallus became the symbol of sovereign desire that was shaped by the notion of the Symbolic – literal or abstract representation and communication. Lacan's work falls broadly into three phases – from 1953–64, when he elaborated a reading of Freud through his seminars and drew from his work in the 1920s and 1930s at the Hôpital Sainte-Anne and concluded that the unconscious was structured like a language. At this time, he theorized the notions of the Symbolic, the Imaginary and the Real, but emphasized the Imaginary – the identification with a specular image. In this phase of his work, gendering was associated with the signification of the phallus. From 1964–74, when he was more concerned with his forumulae and mathematics to explain his findings, he became more focused on the Symbolic. From 1974–81, when he focused on the notion of the Real – that which is outside representability, he developed his notion of sexuation, an understanding of the masculine and feminine position adopted in the unconscious in terms of phallic (masculine) and Other (feminine) jouissance – extreme and anxious pleasure.

In the first phase of his work, which was influenced by Klein and by Rivière, he posited the presence and absence of the Phallus as the organizing force behind the Symbolic (Lacan 1982 [1958]). The Phallus appeared to the infant as if it were something possessed by the father (Lacan 1982 [1958]). Lacan emphasized that everyone was in a relation of lack to the Phallus. Its status as a privileged or primary signifier meant that it came to represent all that the infant, and the Subject more broadly, lacked. The Oedipal structure is writ large through the concept of the Symbolic. In the pre-Oedipal early stages of infancy, which lies outside of the realm of representation, the child lacks nothing. At least, retrospectively, that absence of lack is imagined and projected. At the first moment of recognized need, the child perceives that it lacks something, and begins to perceive its separation from the mother. The child imagines that the mother can no longer fulfil all of its needs because of a rival affection for the father. The mother, as primary object of desire, is in this understanding, the phallus, and the father is in possession of the phallus, creating the idea of being or having the phallus as how sexual difference is perceived. The male is perceived to have the Phallus, the female is perceived to be the Phallus (1982 [1958]). The theory of sexuation from 1972/1973 relied less on identification and more on an asymmetrical and non-complementary notion of the masculine and feminine such that the feminine was the site of the jouissance of the Other. This insight was adapted thoroughly, in spite of their differences in jouissance theory, by Julia Kristeva (1984), Luce Irigaray (1974), and Hélène Cixous (1975).

Much of the scholarship that emerged in the 1970s relating to questions of psychoanalysis and feminism drew on this Lacanian intervention, and in some instances defended psychoanalysis as a crucial mechanism for analyzing patriarchy, rather than as a symptom, defender and labourer for its cause. Juliet Mitchell (1974) and the work of the group *Psychanalyse et Politique* paved the way for an emphasis in feminist psychoanalytic thought on the unconscious manner in which we come to relate to the laws governing society, the relation between production and reproduction in the context of the family, what constitutes a subject in and of society, and how this understanding might help us overthrow the patriarchal family. Similarly, Gayle Rubin's notion of the sex/gender system (1975) focused on how biological bodies became gendered through kinship patterns, which are about forms of prohibition and the heterosexist norms of subjectivation. Whether such prohibition would be all encompassing or whether it could give rise to unconscious resistance to the perils of identity became a topic of debate among psychoanalytic feminists (Rose 1986). Luce Irigaray (1974) developed a notion of the economy of the same through a psychoanalytic paradigm that thought with and against Jacques Lacan. Her theory of sexual difference describes an economy of the same (the *hommo-*) that dominates phallic thinking and sexual relation. The less than full subject 'woman' lives alongside this phallic economy but does not fully inhabit it, giving those who experience life as women access to an alternative economy of difference (the *hetero-*). In this understanding, man and woman are not biological entities necessarily, but the manner in which they are positioned as such materially by a phallic economy presents them in a binary relation within an economy of the same. Man-same and woman-same then, exist within a masculine phallic economy of sameness. Difference, understood as the *feminine* (that not captured by an economy of the same), may be accessed more easily by partial subjects of a phallic economy that cannot fully subjectivate. This theory of gender, then, gives rise to a concept of the one (phallic) that dominates, and the possibility of the more than one understood through the terminology of the feminine but not tied to any notion we already have of that.

It would be a misreading of Irigaray to think of her as essentialist, and too swift to see her as ahistorical even though she finds a common thread of a phallic economy from Plato to Freud. Her theories provide an opportunity to consider different and specific unconscious relations to the phallic economy through the particularities of clinical life, class and geographical difference and distinction, varied moments of alternate relations to the dominant depending on colonial relation, class position, familial structure etc. as differentiated access to the economy of the same. This opens up not an intersectional approach but one that rather understands the specificities of relation to the dominant – how gendering functions in the specificities of unconscious life in any given context even if the notion of the subject is entirely different from that developed in Vienna in the 1900s (Spillers 1987; Spivak 1993; Khanna 2003; Weinbaum 2004).

Further Reading: Dimen and Goldner 2002; Moore 2007; Ragland-Sullivan 2004; Salecl 2000; Schor and Weed 1997.

FEMINIST ECONOMICS

Kanchana N. Ruwanpura

Introduction

Feminist economics is increasingly accepted within mainstream academic circles as a key intervention made by feminists to challenge and question the assumptions underlying orthodox economic thinking. Its accomplishments are many. A high-profile academic journal entitled *Feminist Economics*, influences in diverse international organizations, and an annual conference lay testimony to its success. Moreover, these various mediums together offer a platform for representing the diversity of feminist economics.

While feminist economics has gained increased currency in recent times, feminist emergence within economics is not new. Healthy debate from feminists on the nature and value of economics to understanding gender relationships and issues started emerging in the 1970s. Many of these interventions were limited to challenging the premise of heterodox economics – in particular Marxist thought – rather than the orthodox and other heterodox paradigms. Yet it is important to remind ourselves that even prior to this a few women economists were making pioneering inroads within economics, as scattered and infrequent as they may have been (Pujol 1992, Dimand et al. 2000, Best and Humphries 2003).

Feminist contributions since these times have shifted to tackling head on mainstream and orthodox economic theories. With a growing group of liberal feminists registering their disenchantment at the ways in which particular research agendas are side-lined within the economics discipline, the journal *Feminist Economics* lay testimony to the disquiet within economics. The need to recognize feminist concerns within economics had firmly established itself and feminist scholarship had made inroads into yet another academic field. This entry starts with an outline of values embedded within feminist economics and provides some discernible attributes of the feminist economic paradigm. After this précis, it offers a brief synopsis of the evolution of feminist thought within economics to its maturity today by way of concluding this entry.

Feminist values

Economics, contrary to common understanding, is a pluralist social science with a diversity of standpoints. Austrian, Neoclassical,

Classical, Keynesian, Institutionalist and Marxist economics are some key schools of thought, reflecting an ideological spectrum that spans from the right-wing to left-wing. Yet it is also the case that there is a dominant view within economics, which at this current juncture is neoclassical economics that emphasizes the primacy of the market place and market-led values to shape social life. Contradictorily, however, it frustrates the space for a market place of ideas and diverse standpoints. Since neoclassical economics dominate spheres as disparate as academic departments and influential policy-making circles as the World Bank and the International Monetary Fund (IMF), it is this paradigm that has been subject to much feminist criticism and interventions in the past two decades. What are some of the main concerns of feminists with mainstream economics? This section offers a brief outline of the essential underpinnings of feminist values that inform feminist economics.

Neoclassical economics operates on the premise that people operate as detached and rational agents that engage in market relationships on the principle of self-interest. The values of self-interest and rationality coming together is claimed to lead to competitive behaviour for scarce resources, with this allegedly leading to the efficient allocation of scarce resources. This story line adopted and promoted by neoclassical economics, feminist economists argue, suffers from a partial understanding of human behaviour and social relationships. We point out how these assumptions informing neoclassical economic theorizing neglect the ways in which human beings are connected to each other (Waller and Jennings 1990, Ferber and Nelson 1993, Ruwanpura 2008). Consequently, it overlooks cooperative behaviour that exists between people, within communities and social groups, with the paramount focus of the mainstream economic paradigm becoming about efficient outcomes rather than equity issues.

These facets, however, are not the only anxiety that feminist economists have with mainstream economics. Feminist economists also point out that economics as a discipline emerged at a particular historical juncture and in a particular spatial setting – that of Enlightenment Europe, which was a project dominated by men. They argue therefore that the social construction of economics reflects ideals of this period and of the men in charge of the enlightenment project. Masculine values get valorized and are represented as leading to detached, autonomous and hence objective social science research inquiry. Feminist economists using 'scholarly work on the social construction of science suggests that objectivity is more of a social than an individual phenomenon' (Ferber and Nelson

1993: 11); hence, they point out, many of the values that are purported to reflect objective science are 'emotionally loaded and culturally constructed' (ibid.: 12). By uncovering the ways in which scientific practice is deeply embedded in gender ideals, the purpose of feminist economists is to 'investigate and remedy the biases that may arise from an unexamined emphasis on masculinity' (ibid.: 11).

Feminist economists' challenge to mainstream and neoclassical economics then is that its use and deployment of mathematical models, its assumptions of economic agents as 'separative selves' and the penchant for modelling are reflective of androcentric biases inherent in both the ways in which the discipline is designed and operates. They point out that these assumptions and methods in orthodox economics reveal masculine values and consequently the topics researched tended to reflect these biases. Because of this particular form of theorizing, other values and narratives, that incorporate women's realities of nurture, altruism, cooperative behaviour, negotiation of power relationships and so forth, are excluded in neoclassical economics. Feminist economics, therefore, seeks to rectify this imbalance through its research and scholarship agenda. Therefore, in an effort to reflect more fully the diversity, complexity and richness of human life and social relationships, it seeks to research into the intersections between different spheres of feminist values, interests, themes and methods.

Feminist economists also acknowledge – sometimes implicitly while at other times explicitly – that it is not simply women's voices, interests and values that are disregarded by economics. Interests and values of other women and men (i.e. African-American communities for instance, people of the Global South, etc.) are also denied a fair hearing within the field of economics (Charusheela and Zein-Elabdin 2003). In this regard, neoclassical and mainstream economics is not simply guilty of masculinist biases but also of race, ethnic and class predispositions (Saunders and Darity 2003, Albelda et al. 2004); hence, the particularity of its paradigm and its consequences for social life is brought to bear by feminist economics.

Given the plurality of economics it is not only neoclassical economics that was and is challenged by feminist economists. Feminists similarly scrutinize Marxist and Institutional economics. Marxist or socialist feminist economists point out that while Engels (2010) was a pioneer in identifying the oppression faced by women in and outside of family relationships, it also remained the case that feminist concerns were not the pivotal point of interest for Marx and Engels. Since their aim was to establish political economy and scientific socialism as a science, they downplayed feminist and women's rights issues that were raised by utopian socialists during the time (Folbre 1993). Yet feminists working within the tradition of Marxist and socialist economics were much earlier in debating rigorously the need to pay attention to women's issues and gender relationships within their paradigms (Humphries 1977, Barrett and McIntosh 1980).

The resurgence by liberal feminist economists challenging neoclassical economics is more recent in comparison: kick started a mere two decades ago. Institutional economists too have been similarly slow to respond to feminist issues. As Jennings (1993) points out, while Thorstein Veblen recognized feminist themes in his appreciation of culture at the turn of the twentieth century, later institutional economic scholarship did not take on board this particular thread and expound upon it. It is more recently that institutional economics has elaborated on the convergence of thinking between Institutionalism and feminism (Waller and Jennings 1990). Jennings (1993) thus points out that given Veblen's insights and criticisms of the dualistic thinking inherent in mainstream economics and his development of the need to acknowledge the role culture plays in economic processes, his framework lends easily to feminist economic concerns. Similar shifts are at play within Keynesian economics, with feminist economists making arguments for enriching the existing paradigm by making a case for the incorporation of core concerns of feminists (Todorova 2009). Feminist economics at this juncture therefore spans politically from the right to left, from the Global North to the Global South, and is informed methodologically from diverse standpoints.

The trajectory of feminist economics

Even as feminist economics started establishing itself from the early 1990s, and many of the successes now known can be traced to these efforts, economics has had its fair share of early feminist pioneers. It is only recent research that is uncovering the important contributions these women made to the disparate fields within economics (Pujol 1992; Dimand et al. 2000; Best and Humphries 2003). Yet their fundamental discomfort with the public/private distinction underpinning much economic thinking and the ways in which this led to neglect or devaluation of women's role in the political economy gets emphasized in these interventions. An appreciation of the real world and pursuing theoretical advances through empirical work (rather than vice versa) are hallmarks of this early scholarship. In this way they expounded an alternative view of human nature – one that recognized that humans are not always and necessarily bound by the false dichotomies that separate the individual self from other social connections and relationships.

Early women economists contributed theoretically in fields as varied as imperfect competition to capitalist imperialism and growth of the firm within economics; some important feminist contributors from yesteryear are Millicent Garrett Fawcett, Harriet Taylor, Rosa Luxemburg, Edith Penrose and Joan Robinson. Their important contributions to the discipline are worth reminding ourselves of because they show that feminist strands in economics are not recent and women economists from early on felt deep-seated disquiet at the way in which the discipline was fashioning itself (Pujol 1992). While many of these women economists are gaining prominence through research done by contemporary feminist economists today, it underscores the need for an alternative framing of economics.

Since that time, it took until the 1970s for a perceptible feminist strand of debate to enter economics. Much of these discussions were largely limited to the challenges by feminists to heterodox economics, in particular to Marxist economics. Their main complaint was the ways in which the sexual division of labour (paid and unpaid) was neglected or downplayed; the debates by Humphries (1977), Hartmann (1979) and Barrett and McIntosh (1980) were an effort at invigorating these key concerns. Once these themes were brought to the fore, feminist economists gravitated towards unpacking the contributions of reproductive labour and carework to society and economic life. Issues to do with prevailing gender inequalities in terms of lower pay, occupational segregation and gender budgeting are all areas in which feminist economists have made significant contributions since then (Albelda et al. 2004).

However, women working on development economics were starting to confront the limitations associated with the dominant paradigm and the policies that stemmed from alongside it. Esther Boserup (1970) was pivotal in this regard. She brought to the fore the notion that economic modernization in the Global South was actively detrimental to the welfare of women because economic development policy stemmed from androcentric biases. Yet women economists like Krishna Bharadwaj were also making their mark felt through their involvement in the policy-making sphere in early post-colonial India (Dimand et al. 2000), while Gita Sen's contributions towards a gendered perspective on development was an important catalyst for feminist economists. She (together with Caren Grown) through research and action sought to mobilize women in the South to challenge inequitable social, economic and political relations at global, regional and national levels. Their network (DAWN – Development Alternatives with Women for a New Era) mobilized feminists to create the space for feminist alternatives in the spheres of livelihoods, living standards, social justice and rights (Sen and Grown 1987). Their contributions led the way for sustained feminist economic engagement in spheres of economic development, growth and sustainability and its implications for women and children. Current debates within feminist economics extend within and beyond the different schools of economic thought to connect to interdisciplinary conversations, with influences ranging from post-colonial studies to intersectional legal theory (Brewer et al. 2002, Ruwanpura 2008).

Recent liberal feminist challenge to neoclassical economics then is part and parcel of a reputable trajectory, with them joining a vanguard of feminist economists, such as Randy Albelda, Teresa Amott, Lourdes Beneria, Nancy Folbre, Heidi Hartman, Jane Humphries, Julie Matthei and Gita Sen, who have been in the forefront recording their uneasiness with a patriarchal construction of economics. Their confrontation began well over three decades ago. By now orthodox economics has to accept that feminist economics is an undisputed player within the discipline, academia, scholarship and policy circles. For these and other reasons, it remains the case that there are many women economists who would shy away from the label of feminist economics, while there are men economists who would associate with and identify themselves as feminist economists (Ferber and Nelson 2003).

Feminist economics is no longer an emerging paradigm within economics; while it is still a growing field, most feminist economists would confidently state that it is no longer in its infancy. The existence of this entry as a conceptual piece lays testimony to its strength within academic circles and scholarship.

Further Reading: Agarwal 1995; Charusheela and Zein-Elabdin 2003; Elson and Pearson 1981; Klasen 1994; Sen 1990.

FEMINIST EPISTEMOLOGY

Alessandra Tanesini

Epistemology is the study of knowledge and justification. It is concerned with delineating their scopes, limits and natures. In the twentieth century analytic philosophers focused their attention on a very narrow range of definitional questions, whilst feminist epistemologists have been much broader in their concerns. Feminist work has covered ground in the philosophy, history and sociology of science and has raised questions concerning the relations between knowledge and ethics, science and values. Besides the notions of knowledge and justification, feminist epistemologists have addressed issues of trust, epistemic authority, silencing, ignorance and intelligibility. Often they have put issues of justice and power relations at the centre stage of their enquiries.

Some of the earliest work in feminist epistemology was done by practising scientists who highlighted the androcentrism and the sexism that permeates their disciplines. Science, they note, is androcentric in several ways. Researchers commonly consider males as the paradigmatic example of humanity, and females as deviant or inferior; and they ignore women's experiences and needs. Hence, for example, many early trials of drugs for the treatment of cardiac problems were experimented exclusively on male patients. Science also devalues knowledge that is typically associated with women and values knowledge associated with men, granting it the honorific title of science. This fact has been made manifest by Ruth Ginzberg's work on the history of gynaecological medicine (1987). She notes that the knowledge possessed by midwives was thought to be little more than 'old wives' tales', whilst male doctors were considered to have science on their side. For this reason women were strongly encouraged to move away from home births assisted by a midwife to hospital births in the care of a medical doctor, despite the fact that initially this change resulted in a significant increase in the mortality rate of women in childbirth (pp. 98–100).

These early critics also highlight the sexism of scientific institutions. This manifests itself in the widespread and systematic discrimination encountered by women who want to become scientists. Hilary Rose (1994) was among the first to highlight this problem. Fortunately, in recent years some progress has been made on this point with the development of the Athena SWAN Charter for Women in Science. Another aspect of this early feminist research is its focus on uncovering the sexist assumptions that often lay unchallenged in the background of scientific theories and experiments. Thus, for instance, Anne Fausto-Sterling (1985) exposes many problematic presuppositions and errors in the science of gender differences in mathematical and other cognitive abilities. Her analyses have more recently been updated by Cordelia Fine (2010).

Arguably this early work does not challenge head on traditional conceptions of science as aiming to produce knowledge that is objective, impartial and impersonal. Instead, this research endeavours to find where science falls short of the very standards it has set for itself. This approach, which singles out sexist and androcentric scientific knowledge as simply bad science, has been described by Sandra Harding as a form of feminist empiricism (1986).

So conceived, feminist empiricism is only one of the three approaches in feminist epistemology identified by Harding in her *The Science Question in Feminism* (1986). She names the other two as Feminist Standpoint Epistemology and Feminist Postmodernism. Harding's tripartite characterization is still widely used and it informs the best current survey of the topic provided by Elizabeth Anderson in her 'Feminist epistemology and philosophy of science' (2011). In recent years, however, the boundaries between these approaches have become blurred and different methods of classifying versions of feminist epistemology have emerged.

Early feminist empiricism, as I have mentioned, subscribes to the view that knowledge should be value neutral. It also endorses the claim that the identity of the individual knowers and the composition of their community of enquiry should not matter in determining whether knowledge has been gained. For these reasons, empiricism takes knowledge not to be situated or relative to a perspective. All of these points are rejected by all other feminist approaches to knowledge. Feminist standpoint epistemology in particular, at least in its earliest versions, develops the view that some knowers, in virtue of the position they occupy in society, have some forms of epistemic privilege at least with regard to some areas of enquiry.

In its earliest incarnation feminist standpoint models closely Marxist's accounts of the standpoint of the proletariat. For Marx the working class in a capitalist society has privileged access to the facts concerning the mechanisms of production under capitalism. They have such privilege because as workers (as opposed to those that are outside the labour market) they have first hand experience of these mechanisms, and because, due to their underprivileged position (as opposed to that occupied by the capitalist), they have no standing self-interest in the perpetuation of the system. For these reasons, the workers' view of capitalism is more likely to be accurate than the views prevalent among any other social class. Nancy Hartsock's feminist standpoint (2003) is based on an analogy with the Marxist version. Feminists have a privileged understanding of patriarchy because they have experience of the mechanisms of reproduction in the patriarchal system without having a vested interested in its continuation.

This version of standpoint theory has been subject to numerous criticisms raised by other feminists. Two have been particularly prevalent. The first is the observation that standpoint is committed to essentialism or some form of false generalization (Spelman 1998). The second, related criticism, is that standpoint leads to 'clinging to marginality' (Spivak and Rooney 1994: 162). Standpoint epistemology is said to imply essentialism because it presumes that all women share some experience of oppression merely by virtue of being women. In other words, standpoint would wrongly ignore the way in which different dimensions of oppression interact with each other. So it would presume that all women experience sexism in the same way and that the experience of racism is something distinct and separable in the experience of black women. Further, standpoint would lead to the presumption that one can speak only from one's own standpoint. By licensing individuals to speak as a woman, or as a lesbian, it simultaneously licenses others to treat the speaker as having limited epistemic authority. She who speaks as a woman has only the limited authority of women, and can thus be safely ignored by men.

Both criticisms lead to the elaboration of some versions of feminist postmodernist epistemologies. This latter is not really a unified approach but it is more of a tendency which is characterized by a few commonalities. Two are perhaps the most prominent. Postmodernists deny that there is a single standpoint. Instead, they claim that there are many, each corresponding to a different perspective or subaltern group. Postmodernists are also sometimes prone to denying the difference between power and justification. They, therefore, exhibit a tendency towards scepticism about the discipline of epistemology itself (Flax 1990). It would be a mistake, however, to assume as it is sometimes done by their critics that all postmodernist feminists endorse extreme forms of scepticism and relativism. Donna Haraway (1991), for instance, is keen to preserve a role for objectivity once it is properly reconceptualized.

Despite their differences standpoint and postmodernist epistemologies share a commitment to the situatedness of all knowledge because their supporters assert that the locations of the knowers make a difference to the knowledge that they can produce. In this context 'location' is not to be conceived simply as a matter of geography, but also as a matter of history and of power. One's location is thus understood in terms of the whole multiplicity of social phenomena that make up the identities and social positions of individuals. Epistemologically speaking, feminists have promoted a politics of location that requires reflexive awareness of the nature of one's own social and material privilege (Rich 1986). As a result some white feminists have tried to examine how their own whiteness has influenced their politics so as not to leave their privilege unexamined and unquestioned. This notion of location has also been used by other feminists to foster and promote forms of oppositional agency that emerge out of the simultaneous occupation of multiple, both privileged and under-privileged, positions (Mohanty 1992). Reflection on these kinds of multiple locations has informed and refined ideas concerning multiple standpoints.

Standpoint and postmodernist epistemologies also share a common rejection of the early empiricist assumption that values, biases and preferences are always a source of error in scientific and other cognitive enquiries. Instead, their supporters claim that some biases can be a positive resource. Thus, standpoint epistemologists claim that the adoption of some value-laden perspectives are conducive to the development of better science. Feminist values in particular would play a significant role in development of knowledge that is more complete and accurate *because* it is informed by these values (rather than *in spite of* their influence).

Both critics and some supporters of feminist epistemology have pointed out the paradoxical nature of this conclusion. This is what Louise Antony dubbed 'the bias paradox' (1993). Either biases are always bad, and feminists are entitled to criticize others for their biases but are not entitled to defend theirs. Or at least some biases are OK. If the latter, one must provide some good arguments to distinguish the good biases from those that are bad. Much contemporary feminist philosophy of science is concerned with the articulation and defence of this distinction. It often begins by noticing that biases in research are inevitable. Due to the under-determination of theories by the available empirical evidence, the choice of one theory over its rivals that are equally supported by the evidence will have to be based on evaluative considerations such as simplicity, consistency with other accepted theories, explanatory power or technological applicability. Thus, theory choice is dependent on the satisfaction of numerous values or standards, and science is never value neutral.

It might be argued that this defence of the value-ladennesss of science fails to explain how values can be a positive resource. A recent prominent defence of precisely this claim has been developed by Anderson and is based on two broadly pragmatist moves (2011). First, Anderson claims that truth is not the sole goal of enquiry because we are equally interested in information that is relevant and not misleading. Moreover, only values can help to separate relevant from irrelevant or trivial information. In this manner values are a positive resource. Second, values help to individuate the right questions to ask at the start of any investigation. Without values, as a matter of fact, no enquiry would ever start since we would never ask any questions unless we cared about or valued finding an answer.

In recent years questions about ignorance, trust and testimony have been the focus of intense attention by feminist epistemologists. The immediate stimulus of this attention has been Miranda Fricker's *Testimonial Injustice* (2007). In this influential work Fricker considers some of the injustices that are done to women and members of other underprivileged groups because they are not taken to be credible or authoritative. More specifically, Fricker highlights cases of testimonial injustice where the claims of members of subordinate groups are not taken as seriously as they deserve because of prejudice against taking members of that group to be authoritative about the topic under discussion. She also discusses hermeneutical injustice which occurs when a community lacks the interpretative resources to make sense of the experiences of members of a group. Often this lack of resources is due to the epistemic marginalization of the individuals whose experiences are thus made unintelligible. For a long time both the experiences of being sexually harassed and of being raped by one's spouse belonged to this category as the conceptual means to understand them as anything other than banter in one case or sex in the other were generally lacking.

Fricker's work is best seen as the continuation of a thread in early feminist concerns about knowledge and understanding. This thread is exemplified both by Lorraine Code's early work on the identity of the knower (1991) and by Genevieve Lloyd's (1984) history of the concept of rationality. Code in particular focuses her discussion on the importance of paradigm shift in epistemology. This shift is intended to be twofold. First, she suggests that we take knowledge of people, rather than knowledge of propositions, as the central case of knowledge about which one should theorize. Second, she advances a view which she called 'responsibilism' that moves questions of intellectual character, integrity and authority to the centre stage of enquiry. Further, she develops an account of character in terms of the intellectual virtues such as wisdom, courage, prudence and intelligence. This approach, which suffered from early neglect, is now being rediscovered by both feminist and mainstream epistemologists and offers significant promise for future developments.

In conclusion, as I hope this brief entry has made clear, feminist epistemology is a very varied concept. It has fostered different approaches and is currently being developed in novel ways.

Further Reading: Alcoff and Potter 1993; Anderson 2011; Tanesini 1999; Wylie 2003; Zack 2002.

FEMINIST POLITICS

Jonathan Dean

Politics is fundamental to feminism, and yet one of feminism's most important contributions has been to challenge dominant conceptions of politics. Indeed, many feminists argue that politics – broadly defined as the creation, maintenance and contestation of power – is not just one dimension of human life among others, but something that shapes all aspects of our lives. In this sense, feminism could be said to be at core a *political* enterprise: it is concerned with analyzing, critiquing and transforming power relations, particularly those that create and maintain gender inequality. Because of the broad reach of the political dimensions of feminism, feminist politics is a diverse and varied terrain, both within and outside academia. Contemporary academic feminism offers us a fruitful range of perspectives from which to think differently about contemporary political life and – despite widespread claims in mainstream media to the contrary – few aspects of modern politics are untouched by feminism, and political action by feminists is ongoing, and even flourishing, in many parts of the world.

The diversity of feminism notwithstanding, one can identify four particularly crucial issues to which the term 'feminist politics' may refer, which will each be examined in more detail. These are, first, feminist contributions to debates about the meaning of the concept 'politics'; second, feminist analyses of – and influence within – mainstream political practices and institutions; third, feminist movements for political change and, finally, conceiving feminism itself as a site of political contestation. And although in the interests of clarity they have been separated here, they are closely interlinked and are likely to overlap in specific contexts.

Feminist challenges to 'politics'

Perhaps the most crucial aspect of feminist politics is its capacity to challenge and rethink dominant understandings of what politics is fundamentally about. Very broadly speaking, politics is concerned with power, and for most people this means politics is about who is able to exert power and how that power is exercised. At a more prosaic level, the study of politics has traditionally focused its attention on certain kinds of *public* activity, such as the workings of state institutions, relations between states, political decision-making, and certain forms of public participation such as voting or pressure group activity. However, feminists have challenged this conventional, state-centred view of politics in at least two ways. For one, feminists from at least as far back as Mary Wollstonecraft (1982 [1792]) have highlighted how women are frequently excluded from this particular vision of politics. Citizenship – conceived broadly as the right and the capacity to participate in public decision-making – is a *gendered* concept: the archetypal active citizen has historically been seen as male. This meant that the rights of *man* affirmed by the French and American Revolutions were not initially seen as being extendable to women (or indeed other disenfranchised social groups). This was, one may argue, not because of active and conscious discrimination against women. It was instead a consequence of the unexamined belief that women, by their very nature, could not become rights-bearing individuals. In her famous *Vindication of the Rights of Woman* Mary Wollstonecraft contested this picture of 'female nature' by affirming women's capacities for reason and rationality: there could be no basis, other than the spurious social norms of the day, to arbitrarily deny women access to the political realm.

Subsequent generations of feminists have explored further dimensions of the male-centredness of political life. Feminist political theorists such as Carole Pateman (1988) and Susan Moller Okin (1990) have, for instance, highlighted how the traditional liberal divide between the public and the private realm, in which only (specific parts of) the public realm is reserved for the exercise of political citizenship, has excluded women from politics due to the prevalence of cultural norms (e.g. concerning housework and childcare), tying women to the private, domestic domain. The history of feminism is littered with examples of women defying their socially proscribed confinement to the private sphere, and demanding access to the hitherto male domain of political citizenship. These include demands not only for formal, legislative change (such as the provision of equal voting rights), but also for changes in cultural attitudes: indeed, a frustration with widespread sexist attitudes within the male-dominated left was crucial to the emergence of the women's liberation movement in Britain in the 1970s (Segal et al. 1979). But feminists have not only demanded access to public life on equal terms with men: they have also argued for a 'de-gendering' of the public realm. Rather than claiming – as Wollstonecraft did – that women should be allowed into politics on the same terms as men, other feminists have suggested that what is needed is a different vision of public life less characterized by attributes traditionally associated with men (such as rationality, impartiality and objectivity) (Young 1990).

Whilst the transformation of the public sphere has been central to the history of feminism, a further, equally important, feminist contribution to our understandings of politics has been to call into question the view that matters of private life and domesticity fall outside the conceptual boundaries of politics. Central to the eruption of feminist activism that took place in many countries across the world in the late 1960s and into the 1970s was the creation of a shared sense that women's private lives were marked by unequal power relations with men. This led to a flurry of new political and academic work seeking to make sense of the ways in which male dominance shaped all aspects of society. This new 'sexual politics' (to use the title of Kate Millett's famous text from 1970) meant that housework, intimate life, childcare, domestic violence, rape, women's health, beauty and self-esteem (to name but a few) became *politicized* (Millet 1977 [1970]; Brownmiller 1977). These issues, previously understood as non-political, became sites of intense debate and contestation. Historically, this period in feminist history (sometimes dubbed 'second wave' feminism) coincided with the (re)politicization of a range of other issues including class, race, sexuality and the environment. Feminism was thus a crucial part of a broader historical process that substantially increased the range of sites and issues that we might consider to be 'political'. Feminist politics, therefore, brings sharply into view the limitations of thinking of politics as restricted to the activities of state institutions.

Feminism and the state

Despite its emphasis on non-state based forms of politics, we must not lose sight of feminism's important contribution to the study of state institutions. In this sense, 'feminist politics' may refer to feminist influence on, and insights into, the workings of mainstream political institutions such as parliaments, the civil service and the legal system. This understanding of feminist politics invites us to ask questions such as: to what extent are women's political priorities different to men's? Are there significant gender differences in attitudes to specific issues, policies or individual politicians? How receptive are political institutions to a gender equality agenda? What are the gendered impacts of supranational political institutions? And what are the explanations for, and consequences of, the persistent under-representation of women in political institutions in most parts of the world? The latter question has been a particularly topical issue in recent feminist debates, not least because it poses difficult broader questions about the political status of the category 'women', and the relation between theory and practice. Indeed, theoretical reflection on political representation by feminists such as Anne Phillips (1995) and Joni Lovenduski (2005) has fed into ongoing discussions among academics and practitioners about the advantages of using quota systems to move towards a more representative gender balance among elected representatives.

In addition, feminists have devoted considerable attention to analyzing state institutions' responses to feminist demands for gender equality. In many parts of the world, recent decades have seen the development of a variety of institutional mechanisms – including quotas, the implementation of equality legislation, gender mainstreaming, gender budgeting and the establishment of women's policy agencies – aimed at promoting gender equality in state institutions and in government policy (Squires 2007). This is a notable development, as traditionally many feminist political theorists were suspicious of the state, often framing it as a key agent in the maintenance of male domination. And there is no doubt that many states in all parts of the world continue to be actively hostile to women's participation in public life, but the picture is far from uniform. Many feminists have emphasized how, for example, the Scandinavian experience of 'woman-friendly' welfare regimes, along with the willingness of many states to legislate against gender inequality, suggests that states are not simply or uniformly hostile to feminism. In part taking inspiration from Nordic feminist insights into profeminist state institutions, much recent feminist political analysis has consisted of comparative studies of the relative success of 'state feminism' in different national contexts (Outshoorn and Kantola 2007). Again, the interest in 'state feminism' can be read as indicative of the importance of a gender-analysis of state institutions, despite feminism's ambivalence towards 'state-centred' conceptions of politics.

Feminist movements for political change

Part of feminism's ambivalence towards 'state-centred' conceptions of politics can be explained with reference to the history of feminist movements. As indicated above, one might say that, at heart, feminism is a *political* movement that aims at bringing into existence more egalitarian gender relations. To this end, feminist social movements have intervened politically both at state level (e.g. by campaigning for the provision of anti-discrimination law or for changes in legislation relating to sexual and reproductive rights), and in almost all spheres of social life (e.g. by challenging dominant attitudes to female sexuality, critiquing representations of women in popular culture or contesting dominant divisions of labour in the household). Feminist politics – conceived in terms of activist movements agitating for more equal gender relations – is therefore astonishingly diverse.

Many existing accounts of feminist movements (and indeed feminist theory) highlight three dominant strands: radical feminism (emphasizing the structural character of women's oppression and the centrality of male violence against women), liberal feminism (prioritizing legislative reform and women's participation in mainstream political life) and socialist feminism (emphasizing the intertwinement of gender and class inequality). However, this tripartite analysis was always rather too simplistic, not least because many forms of activism and theory took inspiration from more than one strand. This typology also struggled to accommodate various forms of black feminism and lesbian feminism, among others. Since the late 1980s, the liberal/radical/socialist triad has also been called into question by emergence of so-called 'third wave' feminism, a strand of feminist activism and theory initially spearheaded by younger women in the US. Third wave feminists argued that their second wave predecessors (particularly, but not exclusively, radical feminists) were sometimes prescriptive and doctrinaire, insufficiently sensitive to diversity, and had produced a body of feminist theory that was not easily applicable to the different experiences of the generation of women who grew up in the aftermath of the second wave (Baumgardner and Richards 2000). However, 'third wave feminism' has been criticized by some for its alleged lack of critical political awareness, and for unfairly portraying their second wave predecessors as puritanical and unfeminine. But more generally, there is a strong sense that neither the classic radical/socialist/liberal triad, nor the generationally inflected wave metaphor, adequately capture the complexity and diversity of contemporary feminist activism and theory. This is partly because both are firmly rooted in the Anglo-American feminist experience, and thus not easily exportable to other contexts. Perhaps more important, though, is the fact that the vibrant and diverse forms of feminist activism across the globe, and their complex intersections with anti-racist, socialist, anti-imperialist, lesbian and gay and other forms of politics all defy easy categorization into any given theoretical perspective or history of feminism.

But this vibrancy and diversity of feminism transnationally might come as a surprise to some: much recent commentary on feminism, particularly in the global North, has tended to claim that it is in decline, and that we have now entered a 'post-feminist' age in which feminist social movements are no longer influential or relevant. Even those sympathetic to feminism can often be heard claiming that, in contrast to the political fervour and radicalism of the 1970s, contemporary feminist activism is lacking in vitality and influence. Such a view has some truth in some contexts, but many have drawn attention to the continued influence of feminism as a movement for social change across the world. For instance, recent scholarship on feminist activism has explored, among other things, the impact of feminist NGOs, the role of women activists in supranational organizations (such as the EU and UN), promotion of a gender equality agenda, the production of alternative media by young feminists, the presence of feminism in the anti-globalization movement, mobilizations of feminists across national borders, and the extremely complex intersections of feminism with other forms of progressive politics (Mohanty 2003; Eschle and Maiguashca 2010; Basu 2010). The current economic crisis has also seen renewed feminist scholarship and activism, often focused on the ways in which governments' deficit-reduction measures typically impact more adversely on women than men. These ongoing forms of activism refute the sceptical claim that feminist activism's time has passed, and reaffirm the continued centrality of feminism to ongoing forms of protest, resistance and activism around the world.

The politics of feminism

As indicated above, there are of course substantial disagreements within feminism about how to characterize contemporary feminist history, and how to make sense theoretically of contemporary gender relations and movement politics. Because of this, it is important to highlight that 'feminist politics' also refers to the ways in which feminism itself is a site of political debate and contestation.

The crucial point here is that feminism is not simply concerned with intervening into and changing the world around it. Any historical account of feminist theory and activism will also refer extensively to debates *within* feminism. Very often, such debates concern the status of groups who have historically been marginalized within the feminist community, including ethnic minority women, lesbian, bisexual and transgender women and working class women. On occasion, these debates have proved divisive and traumatic, but they have meant that contemporary feminists, for the most part, are adept at critically reflecting on forms of power and inequality within feminism, as well as in society at large. This is evidenced by ongoing discussions about the ways in which hierarchies of race, class and sexuality are present in feminist spaces, and also – within academia – how feminist knowledge production continues to be marked by inequalities in power and resources between academic communities in different parts of the world. Furthermore, debates about the connections between feminism and other kinds of politics, the status of 'gender studies' as an academic discipline, the role of men in feminism and the conceptual status of the sex/gender distinction could all be read as instances of feminism becoming both subject and object of critical reflection. For many, these continued debates have proved challenging, but feminism's willingness to continually tackle them head on is testament to its dynamism in the context of rapidly changing political and intellectual landscapes.

Taken together, these four dimensions of feminist politics all imply a profound interrogation of dominant conceptions of politics both within and outside the academy. The fact that feminism often provokes unease in mainstream political science (and intellectual life more broadly) is testament to this, and underscores the importance of continuing to examine the rich and diverse interconnections between feminism and politics.

Further Reading: Blakely and Bryson 2007; Dean 2010; Hawkesworth 2006; Phillips 1998; Walby 2011.

GENDER AND DEVELOPMENT

Kalpana Wilson

'Development' is frequently viewed as originating with President Truman's 1949 speech in which he called for a 'bold new program for the improvement and growth of underdeveloped areas'.

But the concept of development initially emerged in the nineteenth century as a means through which 'order' would be brought to the constant, chaotic and potentially dangerous 'progress' associated with capitalism and accumulation on an ever-expanding scale (Cowen and Shenton 1995: 34). However the notion of constant progress itself was defined in counterpoint to the non-European societies whose resources provided the basis for European capitalism. These societies were collectively constructed as collectively devoid of agency and thus incapable of progress. Only under the direction of benevolent but despotic colonial rulers, it was claimed, could progress be achieved (ibid.). These racialized notions of 'trusteeship' and the civilizing mission thus deeply influenced the elaboration of ideas about development, and continue to do so.

It was in the post-1945 Cold War era, however, that development came to be the dominant framework through which unequal relationships between the global South and the global North were understood. Although this was a period in which contesting models of development struggled for dominance, the focus of initial feminist critiques of development was the modernization approach that was integral to the promotion of US economic and geostrategic interests in the global South. Modernization theory was structured around a series of differences – urban/rural, modern/traditional, productive/unproductive – which reproduced both the hierarchies of 'race' (Kothari 2006) and the gendered dichotomy between the public and the private. 'Third World women' were associated with the 'backward', unproductive element and targeted by development initiatives focusing on their reproductive roles, notably population policies (Hartmann 1995)

Ester Boserup's seminal study 'Women's role in economic development' (Boserup 2007 [1970]) questioned the way development theory, policy and practice ignored and marginalized women's role as producers. Even in the context of sub-Saharan African farming systems where women played a central part in cultivation, she argued, colonial and post-colonial administrators assumed women's place was in the home. These preconceptions meant that policies such as those relating to the introduction of cash crops and the promotion of new technology in agriculture 'promoted the productivity of male labour' while excluding women.

This notion of exclusion was the starting point for the Women in Development (WID) approach, which combined equity and efficiency arguments to call for women's inclusion in the processes of modernization. WID advocates suggested that prejudice and stereotyping by development planners, employers (and sometimes women themselves) meant that women were excluded from participating in the productive sphere, where they could prove just as efficient and productive as men. WID-based initiatives focused on women's education, training and access to technology that would make them more productive and improve their access to the market. In practice this often meant handicrafts and small-scale income generating projects. The WID approach is rooted in two interconnected sets of assumptions: those of neoclassical economics in which individuals are utility maximizing and economic growth comes from the exercise of individual choice supported by the institutions of private property and the free market; and those of liberal feminism which emphasizes women's capacity for rational thought and action and seeks equality with men in the public sphere. Thus WID identified discrimination against women within the development process, but did not place it in the context of gendered structures of power, or relate unequal gender relations to those of class, race or imperialism. The challenge to this approach mirrored and extended contradictions within feminist movements globally, in particular the debates between liberal and Marxist feminists, and the critiques which Black feminists in North America and Europe, and feminists located in the global South, were articulating in relation to the dominant narrative of liberation and 'global sisterhood' (Sen and Grown 1985).

Crucially, Gender and Development (GAD) theorists argued that rather than focusing on inclusion of women in processes of capital accumulation, these processes and their gendered implications must be problematized (Beneria and Sen 1981). GAD theorists argued for the recognition of reproductive labour that remained invisible or naturalized in WID approaches. For example, income generating projects targeted at women often increased women's overall work burden by failing to recognize the domestic labour they were already undertaking. Within this framework, they critiqued the tendency of WID initiatives to treat 'women' as a homogenous category with shared interests, and to promote policies, which addressed them in isolation. Instead, gender was recognized as socially constructed and an important category for social organization. For example, GAD analysis of women's participation in the labour market looked at how gender relations in the household and beyond both affect and are in turn affected by the nature of this participation and the particular conditions under which it takes place. (For a full discussion of the transition from WID, via 'Women and Development' (WAD) to GAD approaches see Razavi and Miller (1995)). But while the language of gender and development and a stated commitment to gender mainstreaming now pervades development discourse and policy, these debates and the underlying contradictions they reflect continue to be sites of contestation. WID approaches, which were compatible with the neoliberal turn, have remained dominant within development institutions such as states, the World Bank and other international organizations, and the majority of NGOs.

Scholars working in the broad field of gender and development have contributed significantly to the understanding of questions of the gender division of labour, social reproduction and the gendered distribution of resources. Like other feminist thinkers, they focused on the household as an arena of inequality and conflict. Rejecting the neoclassical model of the household as a unit characterized by altruism, in which all members seek to maximize a joint utility function, they highlighted the unequal gender distribution of resources and power within households. It was argued that members of households had differential bargaining power, which depended on the 'value and visibility' of their labour (Kabeer 1994). The work of feminist anthropologists, particularly on agrarian household production, went further in highlighting regional differences in gendered labour processes and household structures which shape 'appropriability, control and autonomy at different stages of household resource management' (ibid.: 117; Kandiyoti 1988). These themes recur in critiques of policies directed at female-headed households which categorize them as the 'poorest of the poor' without taking into account that women may have more control over both resources and decision-making within these households (Chant 2007).

With the rise of neoliberalism, these concerns were increasingly incorporated into a project of developing a gendered critique of the political economy of global capitalism. The gendered impacts of policies of economic liberalization and of the Structural Adjustment Programmes that many states in the global South were compelled to adopt by the International Monetary Fund and the World Bank from the 1980s onwards were explored in depth. In particular, policies, which drastically reduced social provision, were identified as significantly increasing women's reproductive labour as well as their responsibility for income generation (Elson 1991). Gender and Development theorists also highlighted the mobilization and consolidation of gender subordination by global capital in factories employing mainly young women, generating ongoing debates about the implications of this employment for gender relations (Elson and Pearson 1981, reproduced in Visvanathan et al. 2011; for an example of more recent work see Ngai 2004). Later these came to be linked to a wider concern with the 'feminization of employment' understood as encompassing processes of casualization, flexibilization and informalization, as well as the relative growth in service sector and care work (Perrons 2009).

Inevitably, much Gender and Development thought has been marked by ambiguity about whether it is primarily engaging with development policy makers or feminist political movements. For example, Molyneux's important distinction between women's 'practical gender needs' (those which relate to their existing gender roles) and 'strategic gender interests' (those involving a transformation of gender relations) originally referred to women's movements (Molyneux 1985) but was subsequently incorporated into frameworks for development policy planning. This ambiguity has been deepened by the growing emphasis on the role of 'civil society', and of NGOs in particular, as agents of development within the dominant neoliberal development paradigm since the early 1990s.

Post-development approaches, drawing on a post-structuralist theoretical framework, have questioned the notion of development itself, critiqued the hierarchical assumptions and binaries of 'traditional/modern' and 'backward/progressive' within development discourse and sought to revalorize the 'local' as a source of different understandings of the world. In this vein, ecofeminist thinkers highlighted associations between women and nature, linking women's oppression with the degradation of the environment from the colonial period onwards (Mies and Shiva 1993). But it has been argued that this approach continues to essentialize the women to whom it refers, while romanticizing local communities and failing to recognize that social movements may be informed by alternative visions of development rather than rejecting development altogether (Kapoor 2008).

The essentialized construction of 'Third World women' within gender and development has been the focus of postcolonial feminist critiques, notably Mohanty's influential 'Under Western Eyes' in which she argued that 'Third World women' are constructed within gender and development discourses as 'a homogeneous "powerless" group often located as implicit *victims* of particular socio-economic systems' (Mohanty 1984: 338) to be saved by Western feminists. This has contributed to a much greater emphasis on identifying women's agency and promoting empowerment in more recent gender and development work. However, the turn to agency and empowerment is also consistent with a shift in neoliberal development policy in the 1990s. With evidence of deepening poverty resulting from the neoliberal policies of the 1980s, the World Bank and other institutions focused attention on addressing poverty while retaining the neoliberal model, and arguably further extending the gains of global capital. This was variously known as the Post-Washington Consensus, the new poverty agenda, or the New Social Policy. In this framework, empowerment and participation were closely related to ideas of individual responsibility and self-help. The growth of cost recovery, co-financing and co-management schemes along with community participation and voluntary work shifted the burden of responsibility onto poor households, and specifically poor women. At the same time, they were directly subordinated to the disciplines of the market in new ways (Molyneux 2008).

These changes have accompanied a shift from a 'needs-based' to a 'rights-based' discourse in development. Considerable scepticism about the substance of this change has been expressed within the GAD literature, with observers highlighting the fact that, particularly in the global South, many states, to whom rights claims are to be addressed in this model, have been progressively weakened by neoliberal policies, and are frequently not in a position to meet such demands (particularly those for economic rights), being primarily accountable to international financial institutions and donor governments, rather than their citizens (Tsikata 2004).

The contradictions surrounding the emphasis on agency and the accompanying shift to 'rights' in development are evident in the discourse of reproductive and sexual rights, in which gender and development writers are increasingly advocating a greater focus on pleasure and sexual agency, questioning the tendency in earlier development interventions to frame sexuality exclusively in terms of risk. Yet this leaves unanswered questions about who defines the terms of this agenda and about the power relations inherent in all development interventions. Meanwhile, however, other theorists have engaged more critically with this discourse, emphasizing the continuing centrality of the control and regulation of sexualities to global capital accumulation and governance (Lind 2010) and questioning the continuing heteronormativity of gender and development theories and analysis.

Recently the appropriation and transformation of feminist ideas within neoliberal approaches to development has been increasingly highlighted. Kate Bedford (2007) describes how, drawing on the now considerable body of work on masculinities in GAD, some World Bank initiatives are promoting greater involvement of men in household work in order to facilitate women's labour force participation. This is occurring in the context of further shifts away from state and corporate responsibility for social reproduction and the promotion of the heterosexual family as the only remaining 'safety net'. More broadly, there is argued to be a growing instrumentalization of gendered compulsions on women to work harder and spend more of their income and resources on their children's well being. This underpins the World Bank's slogan 'Gender Equality as Smart Economics' (World Bank Gender Action Plan, 2007–10; World Development Report 2012); it is also reflected in the remarkable rise of microfinance models, with their emphasis on women as better borrowers as well as better providers (Cornwall et al. 2008).

While the fact that gender is now much more frequently given prominence in policy pronouncements by mainstream development institutions reflects the impact of the ideas generated by gender and development work, it has given rise to two related concerns. First, these commitments to gender equality remain superficial, limited in scope and unachievable within existing development paradigms – as has been argued in the case of the Millenium Development Goals (Antrobus 2003). And second, feminist concepts are increasingly being incorporated into development models whose long-term effects are to reinforce, rather than challenge, gendered and heteronormative ideologies and relationships as well as other intersecting forms of inequality (Cornwall et al. 2008), necessitating a radical rethinking of the relationship between feminist politics and development.

Further Reading: Chant 2010; Cornwall et al. 2007; Jackson and Pearson 1998; Razavi and Miller 1995; Saunders 2002; Visvanathan et al. 2011.

GENDER-BASED VIOLENCE

Gwendolyn Beetham

Gender-based violence (GBV) refers to the ways in which violence is differently expressed and experienced according to one's sex, race, class, religion, sexuality, ability and other situating factors. This entry first traces contemporary understandings of GBV to its origins in the international violence against women movement of the 1970s. Common approaches to measuring and addressing gender-based violence on both national and international levels are then explored, followed by an overview of critiques of these approaches.

The concept of GBV has its roots in the 'battered women's' movement of the 1970s, which grew out of second-wave feminist organizing (see feminist politics). The United Nations' Decade for Women (1975–85) played a key role in internationalizing the movement, drawing together women activists and scholars from around the globe for conferences that addressed some of the major issues facing women. Two key goals of the nascent movement were first, to name the problem itself since, prior to these efforts, there was no concerted international effort to label the various practices that we now understand to be 'violence against women'. Second, and equally important, was the recognition that violence against women was committed in both the 'private' and 'public' spheres (see feminist politics). Violence against women was viewed as 'universal' in scope, although varied in form, according to cultural and geographic context. For example, domestic violence and rape took precedence in some geographic locations, while dowry murders and honour killings were the main concerns in others. However, it was argued that violence against women could be attributed to the oppression of women under patriarchy – the organization of society according to men's dominance and control – a model that was believed to be the primary form of societal organization in nearly every culture.

The multifaceted ways in which violence against women takes shape led to difficulties in defining violence against women on an international scale. After years of both deliberation and advocacy by women's organizations and scholars, a broad definition of violence against women was included in the United Nations Declaration on the Elimination of Violence Against Women (1993). Article 1 of the Declaration describes violence against women as 'any act of gender-based violence that results in, or is likely to result in, physical, sexual or psychological harm or suffering to women, including threats of such acts, coercion or arbitrary deprivation of liberty, whether occurring in public or in private life' (United Nations 1993). This definition became the normative definition of violence against women in the international realm; an identical definition appeared in the Beijing Platform for Action (United Nations 1995), the outcome document of the United Nations' Fourth World Conference on

Women, which continues to guide much contemporary gender and development policy at the international and national levels.

Activism by women of colour in the global North and women from the global South, along with increased research on violence against women during this period, led to the important recognition that violence against women was experienced differently according to factors such as class, race and cultural difference. For example, Merry (2009: 29) notes that, in China, domestic 'violence' is understood to occur at different levels – bao-li (brute force), nue-dail (cruel treatment or abuse), and qin-fan (violation) – specificities that are not captured under Western definitions of the concept. In the United States, a long history of racism, colonialism and heteronormativity has led to very different understandings and experiences of violence for Black and Native American women, as well as for poor white women, lesbian, bisexual and transgender women, and immigrant women (Incite! 2006; Sokoloff and Dupont 2005). The recognition of the intersectional ways in which violence is experienced – that is, that women experience various and overlapping forms of violence depending on their location within society – eventually led to the broadening of approaches to address GBV, as discussed below.

In addition to the critiques from women of colour in the global North and women from the global South, several theoretical developments in anthropology and women's and gender studies in the 1980s and early 1990s, including 'the shift from sex to gender, from roles to performances, and from essentialised gender identities to intersectional ones' (Merry 2009: 9) were of great significance as international movements shifted their focus from 'violence against women' to 'gender-based violence' (see performativity, intersectionality). These developments were important in that they contributed to an understanding of gender-based violence as resultant from power relationships encased within larger structures of inequality and violence. The move from 'women' to 'gender' is partly one of semantics (for example, the term 'battered woman' conjures up images of victimization). However, far beyond the rhetorical significance, viewing violence as part of the gendered power dynamics in societies allows for a broader – and more complex – understanding of GBV to emerge. That is, not only does the inclusion of the concept of gender allow for the recognition of the diverse realities of women, but viewing violence from the perspective of how it is shaped by power relationships allows for a definition which includes men (as both victims and perpetrators), violence against one's sexuality or gender identity, violence within same-sex relationships, abuse of the elderly, violence against people with disabilities, as well as attention to the structural elements that (re-) produce such violence. The inclusion of global inequalities, as well as racism, classism and heteronormativity, importantly moves beyond the attribution of violence against women solely to patriarchal structures – i.e. gender inequalities – while still recognizing the link between gender and violence. This type of analysis allows for what Cynthia Cockburn (2004: 43) terms a 'gendered continuum of violence' whereby 'gender links violence at different points on a scale reaching from the personal to the international ... battering and marital rape, confinement, "dowry" burnings, honour killings, and genital mutilation in peacetime; military rape, sequestration, prostitution, and sexualized torture in war'.

Additionally, in the international realm, the use of the concept 'gender-based violence' was accompanied by a move towards gender mainstreaming, which attempted to integrate gender analysis into all aspects of policy, which some have argued has taken the focus off of the main victims of gender-based violence: women. In the majority of policy and practice, however, gender-based violence interventions tend to remain primarily targeted at women, leaving the relationship between masculinities and violence, as well as larger power inequalities, unproblematized (Katz 2006; Merry 2009). Further, the concept of 'gender' itself has been contested in some cases, whether due to translation difficulties or because the use of 'gender' rather than 'women' is understood in some contexts to signal a more 'radical' approach that some anti-violence (and other women's rights) advocates see as detrimental to gaining support for their cause (see gender and development and women's studies/gender studies).

In the 1990s, advocates began to frame GBV within the context of human rights discourse (Cook 1994; Merry 2009). The idea that 'women's rights are human rights' not only gave GBV a certain sense of legitimacy, in that the human rights discourse was an already well-established part of the international lexicon, but it also broadened the human rights framework, which was developed in the post-World War II period as a 'gender neutral' framework of protections – that is, the gender-specificity of rights violations was not acknowledged. To date there have been significant questions surrounding the implementation of GBV laws within the human rights framework. At the international level, this is due to limited enforcement mechanisms. At the local level difficulties often arise when translating international standards to conform to cultural and social specificities (Merry 2009); 'cultural differences' and 'tradition' have both been used by some states as a way to side-step the implementation and enforcement of human rights treaties at the local level where gender equality and women's rights are concerned. Recent critiques of including GBV within a human rights framework point to the fact that such measures often work to expand the state apparatus, leading to the criminalization of violence in ways that are harmful to women and men (see below and Bumiller 2008).

Measuring GBV

Gender-based violence has been defined in different ways according to cultural and geographical context. This takes place through the advocacy of women's organizations, the implementation of laws at the national level and, as explained above, international standards. As a result, what counts – and does not count – as gender-based violence is not only dependent on context, but also constantly in flux (Merry 2009). Recent anthologies on gender-based violence have included works on the sexual exploitation of girls at school, gender violence in schools in humanitarian and conflict contexts, militarized rape, environmental violence, trafficking for prostitution, violence against incarcerated women, police brutality, medical violence against people of colour, femicide (the murder of women because they are women), and female genital mutilation (see Incite! 2006; Terry with Hoare 2007).

A key aspect of what gets 'counted' as gender-based violence is captured by the way in which it is measured. Measuring levels and types of gender-based violence has been a major part of the international GBV movement. There are many ways to measure the prevalence of gender-based violence: from counting the numbers of people seeking help at domestic violence shelters, to numbers of rapes prosecuted, to numbers of attacks on LGBT people reported to the police. Some of these methods require a number of elements to be in place for data to be collected, for example, laws against different forms of gender-based violence, as well as a functioning legal system and/or governmental departments in charge of collecting and analyzing data.

It also requires that people both understand their rights and believe that they can turn to the government for help (Merry 2009). Additionally, the collection of this quantitative data only provides limited information about the experience of gender-based violence.

Small-scale victimization surveys conducted by local or national organizations and academic research on GBV fill some of these gaps, as do large-scale victimization surveys such as the Demographic and Health Surveys (used to collect data on population and health in over 75 countries), and those conducted by international organizations, which are also used for comparative purposes. For example, in 2005 the World Health Organization (WHO) published a study that analyzed data on domestic violence collected from 24,000 women in 10 countries (García-Moreno et al. 2005). The study framed violence against women as a health issue (that is, one which affects reproductive health, mental health, leads to drug and alcohol abuse, etc.) and used an adapted version of the Critical Tactics Scale (CTS) to collect its data.

The use of the CTS is important in understanding how GBV is framed. Developed in the 1990s by Murray Straus, the CTS has been widely used to collect data on gender-based violence, including in Demographic Health Surveys in several countries and in the National Violence Against Women Survey in the United States (Straus 2007). The underlying premise of the CTS is that domestic violence results from conflict, and the questions that appear in surveys using the CTS tend to focus on the types of acts committed, framing them within the context of the 'conflict' that brings about the violent act. The structural and gendered power imbalances within which GBV is situated are therefore bypassed, with a focus instead on individual acts of violence (Kimmel 2002). Implementing structures that situate GBV as an individualized act rather than part of a larger system of inequality is a problem also found in common approaches to addressing GBV, as explored below.

Addressing GBV: common approaches and critiques

There are three broad approaches to interventions which follow distinct, yet interconnected, rationales: punishment, which seeks to punish the offender; safety, which seeks to protect the survivor; and reform, which seeks both to reform the offender, as well as help the victim to develop an analysis of GBV as abuse (Merry 2009: 48). Despite the fact that gender-based violence around the globe has been framed in different ways according to cultural specificities, punishment remains the dominant mode of intervention in many contexts, to varying effects.

While enacting legal measures against GBV has been key to the struggles of advocates in many parts of the world, focusing on the criminalization of GBV has also been critiqued by feminist scholars and activists, for various reasons. As noted above, there is a widening of state apparatus that results from carceral approaches to GBV (Bumiller 2008). These apparatuses, including criminal justice systems, are subject to the same power imbalances and structural inequalities that organize societies more broadly and therefore, in many cases, can result in the further criminalization of certain groups of people according to race, class and other factors and the perpetuation, rather than end, of violence (Incite! 2006; Bumiller 2008). Additionally, depending on local legal structures, focusing on criminalization can, in some cases, lead to the prosecution of GBV victims, for example, in cases in which the victims of violence have also committed violent acts (sometimes in defence, sometimes not) and in the context of trafficking for prostitution (Bumiller 2008; Merry 2009). Further, the punishment of individual people for individual acts of violent crime can also contribute to the portrayal of GBV as 'isolated' incidents perpetrated by 'deviants', rather than as part of larger societal structures.

Approaches that aim to protect the survivor include restraining orders and shelter programmes, both of which rely on government intervention. For example, although early shelter programmes developed in the United States (known as 'refuges' in the United Kingdom) by the 'battered women's movement' were based around a radical feminist critique of patriarchy which eschewed government involvement, over time these programmes became increasingly dependent on the state for government funding and other support, leading to a shift in the way that GBV was addressed and greater government control over women's lives (Bumiller 2008; Merry 2009). In other contexts, however, shelter programmes were never a key part of strategies to address gender-based violence. Narayan (1997) argues, for example, that building shelter systems was not a viable option in India, a country without a social welfare state, and where it is not culturally feasible for many women to leave their homes and/or communities.

Approaches to GBV that are aimed at reform include, among others, anti-violence educational programmes that aim to 'sensitize' individuals and communities about GBV, programmes aimed at analyzing the connection between masculinities and violence, and therapeutic programmes for offenders and victims (Merry 2009). These programmes vary widely in terms of focus and type of analysis of GBV, according to the organization or government agency in charge of implementation. Therefore, while some therapeutic programmes may connect GBV to wider societal structures, others may focus on the actions of individuals, while others may integrate both. Some have argued, however, that reform approaches have contributed to the medicalization of GBV (that is, the idea that GBV is an individual, 'treatable' problem) (Bumiller 2008; Incite! 2006). Like the other common approaches to GBV, then, the effectiveness of this approach is highly contingent on a number of factors.

Research on approaches to GBV has led to interesting findings about the effects of GBV interventions on subjectivities. In the United States, Bumiller (2008) found that the medicalization of GBV, combined with the increased reliance of domestic violence shelters on the state, led to the construction of 'good' and 'bad' victims. 'Good' victims completed certain actions and understood their victimization in the 'right' way so that they could receive services from the government, while 'bad' victims did not receive services and were even punished for their actions by having their children taken away, housing denied or, in some cases, being sent to jail. Although Bumiller (2008) notes that victims in both cases asserted a considerable amount of agency in resisting these constructions in various ways, her findings echo those in other contexts. For example, Caple James' (2010) study of violence in Haiti describes a 'political economy of trauma'; whereby accounts of victimization (real or fabricated) are tailored to fit the development and humanitarian industries' expectations, becoming the currency through which Haitian women (and men) secure development services. Men's subjectivities are also affected (Katz 2006), as male perpetrators of GBV become 'pathological' or 'deviants', identities that are raced and classed according to context, for example, as is the case with the stereotype of the 'Black male rapist' in the United States (Incite! 2006). As these findings illustrate, although the concept of GBV has broadened over the past three decades to be more inclusive of intersectional ways in which GBV is experienced, more can be done to ensure that approaches to GBV targeted at women – and men – address both larger social, economic and political power inequalities, as well as those between providers of services and recipients. Gender-based violence will only be eradicated when these overarching power imbalances are addressed.

Further Reading: Dobash and Dobash 1998; Friedman and Valenti 2008; Kelly 1988; O'Toole, Schiffman and Edwards 2007; Radford, Friedberg and Harne 2000.

GENDER IDENTITY

Silvia Posocco

Introduction

Gender identity has been the object of research and theorizing across a range of disciplines in the humanities and social sciences. It is central to the interdisciplinary field of academic gender studies, where a range of critical perspectives on this concept has been developed. Theory, analysis and critique in gender studies have challenged understandings of the acquisition of gender identity as a teleological and unilinear process of human development leading to gender binarism and dimorphism, that is, ideas of distinct and opposite feminine and masculine identities and embodiments. Ethnocentric assumptions about the stability, coherence and direct and unproblematic translatability of the experience and expression of gender identity cross-culturally and trans-historically have also been systematically unpacked. Traditions of anthropological research, for example, have documented ethnographically the plural, complex and situated articulations of discourses and practices relating to gender identity cross-culturally, and in non-Western contexts in particular (for example, Blackwood 1998; Moore 1994). In turn, this pluralizing and relativizing intellectual effort has worked towards bringing into view and provincializing the colonial epistemologies and relationalities in play in shaping the articulation of knowledge and experience of gender identity in a variety of colonial and postcolonial settings. As Morgensen (2011) argues, this critical task therefore also crucially entails denaturalizing settler colonialism and other colonial formations, as well as decolonizing indigenous understandings and perspectives. Since the 1990s, Queer Theory and Transgender Studies have further problematized assumptions about the assumed coherence and permanence of gender identity, carefully teasing out the specificities and nuances inherent in gender variant experience, and providing compelling accounts of the complexity of gender identities and identifications, as well as of the variability of the relations between gender identity and embodiment (Butler 1990; Halberstam 1998; Prosser 1998; Salamon 2010; Stryker and Whittle 2006).

Identity, identification and disidentification

Debates in the field of psychoanalytic studies have offered theories of the development of gender identity centred on the Oedipal drama and the related establishment of a differential relation to the phallus, as both a symbolic and material marker and a gendering device. From this perspective, masculinity develops through the boy's desire for the mother and rivalry for the father, whilst femininity results from the girl's realization of her own 'castration' and lack. Feminist critics have questioned and radically problematized the reductionism, essentialism and phallocentrism inherent in psychoanalytic accounts, whilst at the same time harnessing the analytical and critical possibilities opened up by psychoanalytic theory for theorizing the processual, ambiguous, partial and shifting character of gender identifications. Feminist psychoanalytic perspectives show that gender identity is not exclusively a matter of social regulation, but rather is produced relationally (see, for example, Benjamin 1995) in and through desire. In this view, desire's ontological and epistemological valence is central to the production of a range of dynamic, ambiguous and fundamentally unstable gender identifications. Further, Rose (1986) argues that the psychoanalytic emphasis on the unconscious radically disrupts and undermines the cultural fantasy of the existence of stable, univocal and discrete gender identities.

For Sedgwick (1991, 1994), the tensions between constructionist and essentialist articulations of the notion of identity represent a recent iteration of a long-standing impasse in which academic and popular models are equally implicated. The significance of this recurrent and ultimately unresolved debate is that it brings into view the workings of identification and desire specifically in relation to tropes of homosexual gender. Sedgwick makes this argument in the celebrated book *Epistemology of the Closet* (1990), in the context of an analysis of how two key tropes of gender have provided frames for the understanding of same-sex desire in Western contexts (Sedgwick 1991, Ch. 1). First, Sedgwick identifies the trope of inversion, where an essential heterosexuality regulates desire between differently gendered selves, regardless of the sexed bodies they inhabit. Second, Sedgwick highlights the trope of gender separatism, whereby desire is not seen to cross boundaries but rather is articulated between selves brought together by ties of commonality, rather than difference. These different models, which can be in part genealogically connected to early sexology, but that are also prominent in a range of contemporary academic and popular imaginaries, hold different consequences for the ways in which the relations between gender and sexuality are understood. Tropes of homosexual gender, forms of cross-identification and alliance, and their articulation through appeals to transitivity, liminality or separatism are particularly significant in that they reveal a multiplicity of possibilities, and invariably lead to the 'impasse of gender definition' (Sedgwick 1991: 90). For Sedgwick, the deadlock resulting from the models is a key feature of the epistemologies and relationalities in which gender is mobilized to instantiate a distance between homosexuality and heterosexuality, as this foregrounds the incoherence and contradiction that lie at the heart of debates over the status of sexual identity. As Sedgwick argues, 'the impasse of gender definition must be seen first of all in the creation of a field of intractable, highly structured discursive incoherence at a crucial node of social organisation, in this case the node at which *any* gender is discriminated' (Sedgwick 1991: 90, Sedgwick's emphasis). In turn, the focus on the dynamics of identification shows the nonlinear processes that mark identities as tenuous, precarious dynamics, unstable and always unfinished.

Racialization and racism, as Frantz Fanon has powerfully argued in *Black Skin, White Masks* (1952), are also fundamentally entangled in the articulation of desire. Fanon shows that the articulation of identifications is always already fully marked by historicity, context and location – and by the historical experience of coloniality and empire. Fully acknowledging that racialization and racism fundamentally structure gendered and racialized identifications, Muñoz (1999), in a deft analysis of the cultural and artistic production associated with migrant, diasporic and racially and sexually minoritized communities in the United States, highlights the disidentificatory and transformative potential of marginal social and cultural practices. As an inherently partial and open-ended process, identification therefore entails the possibility of counter-identification and disidentification and the realignment of gender, sexuality and 'race'.

Performativity, citationality and melancholia

A major shift in the theorization of gender identity in interdisciplinary gender studies is associated with the work of Judith Butler. In the groundbreaking text *Gender Trouble: Feminism and the Subversion of Identity*, Butler argues that '[t]here is no gender identity behind the expressions of gender; that identity is performatively constituted by the very "expressions" that are said to be its results' (1990: 25). The emphasis on the performative character of gender does away with notions of interiority and posits both identity and embodiment as tied to processes of repetition and iteration of culturally intelligible stylized acts. Combining references to Austinian speech act theory and Derridean deconstruction, Butler's understanding of 'citationality' makes clear that gender performativity is radically unhinged from a voluntaristic subject freely choosing modes of gender presentation and performance. Rather, citationality specifically references the 'regulatory power of discourse to produce the phenomenon that it regulates and constrains' (Butler 1993: 2). Citationality and iteration are linked to the regulation of gender identifications, and crucially, to the very materialization of bodies (Butler 1993). However, far from amounting to discursive determinism, citationality and iteration place emphasis on the constitutive re-articulatory dimension at the heart of gender identity and embodiment. Butler argues that gender may appear as an identity, but is in fact a citational effect (Butler 1993). As Butler explains,

> gender ought not to be construed as a stable identity or locus of agency from which various acts follow; rather, gender is an identity tenuously constituted in time, instituted in an exterior space through a stylised repetition of acts. The effect of gender is produced through the stylisation of the body and, hence, must be understood as the mundane way in which bodily gestures, movements and styles of various kinds constitute the illusion of an abiding gendered self.
>
> (Butler 1990: 140)

Butler's groundbreaking work on the psychic dynamics of gender identification should also be noted. In *The Psychic Life of Power*, Butler (1997b) asks whether gender identifications may be thought through an analogy with melancholic identifications, as theorized in psychoanalysis. Melancholic identifications entail a sustained emotional investment in a lost object through the mechanism of internationalization (see Butler 1990, Ch. 2; Butler 1997b, Ch. 5). Butler notes that for Freud, the prohibitions that structure the emergence of gender identity are linked to the establishment of heterosexuality. This 'heterosexual matrix' (Butler ibid.), and the gender identifications that coincide with it, are dependent upon the repudiation of homosexual attachments. As Butler explains

> gender is acquired at least in part through the repudiation of homosexual attachments; the girl becomes a girl through being subject to a prohibition which bars the mother as an object of

desire and installs the barred object as part of the ego, indeed, as a melancholic identification.

(Butler 1997b: 136)

From this perspective, gender identifications are fundamentally melancholic identifications. Gender identity in this sense is not, strictly speaking, expressive, but rather, 'gender itself is here understood to be composed of precisely what remains inarticulate in sexuality' (Butler 1997: 140). Hyperbolic masculinity and femininity emerge through these compulsory dynamics and signal the culturally barred and ungrievable loss of homosexual attachments.

In an influential book, Halberstam (1998) challenges psychoanalytic readings with a view to theorizing gender identity through a specific focus on 'female masculinity'. Halberstam (1998) moves from the premise that unhinging the relation between masculinity and men can yield important insights into the social and cultural production of masculinity. This theoretical move reveals a spectrum of female masculine-inflected subject positions, identities and identifications. Building on Rubin's (1992: 467) classic definition of butch as 'a category of lesbian gender that is constituted through the deployment and manipulation of masculine gender codes and symbols', Halberstam (1998) aligns this spectrum of gender identifications of female masculinities firmly with lesbianism. In his analysis of transsexual autobiographies, however, Prosser (1998) contests this point and speaks of butch identity as a 'propeller' (Prosser 1998) towards a transgender identification, while also highlighting the often unacknowledged centrality of transgender themes in theories of gender identity.

Regulation, biopolitics and assemblage

Contemporary innovative conceptual trajectories of research and theorizing on gender identity also deal with a sustained analysis of the regulatory domains through which gender identity is instantiated. The question of regulation is addressed not only in relation to discourse, but it also brought to bear on the specific institutional arrangements, policy domains, and legal technologies through which gender identity is produced. In a bold theoretical move, Spade (2008) shifts the analytical focus to the political and legal administrative technologies that govern and realize gender reclassification policies in a range of administrative contexts in the United States. Spade highlights contradiction and inconsistency in these administrative and regulatory practices and shows the fundamental instability of gender as a category of identity verification. This point also emerges in a compelling analysis of contemporary micro-practices leading to the increased securitization of gender in everyday life. Currah and Mulqueen (2011) focus on technologies of surveillance used in border control and airport security. They argue that gender identity is fully within, and not outside or beyond political arrangements and show that different securitizing practices produce contradictory and conflicting accounts. Currah and Mulqueen (2001) also show that gender, rather than a stable marker of identity is in fact a fundamentally unreliable and inconsistent measure through which gender variant and gender non-conforming subjects are policed in and through increasingly violent and oppressive practices of securitization. In this view, gender, sexuality, 'race', ethnicity, class, age, religion and nation are no longer understood to constitute separate analytics, but an 'assemblage' (Puar 2007, Chapter 4) produced in and through biopolitical regulation. As Puar explains, '[t]he assemblage, as a series of dispersed but mutually implicated and messy networks, draws together enunciation and dissolution, causality and effect, organic and inorganic forces' (Puar 2007: 211). Assemblage analytically displaces identity in favour of a focus on 'affective conglomerations' and 'contingencies of belonging' (ibid.), and ever-shifting fields of possibility, whilst simultaneously bringing into focus the place of a multiplicity of identity markers in contemporary regulatory practices connected to violence, surveillance and control.

Further Reading: Mattilda aka Matt Bernstein Sycamore 2006; Fuss 1994; Moore 2007; Stryker and Aizura 2012.

GENDER MAINSTREAMING

Emanuela Lombardo

Gender mainstreaming is 'the (re)organisation, improvement, development and evaluation of policy processes, so that a gender equality perspective is incorporated in all policies, at all levels, and at all stages, by the actors normally involved in policy-making'. This definition of gender mainstreaming, developed by gender experts of the Council of Europe (1998: 15; Verloo 2005), is the one that has travelled most among scholars and practitioners. Gender mainstreaming includes attempts to inform all public policies that are not specifically on gender, such as for example transport or agriculture policies, so that they counter gender bias in society and policies and produce gender equal policies.

The theoretical origins of this political strategy lie in the work of gender scholars who have shown that public policies and political and organizational processes and structures, are androcentric in that they tend to reproduce the male norm masqueraded as 'neutral' while they systematically disadvantage women (Rees 1998; Hawkesworth 1994). Feminists involved in international development planning have been pioneers in placing gender into the mainstream political agenda; to confront the marginalization of women's needs in international development programmes (Jahan 1995; Moser 1993). To challenge the existence of androcentric policy norms and structures and to promote gender equality in all processes and policies, feminists have proposed gender mainstreaming as a strategy that envisions the transformation of existing unequal gender roles and practices (Rees 1998; Verloo 2001, 2005; Squires 2005).

At the Fourth UN Women's Conference of Beijing in 1995 the strategy of gender mainstreaming was launched and endorsed by all governments and civil society actors participating in the forum. The commitment included in the Beijing Platform is that of mainstreaming a gender perspective into all policies, so that the potential impact that policy proposals could have on, for instance, finance or education, on women and men is analyzed before policies are adopted. 'The ultimate goal is to achieve gender equality' in society by formulating, implementing, and evaluating all policies 'so that women and men benefit equally and inequality is not perpetuated' (UN 1997: 1).

The broad definition of the strategy has made of gender mainstreaming a particularly 'contested concept' which has generated a variety of feminist 'productive tensions in theory and practice' (Walby 2005: 321). Feminist debates on mainstreaming – Walby (2005) argues – include discussions concerning different visions of gender equality (sameness, difference, and transformation, see Squires 1999; Rees 1998), intersectionality (Squires 2005), and the relation between expertise and democratization (Rai 2003). Other debates assess the extent to which feminist ideas about transformation of inequalities are incorporated into mainstreaming policy practices. Lombardo and Meier conceptualize five policy shifts or criteria that can indicate the extent to which gender has been mainstreamed into policymaking (Lombardo 2005; Lombardo and Meier 2006): first, a shift towards a broader concept of gender equality that focuses on gender and targets the multiple interconnected causes of gender inequality in all domains (Walby 1990; Verloo 2001); second, a reorientation of the mainstream political agenda by rearticulating policy ends and means from a gender perspective (Jahan 1995); third, an equal political representation of women and men; fourth, a shift in the institutional and organizational cultures, which requires changes in the policy process, mechanisms and actors (Council of Europe 1998); and fifth, an increased diversity of the actors involved in policymaking, through a greater participation of civil society (Squires 2005; Verloo 2005). These shifts seek to clarify what has to be understood by the incorporation of a gender equality perspective in the mainstream so that gender mainstreaming is no longer an 'open signifier' that could be filled with different meanings, but rather reflects concerns that are present in feminist agendas (Lombardo 2005; Lombardo and Meier 2006).

Other scholarly debates have focused on the different political approaches to mainstreaming. Jahan (1995) distinguishes between 'integrationist' and 'agenda-setting' approaches. 'Integrationist' approaches to gender mainstreaming introduce a gender perspective into existing policy paradigms without questioning them (Jahan 1995). This has been associated with more 'expert-bureaucratic' models of mainstreaming, based on the inclusion of gender experts in policy machineries, which have been adopted in a number of European countries, Australia, New Zealand and Canada (Barnett-Donaghy 2004a; Council of Europe 1998). 'Agenda-setting' approaches imply changing decision-making structures and processes, prioritizing gender objectives among competing issues, and reorienting the mainstream political agenda from a gender perspective (Jahan 1995). This has been associated with more participatory and democratic forms of mainstreaming (Rai 2003), which, if implemented through practices of citizens' forums – Squires (2005) argues – could promote diversity mainstreaming and potentially transform unequal relations not only in gender but also other inequalities. Northern Ireland is one of the few examples of a 'participatory-democratic' approach, which involves the consultation, before policies are adopted, by state authorities of civil society groups representing different equality concerns that could be affected by policy proposals (Barnett-Donaghy 2004b; Beveridge, Nott and Stephen 2000).

Whatever the approach taken, gender scholars agree on the largely ineffective policy implementation of gender mainstreaming, a strategy based on voluntaristic efforts rather than binding commitments

(Verloo 2005; Walby 2005; Behning and Serrano 2001; Council of Europe 1998; Rees 1998). Reasons for this lack of implementation vary. One reason has to do with policy actors' treatment of gender mainstreaming as 'everybody's – and nobody's – responsibility' (Mazey 2002: 228). Although scholars see the role of gender equality institutions and experts as key to ensuring that policy-making is based on 'gendered' knowledge (Beveridge and Nott 2002; Rai 2003; Woodward 2003), the introduction of gender mainstreaming risked the dilution of gender expertise and dismantling of the infrastructures and specific actions created to support women's policies, based on the mistaken assumption that gender equality is already in the mainstream (Stratigaki 2005; Mazey 2002). Another reason for ineffective implementation is the organizational resistance to change (Benschop and Verloo 2006). Successful implementation of gender mainstreaming requires a high level of gender awareness among policy makers who are not gender experts, but the paradox of gender mainstreaming is that – in the words of Roggeband and Verloo (1996: 629) – the 'actors trapped in gender discourses [gender-blind civil servants] are held responsible for transforming these discourses'.

Yet, gender mainstreaming has produced changes, which will be easier to recognize if, as Van Eerdewijk and Davids (2010) suggest, gender scholars escape a utopian framing of mainstreaming as a 'mythical beast' that will produce social transformation, and rather begin to scrutinize both the resistance to change and the margins for change that exist in specific policy-making contexts. Room for change exists, for instance, in the discursive shifts that gender mainstreaming produces. In the European Union (EU), where mainstreaming has mainly been promoted through 'soft' instruments, scholars have detected policy changes that are due to the facilitation of gender norm diffusion that mainstreaming encloses (Beveridge and Velluti 2008), though they have also highlighted the limitations in achieving progress that persuasive incentives might have (Hafner-Burton and Pollack 2009).

Some studies seek to explain cases of successful implementation of gender mainstreaming in specific contexts considering a combination of factors. According to Hafner-Burton and Pollack (2000), who have applied a social movement theory approach to analyze the implementation of gender mainstreaming in five areas of EU policy, three factors can explain such success: political opportunities opened by EU institutions, networks of gender advocates, and the strategic framing of gender mainstreaming (emphasizing gains in terms of efficiency) to make it fit with the dominant frame of a given Directorate General (e.g. Competition), to avoid potential resistance from policy makers that are more market-oriented and less familiar with gender issues. Beveridge, Nott and Stephen (2000), analyzing shifts in political opportunities, showed how government decentralization opened up opportunities for implementing gender mainstreaming. They find that the devolved governments of Scotland, Wales and Northern Ireland have integrated the commitment to mainstreaming equality into policy-making more than at the central UK level by requiring gender impact assessment of all policies and by adopting a more participatory approach to mainstreaming that incorporates wider concerns of the population. Finally, feminist alliances and deliberative forums emerge as key factors for implementing more transformative mainstreaming, and monitoring such implementation (Lycklama à Nijeholt et al. 1998; Woodward 2004). Verloo (2005) argues that for mainstreaming to be a transformative feminist concept, it must be a strategy that displaces the continuously arising and diverse forms of inequality by creating spaces for the expression of ongoing feminist struggles.

Recent developments in gender mainstreaming include the increasing use of gender budgeting and the emerging practice of gender training for public administrations personnel. Feminist economics has defended gender-responsive budgeting as a means to integrate gender priorities into governmental plans by analyzing the differential impact that budgets have on women and men, and introducing the changes necessary to answer the needs of both groups (Budlender, Sharp and Allen 1998; Elson 1999). Thanks to the efforts of international organizations such as the UN and the Commonwealth Secretariat and domestic policy actors, more than 60 countries have implemented gender-sensitive budgets (Rubin and Bartle 2005). A rising practice to mainstream gender into policy-making is the training of civil servants and politicians. Experiences of gender training processes are emerging in different countries and reflections on how to improve such training as part of wider strategies to gender policy-making are growing among trainers, consultants, development and policy experts (Oxfam 2007; QUING and TARGET research projects).

Although gender tools are important for promoting gender equality (Villagómez 2004), feminists have also denounced the pitfalls of the 'gender tools business' for the de-politicization of the feminist project. The increasing governmental use of gender tools such as gender impact assessment, targets and indicators, might involve a normalization of the political project of gender equality into a technical and apolitical project where it is assumed that gender equality will be achieved through the compliance of a few procedures, such as ticking a 'yes' answer in the box if a policy proposal is deemed gender friendly. This toolkit approach might involve a 'de-radicalization' of feminism in terms of losing the **power** dimension of the gender struggle (Currie 1999) and leave the prevailing unequal gender relations untouched (Mukhopadhyay 2004).

Governments' gender mainstreaming policies have also been criticized for normalizing and reproducing the heterosexual and white cultural hegemony, thus perpetuating the unequal status quo while they create the illusion that equality has been achieved and mainstreamed (Butler 1990; McRobbie 2009).

Feminists face the challenge to bring back the power dimension into policy-making and 'change discourse, values, and power relations' (Eyben 2010: 56) within institutional and organizational contexts that appear mainly concerned with changing 'procedures'. Eyben (2010: 56) suggests focusing 'less on organisations' and more on what the 'agents' within organizations 'can do to realise some of the more radical potential of gender mainstreaming'. Institutions and organizations offer discursive and material opportunities that feminist bureaucrats, activists and academics can exploit to further transformative agendas of gender mainstreaming. Alliances and networks can make mainstreaming serve ongoing feminist transformative causes. Despite the dangers of 'cooption' of feminist agendas by the state, the collaboration of feminist activists and experts with state actors, the so-called 'velvet triangles' (Woodward 2004) or 'pentangles' (van Eerdewijk and van der Vleuten 2010), and the creation of spaces for the empowerment of subaltern voices (Verloo 2005; Mukhopadhyay 2004; Fraser 1989) have all proved key to voicing different women's concerns and further gender equality goals into mainstream policy-making (Subrahmanian 2004; Eyben 2010).

Further Reading: Mazey 2000; Rai 2003; Rees 1998; Verloo 2005; Walby 2005.

HETERONORMATIVITY

Carolyn H. Williams

Although rather an unwieldy term, heteronormativity is rapidly gaining ground as a conceptual tool for social science theorists and researchers of sexuality and gender. The foundations of this concept can be traced back to feminist theories of the relationship between gender, sexuality and heterosexuality in the 1970s and 1980s. Anthropologist Gayle Rubin, for example, examined the underlying logical structure of kinship, arguing that this form of social organizsation of sex '… rests upon gender, obligatory heterosexuality, and the constraint of female sexuality' (1975: 179). Rubin's critique of heterosexuality as an institution introduced the notion of the sex/gender system, within which individuals are engendered in order that marriage is guaranteed. In this system, gender is not only an identification with one sex; it also entails that sexual desire be directed towards the other sex (ibid.). Monique Wittig developed explorations of 'obligatory heterosexuality' and its relationship to gender further in her reflections on fundamental questions of human knowledge and 'the straight mind' (1992 [1980]). Wittig identified the heterosexual relationship as a central problem in social analysis that resisted examination: 'With its ineluctability as knowledge … as a given prior to any science, the straight mind develops a totalising interpretation of history, social reality, culture, language, and all the subjective phenomena at the same time' (ibid.: 27). According to Wittig, 'straight society' cannot work economically, symbolically, linguistically, or politically without the different/other at every level, but, crucially, this 'othering' of the straight mind '… not only oppresses lesbians and gay men, it oppresses many different/others, it oppresses all women and many categories of men, all those who are in the position of the dominated'. Wittig understood this constitution and controlling of difference as a normative act, and as such essentially an act of power (ibid.: 29).

Wittig's idea that 'obligatory heterosexuality' oppressed many 'others', and not only lesbians and gay men, was soon explored in more depth by Rubin, who developed the notions of the 'erotic pyramid' and the 'charmed circle of sexuality' of modern Western societies based on a hierarchical system of sexual values stemming from religion, medicine, psychiatry and popular culture (1991 [1984]). In this system:

> … marital, reproductive heterosexuals are alone at the top of the erotic pyramid. Clamouring below are unmarried monogamous heterosexuals in couples, followed by most other heterosexuals. Solitary sex floats ambiguously. … Stable, long-term lesbian and gay male couples are verging on respectability, but bar dykes

> and promiscuous gay men are hovering just above the groups at the very bottom of the pyramid. The most despised sexual castes currently include transsexuals, transvestites, fetishists, sadomasochists, sex workers such as prostitutes and porn models, and the lowliest of all, those whose eroticism transgresses generational boundaries.
>
> (Rubin 1991: 279)

According to Rubin, society and culture reward those standing high in this hierarchy with certified mental health, respectability, legality, social and physical mobility, institutional support, and material benefits. However, individuals who practice sexual behaviours or occupations lower on the scale are subjected to a presumption of mental illness, disreputability, criminality, restricted social and physical mobility, loss of institutional support, and economic sanctions (1991: 279). As society and culture change over time, arguments are then conducted over where to draw the line between 'good' and 'bad' sex, and to determine what other activities, if any, may be permitted to cross over into acceptability (1991: 282). The sexual hierarchy therefore was no longer understood to represent heterosexuality and its unequal 'other' homosexuality, based on socially and culturally valued forms of masculinity and femininity and gender roles, but instead was more complex and far-reaching.

While Wittig and Rubin directed their critiques of the 'straight mind' and sexual hierarchies at hegemonic social institutions, theories, cultures and values, Adrienne Rich took up the challenge of the unexamined 'economics of prescriptive heterosexuality' and consequent 'compulsory heterosexuality' of feminist thought in particular (1980: 634). Rich called for feminism to move beyond the acceptance of lesbian existence as mere 'sexual preference', and to critique compulsory heterosexual orientation for women, since heterosexuality, like motherhood, needed to be recognized and studied as a political institution (ibid.: 637). Here Rich drew attention to the problem in feminism of the assumption that 'most women are innately heterosexual' and called for an analysis of the ways in which for women heterosexuality may be something that has had to be imposed, managed, organized, propagandized and maintained by force, including both physical violence and false consciousness (ibid.: 648). For Rich then, feminist analysis needed to challenge the imposition of heterosexuality rather than accept and even celebrate lesbians as a sexual minority. It also needed to recognize that the assumption of the heterosexuality of the majority of women among heterosexual feminists was as important to overcome as the imposition of heterosexuality by the patriarchal societies they were themselves critiquing. A decade later Judith Butler (1990) drew on the work of Wittig and Rubin (and Foucault's *The History of Sexuality* (1978) among others) to develop her critique of the pervasive heterosexual assumption in feminist theory, and to counter feminist views that restricted the meaning of gender to received notions of masculinity and femininity within the framework of a 'heterosexual matrix'. Butler sought to establish that normative sexuality fortifies normative gender, foregrounding the causal and structural links between sexuality and gender. According to this normative framework, 'one is a woman to the extent that one functions as one within the dominant heterosexual frame and to call the frame into question is perhaps to lose something of one's sense of place in gender' (Butler 1999: xi). In her exploration of normativity and the power of social norms, including the role of psychic as well as social processes, Butler refers to her 'strong desire both to counter the normative violence implied by ideal morphologies of sex and to uproot the pervasive assumptions about natural or presumptive heterosexuality that are informed by ordinary and academic discourse on sexuality' (ibid.: xx). In this context, Butler's study of normativity seeks to answer the question of which expressions of gender and sexuality are acceptable, and which are not, and furthermore, how do presumptions about normative gender and sexuality determine in advance what will qualify as the 'human' and the 'liveable'? (ibid.: xxi–xxii). This work incorporated poststructuralist approaches to the destabilization of subject and identity categories, such as gender, heterosexuality, lesbian, and the discursive structures within which they are formed, in order to expose the limitations and instability of social and cultural norms regulating gender and sexuality.

From the 1990s onwards these early feminist critiques of sexual norms, values and hierarchies and their relationship to gender have been developed by a wide range of scholars, particularly in the fields of gender, sexuality, feminist and queer studies. Theorizing compulsory, institutionalized and normative accounts of sexuality and gender led to a shift from the deployment of the concept of homophobia to that of heteronormativity, a term first coined by Michael Warner (1991). The limitations of homophobia as an analytical category were outlined by Plummer (1998: 89), first for its reference to 'homosexuality', often assumed to be male only, thus perpetuating a male bias which ignores female experience and agency. To a certain extent, politically if not academically, this male bias has been addressed in recent years by the adoption of the term 'lesbophobia', notably by lesbian feminist activists across the globe.[1] However, Plummer argued that the concept of homophobia also fails to address how sexuality intersects with other vectors of power and elements of subjectivity, such as race, ethnicity and class. Moreover, it reinforces the notion of violence and hatred expressed by individuals due to their psychological problems, rather than addressing the underlying structural, social and cultural conditions and discourse of sexuality (Plummer 1998: 90). The concept of homophobia is also therefore considered politically limited in that if we address homophobia as the problem, then we imply that the solution depends solely upon changing individual attitudes and behaviour (Chambers 2007: 664). Moreover, a reliance on the concept of homophobia compresses the insights of feminist and queer critiques within the framework of interest-group liberalism and pluralism within modern democratic politics, and the relationship to gender slips out of sight. Specifically, sexuality is not thoroughly problematized (or theorized) but is instead conceptualized as 'sexual orientation', and the proposals for the solution to homophobia focus on criminalizing violence and discrimination against homosexuals as minorities and ensuring their equality in law (ibid.). This political identity and rights-based approach, characteristic of the advocacy and lobbying initiatives of many LGBT (lesbian, gay, bisexual and transgender) organizations, has yet to address, therefore, how to transform social and cultural norms that continue to value and promote heterosexuality as the most natural, normal and healthy sexuality.

The emergence of heteronormativity as an analytical category in gender and sexuality studies has therefore provided an important shift towards understanding the workings of cultures and societies beyond individual attitudes and behaviour. It is also particularly useful when it is deployed to deconstruct the heterosexual/homosexual binary, by examining heterosexuality as an institution and epistemology that constructs and regulates both homosexuality and heterosexuality on the basis of normative notions of sexuality and gender. This understanding of heteronormativity therefore provides the potential for uniting people across the heterosexual/homosexual divide, recognizing that heteronormativity and heterosexuality are not one and the same. Moreover, the optimal operation of a norm is as an invisible and silent operation, most effective when it is never exposed (Foucault 1978), thus a focus on norms opens up the space to examine hidden, unconscious and even unintended workings of power beyond explicit forms of violence, rejection and exclusion.

The different terms for analyzing social inequalities and exclusions pertaining to sexuality and gender consequently lead political action in different directions, often categorized as the difference between queer and LGBT politics. Queer theorists, such as Warner (1991) argue that deploying heteronormativity as a concept to name, make known and critique the effects of sexual norms can be a powerful political tool for subverting them and creating a radically different understanding of and strategies for the processes and desired outcomes of social transformation. These norms may overtly promote certain valued expressions of heterosexuality or they may be enacted through assumptions and unconscious processes of even the most radical campaigners for human rights and social justice. This approach differs from one that conceptualizes LGBT people as minorities who need legal and social protection and their own specific rights in order to attain citizenship. It also contrasts with current political activism on sexuality in which gendered and sexual identities are multiplied (LGBT becomes LGBTQI and so on, adding 'queer' and 'intersex' to the mix, for example), creating the 'alphabet soup' phenomenon (Petchesky 2009). In the field of queer theory, for example, Berlant and Warner (1998: 548) state that they

> … want to promote as the radical aspirations of queer culture building: not just a safe zone for queer sex but the changed possibilities of identity, intelligibility, publics, culture, and sex that appear when the heterosexual couple is no longer the referent or the privileged example of sexual culture.

More recently, forms of sexuality politics that do not contest the dominant heteronormative assumptions and institutions but uphold and sustain them have been described as 'the new homonormativity' (Duggan 2003: 50).

Studies of heteronormativity have also extended analysis to different contexts outside the West, opening up the exploration of broader understandings of subjectivity and difference, and connecting sexuality and gender norms with historical processes of colonization and decolonization, race, ethnicity, class and modernity, for example. Alexander's (1994) study of Trinidad and Tobago and the Bahamas examines the ways in which the governments of these newly-independent states established powerful signifiers about appropriate and decent sexuality in contrast to kinds of sexuality that were seen to imperil the new, decolonized nation state. Powerful feelings about sexuality, femininity and masculinity were mobilized by the state to embody and represent 'the nation'. One of the preconditions for this was the construction that the nation itself is in a process of disintegration and moral decay that incorporated both same-sex and opposite sex sexual practices and identities. In the field of international development, the concept of heteronormativity has also been deployed to analyze the 'heterosexist bias and gender normativity' in post/neo colonial state planning traditions and technologies, heavily influenced by international development theories, institutions and policies funding criteria (Lind 2010: 1). These narratives share either a conscious or an unintended complicity with reproductive heterosexuality and its central place in modernist international development conceptions of family life and the nation-state (ibid.: 10). The channelling of development aid to heterosexual couples by the World Bank is one example of more 'conscious' heteronormative development and social policies (see Bedford 2007). Meanwhile, feminist and international development NGO efforts to promote women's empowerment and rights, including sexual rights, have been found to unintentionally reinforce race, ethnic and class-based normative notions of the sexual and gendered subjectivities of indigenous, afro-descendent and mixed-race low-income women in Latin America, for example. In this context, lesbian subjectivity has come to represent a modern, urban subject of rights, in contrast to the traditional, heterosexual 'poor Third World woman' (Williams 2012). Norms vary across time, place and culture, and are reproduced, resisted and transformed by institutions, groups and individuals from the most progressive to the most conservative. They therefore serve to remind us of the importance of examining the nature of heteronormativity as the starting point of research, in order to understand the complexities of its workings of power, whether hidden, unintended, contradictory or explicit in any given context.

Further Reading: Chambers and Carver 2008; McClintock 1995; Moore 2007; Sedgwick 1990.

Note

1 See for example, the International Lesbian and Gay Association: 'Lesbophobia in France, 18/12/2006 *What is "Lesbophobia"?*'. Available at http://ilga.org/ilga/en/article/997. Accessed 16 January 2012.

INTERDISCIPLINARITY

Gabriele Griffin

From its inception in the late 1960s and early 1970s, Women's and Gender Studies as a subject in universities regarded itself as interdisciplinary. Interdisciplinarity here means that the study of women and gender draws on the knowledges and methods of a whole range of disciplines as well as developing its own knowledges and methodologies. Inaugurated by academic staff from the humanities, particularly literature and the social sciences, the study of women/gender did not arise as an abstract body of knowledge such as mathematics or history, but from an identity category: initially women, later increasingly gender (Evans 1991). One might thus argue that it was its focus – an identity category – that made the study of gender interdisciplinary in the first instance. Thus its field of enquiry encompassed not only the disciplines such as sociology and literature in which it first gained ground, but increasingly it moved across the boundaries of human and natural sciences as well. This is strikingly indicated in one of the early volumes on the topic, *Theories of Women's Studies* by Gloria Bowles and Renate Duelli Klein (1983), which included chapters with titles ranging from 'Feminism: a last chance for the humanities?' to 'The value of quantitative methodology for feminist research'. Here the first title points to the Humanities and to the ideological disposition (feminism) underpinning Women's/Gender Studies, and the second points to the issue of methods (here drawing on the social sciences and statistical, numbers-based methods). Together these indicate the concerns that occupied academics in Women's/Gender Studies as they sought to establish what the study of women/gender actually entailed, how it should be done (methods) and from what ideological perspectives. These concerns were partly a function of the issue of if, and how, Women's/Gender Studies should become part of the academy, rather than being only activist, for instance, in other words, a matter of the institutionalization of the subject (Morley and Walsh 1995).

Much of the early debate about the study of gender (which until the mid-1980s at least was very much conceived as the feminist study of women) concerned the extent to which such study should occur within traditional academic disciplines and therefore be discipline-specific, or if it should become established as a discipline in its own right (Aaron and Walby 1991). One side of the argument was that the study of gender should be an integral part of all disciplines and therefore should not be hived off into a separate arena. Knowing about women's literary legacies, for example, was as significant as giving due attention to gender-specific medical needs, and this would not be achieved if gender did not become an integral matter of consideration in all disciplines. The other side of the argument was that without being a named discipline in its own right, the study of women/gender would remain invisible and a matter of individual passionate advocates within traditional disciplines rather than a recognized domain of knowledge and object of enquiry. Establishing Women's/Gender Studies as a discipline in its own right also appeared to contradict the notion of it being an interdisciplinary subject. However, drawing on a range of disciplines and transforming their knowledges and methods to pursue the study of gender could of course occur more easily if this study was accepted as a discipline in its own right since it would enable its practitioners to decide how the discipline should operate.

These debates about Women's/Gender Studies as a discipline also had to contend with the realities of academic institutions which are quite diverse. In many countries women who were the main proponents of the study of gender found it easier to propagate such study within traditional disciplines than to set up new degrees, either undergraduate or postgraduate, in Women's or Gender Studies. In Spain, for example, new academic degrees are established by royal decree, which makes it very difficult to introduce a new discipline. In the UK, on the other hand, higher education since the 1980s has become increasingly market-driven and, provided there are students interested in taking the degree, one can introduce new degrees with relative ease. In 2012 the situation is that in many countries, especially in Europe, the USA, Australia, Canada, South Africa, India and Latin American countries, the study of gender is both significantly embedded in traditional disciplines where topics such as 'Women's writing' or 'Queer sexualities' which were unthinkable in the 1960s are routinely taught, and, on the other hand, in these same countries there are also a number of research centres and degree programmes devoted to the study of gender as a discipline.

The introduction of gender as an object of explicit and critical study in traditional disciplines during the 1970s coincided with significant debates, the so-called 'canon wars', about the content of university curricula and their lack of inclusivity (see Hull, Scott and Smith 1982). Not only gender, but class and ethnicity too became new categories of inquiry, and these put traditional disciplines under pressure to reframe their knowledge and methodologies, in particular to recognize how these traditional disciplines worked through their content and methods to exclude certain kinds of knowledge, for instance popular knowledge (see Hinds, Phoenix and Stacey 1992). The study of gender brought with it a recognition, for example, that women and men are encouraged to consume culture differently (Mills and Boon romances for women, football for men); inflected by class, this also showed that certain forms of culture were considered an appropriate object of study whilst others were not (so-called classic writers such as Shakespeare, and genres such as poetry were appropriate but soap operas on television were not). As different groups of women and men in the academy fought to change the traditional disciplines to become more inclusive of hitherto marginalized voices and socio-cultural practices, their disciplinary boundaries loosened and as part of this interdisciplinarity was increasingly claimed both by traditional disciplines and by newly emerging ones such as Gender Studies and Black Studies.

These claims led to debates about the nature of disciplinarity as such. Some claimed that all disciplines were interdisciplinary, at least to some extent, whilst others maintained that each discipline has its own knowledge domain and methodological practices, and that deep knowledge of a particular discipline required proper sustained study of that discipline which could not be gleaned from simply 'reading around' in a subject one had not studied. There were also increasing studies and reports of the difficulties inherent in interdisciplinary work, raising questions such as what is interdisciplinarity, how easy is it to work with people from very different disciplines who may understand concepts and methods in quite different ways from oneself, or what kinds of transformative knowledge can really be achieved through interdisciplinary work? (Griffin, Medhurst and Green 2006).

From the late 1990s onwards a number of terms – interdisciplinarity, transdisciplinarity, postdisciplinarity – entered the debate in an effort to theorize shifts in knowledge production and the loosening of previous disciplinary boundaries referred to above. These terms were concerned both with what was happening to disciplines and with what was happening in academic institutions and in research, where collaborations across disciplines were increasingly fostered, for example, by the kinds of thematic research programmes funders set up to deal with the complex problems of the contemporary world. So, for example, sociologists found themselves working with engineers and computer designers to understand the world of social networking online.

Whilst terms such as 'transdisciplinarity' were the objects of academic debate, prompted by a desire to understand how knowledge production was changing in an increasingly globalizing world and under the impact of new technologies, the question of the interdisciplinarity of Women's/Gender Studies receded during the 2000s. This is because issues of the institutionalization of Women's/Gender Studies were no longer so prominent, since that process had occurred in many countries. Instead, the focus shifted to a different term, 'intersectionality'. One of the debates within Women's/Gender Studies had been the extent to which gender was the key determining category of experience and knowledge, and to what extent experience and knowledge were shaped by the intersection of gender with other identity categories such as race, class, sexuality, religion or able-bodiedness. That debate went back to the 1970s when the feminist claims of that period made for women as equally oppressed and thus forming a 'global sisterhood' had been contested by diverse groups of women such as working-class women, lesbians and black women. They suggested that not all women's experience is the same, and that there were differences of power between, for instance, working-class and middle-class, and black and white women, women who employ female cleaners, and women who do the cleaning. Their experiences of oppression, for example, or of exclusion from the labour market or of differential access to resources were not only shaped by their gender but also by their colour, by their sexual identity, indeed, by a combination of multiple factors. Already in 1979 US legal scholar Kimberlé Crenshaw proposed the term 'intersectionality' to reference this complex interplay of multiple factors that effect women's experiences but it was not until the 2000s that it was widely taken up. In 2012 'intersectionality' has become a term widely used and theorized to discuss the complex structures underpinning the study of gender. It is not a term, however, as interdisciplinarity is, that addresses the issue of the study of gender as a discipline within academic institutions. Rather, it describes a theoretical position within the study of gender, one which has become increasingly prominent just as the practice of interdisciplinarity in the field of Women's/Gender Studies has also become more prominent.

The interdisciplinarity of the study of gender, much discussed between the 1970s and the 2000s as part of the effort to institutionalize that study, has become widely accepted in the 2000s, and is evident in new sub-fields of Women's/Gender Studies such as feminist science studies which brings together gender knowledge, feminist theory, feminist ethics and science to understand and critique how science practices are shaped by and shape gender. Here fields such as microbiology, nanotechnology and engineering that are conventionally considered to be discrete disciplines or sub-fields of science areas, are engaged with by gender scholars, to examine for instance how technologies such as ultrasound that make the foetus prenatally visible have changed debates about abortion, or the relative rights of the 'mother' and the 'child'. Gender scholars have shown, for example, that the possibility of viewing the foetus on-screen as a discrete entity has led to a diminution in concern for the woman carrying the foetus and her bodily integrity. Gender scholars have also been critical in analyzing the ways in which science through its technological presentation encourages certain narratives about the relation between the human and the non-human, conventionally regarded as distinct. Such narratives of distinctness deny the complex inter-relation and the inter-dependence between the human and the non-human, for instance in the ways in which women are encouraged to consider, even desire breasts implants to achieve a particular body shape that is highly normalized and to which their bodies may show, for example, anti-immune reactions. In her interdisciplinary work on the relations between the human, animals and technology, American feminist scholar Donna Haraway (1991) has coined the term 'cyborg' to describe the merger or fusion of human and machine that has become highly prevalent in contemporary culture, from its depictions in sci-fi and horror movies such as the *Aliens* film series, to people with implants and in constant contact with technology through the use of iPods, mobile phones, etc., which many people increasingly describe as being unable to live without. Working interdisciplinarily at the interface of gene technology, ethics and anthropology, gender researchers have shown how new reproductive technologies are on the one hand presented as 'natural' extensions of traditional heteronormative families and simultaneously, on the other, as putting these families into question as new kinship formations emerge. One example of this is the possibility of being pregnant with a child to whom one has no genetic relation since both the egg and the sperm were donated.

In the 2000s the claim of interdisciplinarity became commonplace, and it has been fostered in academic institutions through having thematic (rather than discipline-specific) research centres that focus, for example, on Applied Human Rights, say, drawing on the expertise of scholars from disciplines such as Gender Studies, Law, Economics and Religion, to provide new insights into how such rights might be practised. As this last sentence indicates, scholars working in academe in the 2000s were for the most part educated in traditional disciplines, often only in one, since the American concept of liberal arts colleges, where one takes a range of courses from diverse disciplines, is not widespread elsewhere. However, the complexities of the contemporary world, and technology-based shifts in the production of knowledge suggest that over the next decades, disciplinary and institutional practices will also shift to accommodate the drive towards interdisciplinarity that has now become widespread, and which has always been evident in Women's/Gender Studies.

Further Reading: Jackson 2004; Karlqvis 1999; Moran 2002; Anon: European Reports on Interdisciplinarity 2012; Tait and Lyall 2000.

INTERSECTIONALITY

Wendy Sigle-Rushton and Elin Lindström

Introduction

Intersectionality is a key concept in gender studies both because feminist scholars played a key role in its early development and because, once articulated, it has provided an enormously challenging critique with extensive theoretical and political implications. It is a concept with a rich and diverse genealogy, one in which gender studies figures prominently, not least because intersectionality can been seen as a logical extension of critical feminist approaches.

An important early contribution of feminist scholarship was its critique of mainstream research for not acknowledging or incorporating the experiences of women. Feminists developed tools to uncover strategies of power and exclusion that were hidden in mainstream, male-dominated and male-centred research. In an attempt to understand what it means to be oppressed 'as a woman', some feminist scholars sought to isolate gender oppression from other forms of oppression and as a direct consequence their work tended to be either preoccupied with the experiences of white middle-class women or to ignore completely the experiences of other women. It is from critiques of this (largely feminist) work that the development and articulation of intersectionality began to take shape. However, it wasn't until just over two decades ago that the theoretical concept found its name.

The term intersectionality was coined by Kimberlé Crenshaw (1989) in her seminal critique of US antidiscrimination law and its failure to acknowledge Black women's unique experiences of racism and sexism as simultaneous and inseparable. As Crenshaw argued, if there is no unified group of women that experience gender discrimination in the same way, it makes no sense to treat sexism and racism as if they could be isolated and then understood and redressed separately. Legislation that proceeds in this way fails to provide equal protection to Black women. While the concept did not represent a new way of thinking, its articulation gave voice to long-standing and widespread theoretical preoccupations and provided a much-needed frame of reference for the comparison and negotiation of various endeavours, opening up space for critical dialogue.

Described as '… one of the most important theoretical contributions that Women's Studies, in conjunction with related fields, has made thus far' (McCall, 2005: 1771), it did not take long for intersectionality to enter the feminist lexicon. Despite, or perhaps because of, its continued pervasiveness, intersectionality is understood in a wide variety of ways, as both a theoretical and an analytic tool. Nonetheless, relative to its theoretical sophistication, its methodology remains poorly specified and underdeveloped (McCall 2005; Nash 2008). With these two points in mind, rather than attempt to catalogue the myriad ways in which the concept can be formulated (both explicitly and implicitly), which would extend well beyond our limits of size and scope, we have chosen a more modest but more tractable strategy for our contribution. In what follows, we briefly present intersectionality's main theoretical premise and trace out its implications.[1] We pay particular attention to what the implications mean for how we analyze gender and gender inequalities. In recent years, researchers have expressed concern that 'there has been little discussion of how to study intersectionality, that is, of its methodology' (McCall 2005: 1771; see also Nash 2008). By illustrating some of the issues that must be grappled with when we seek to use intersectionality to rethink how we go about analysis, we aim to contribute to the development of this discussion.

Intersectionality: theoretical premise and critique

Intersectionality is, by all accounts, a loosely specified theoretical concept – an umbrella term – that brings together a set of ideas about the complex multidimensionality of subjectivity and social stratification and the consequences of its mis-specification. At its root, intersectionality posits that different dimensions of social life (hierarchies, axes of differentiation, axes of oppression, social structures, normativities) are intersecting, mutually modifying and inseparable. They 'fuse to create unique experiences and opportunities for all groups' (Brown and Misra 2003: 488). If we accept this basic premise, the implications are both extensive and profound. First, any (unqualified and unreflective) references to analytic categories such as gender, class, sexuality or ethnicity are deemed problematic. We cannot, for example, 'think of a woman's "woman-ness" in abstraction from the fact that she is a particular woman, whether she is a middle-class Black woman living in North America in the twentieth century or a poor white woman living in France in the seventeenth century' (Spelman 1988: 13). Second, because multidimensionality cannot be understood or assessed as a series of additive and separable relationships, we cannot, for example, understand Black women's experiences of discrimination by thinking separately about sex discrimination and race discrimination. Additive thinking of this sort, assumes away, for example, the possibility that Black women experience different kinds of gender oppression than white women or different kinds of racial oppression than Black men.

Taken together these two corollaries require that we take on and take in an enormous amount of complexity. Instead of a vector of social structures, each of which can be assessed in its own right, we are confronted with a 'matrix of domination' in which each cell represents a unique position (Collins 1999). But if we sacrifice complexity, we also sacrifice inclusion. Failing to account adequately for complexity means that the experiences of the multiply marginalized are likely to be overlooked or obscured, bringing issues of power and privilege within feminist theory and politics into stark relief. For example, consider the claim, common in Anglo-American feminisms during the 1970s, that gender inequality is rooted in women's exclusion from the public sphere of work and politics and that to redress gender inequality, feminism should promote women's entry into the public sphere by facilitating (or at least removing obstacles to) their labour market participation. This account tended to universalize the experiences of certain women, most of whom were white, middle- or upper-class women in heterosexual marriages. It was not necessarily relevant to all women, as Patricia Hill Collins' (1999: 45–67) overview of studies of Black women's experiences in the United States demonstrates. Rather than being confined to 'the private', there is a long history of Black women's paid or bonded work in the US 'public'. But instead of being a route to empowerment, it was, and for many remains, hard work for low pay, often in the low-status service sector. In addition, rather than 'the private' home being a source of subordination, it has been described as a site of respite from and resistance to the discrimination experienced in public (ibid.: 46).

Accepting the basic premise of intersectionality means acknowledging that power hierarchies not only stratify two supposedly homogenous groups – 'women' and 'men' – but that power hierarchies are also involved in determining whose experiences count and who gets to speak on behalf of 'women' (Spelman 1988: 77–79). It not only calls to mind analyses focusing on power, both in relation to sexuality and in relation to racialization, that document the ways in which the essentializing assumptions and perspectives of privileged women permeate much of feminist discourse. These concerns also resonate with postmodern and postructuralist arguments that the act of categorization itself is part of the workings of power, producing, policing and stratifying subjects.

Because it provides a powerful and salutary critique of how feminism has conducted itself, intersectionality raises some troubling questions. If we cannot somehow conceptualize or name women as a group, does feminist politics become meaningless? This leads to a commonly identified dilemma: '... how simultaneously to hold on to a radical and contingent account of knowledge claims and knowing subjects, thereby dissolving the false "we" of the feminist standpoint, while maintaining solidarity, across differences, among women in the name of a long-term or wide-ranging feminist movement' (Dietz 2003: 410).

Intersectional analysis

Thus far, we have discussed how intersectionality has provided a critical tool that was used to uncover important weaknesses in how we have gone about trying to understand and analyze gender. In this section, we consider how, taking the implications of intersectionality into account, we might modify the ways we analyze gender and gender inequality.

Broadly speaking, intersectionality requires that we sacrifice simplifying assumptions and embrace a good deal more complexity, while at the same time paying close attention to issues of power.

At present, there is no clear or straightforward solution for how that complexity can effectively be managed (McCall 2005). Clearly, an intersectional analysis should aim to treat different social dimensions as mutually modifying or reinforcing, but that is difficult, if not impossible, to accomplish in its entirety. If the theoretical premise is taken to its limit, 'this strategy can generate an infinite regress that dissolves groups into individuals' (Young 1994: 721). Collins (1999) suggests that researchers should focus on 'a concrete topic that is already the subject of investigation and ... find the combined effects of race, class, gender, sexuality, and nation, where before only one or two interpretive categories were used' (278). Even if we follow that pragmatic strategy and try to consider a limited but greater number of dimensions (and build on the findings of previous analytical endeavours), analyzing all of the permutations of even three or four categories can be daunting. It may dissolve into 'just a listing of people and a description without any analysis as to how their particular conditions are located within structures of power' (Crenshaw quoted in Guidroz and Berger 2009: 70).

To both deal with complexity and allow a greater balance between description and analysis, one strategy is to narrow the analysis to a particular set of intersections and focus intensively on marginalized or neglected groups located at the interstices of several social dimensions (McCall 2005). Comparisons with analyses that treat as homogeneous the more broadly defined category to which that group belongs provides opportunities to explore the diverse experiences of differentially located subjects. Nonetheless, to the extent that this approach is only the first stage of a larger project – one which seeks to redress previous oversights and the impact of previous exclusions on theory and practice – it is a strategy that defers rather than obviates questions about how to deal with complexity. Methods for dealing with complexity, including how to present it (a particularly vexing issue when faced with the constraints and space and scope imposed by some scholarly outlets like journals), remain limited and underdeveloped (Sigle-Rushton and Perrons 2007).

Both the broader and the narrower approaches to analysis that we have just described begin with the use of analytic categories. They both draw attention to the importance of heterogeneity within broadly defined analytic categories. But intersectionality highlights dilemmas that may lead us to ask whether (or at least when) it is possible to justify the use of categories in this way (McCall 2005). If categories will never sufficiently capture complexity and if the act of categorization is an exercise of power that disciplines and manages difference (Dietz 2003; 411–14), any approach that uses categories must proceed with great care. The choice of categories matters for how inequality comes to be understood, shapes whose situation is highlighted and obscured, and produces specific subject positions. Although methodological approaches which aim to deconstruct categories and those that provisionally and pragmatically make use of them might be understood as mutually exclusive and incompatible, we think this interpretation should be resisted. Intersectional analyses should aim both to document patterns of inequality and to explore how groups and categories are produced – and here we see the potential for intersectionality to build bridges across the material-discursive divide.

Concluding thoughts

In the past two decades, intersectionality has transformed the way we think about feminist theory and politics. Intersectionality illustrates the need for feminist scholars to pay greater attention to issues of inclusion, privilege and power. By drawing attention to processes of exclusion and its consequences, intersectionality highlights the need to critically question our own position and assumptions. It provides a salutary reminder that the conceptual models we employ determine not just what we ask but also what we are able to find, that our definition and use of categories, our underlying assumptions, and our modes of analysis all work to focus attention to some areas and divert it from others. Because intersectionality provides a set of critical questions and challenges that cannot be resolved, but must be made part of reflective approaches to feminist theory and practice, we expect it will remain both prominent and influential for years to come.

Further Reading: Brah and Phoenix 2004; Brewer et al. 2002; Lutz et al. 2011; Shalev 2008; Steinbugler et al. 2006.

Note

1 We acknowledge that space limitations mean our treatment of the underlying theoretical premise is both cursory and incomplete, and does not acknowledge the discussions and debates that surround its meaning and interpretation. However we are more concerned with the implications, the substance of which would remain generally unmodified were we to examine the core theoretical premise in more depth and detail.

LGBT POLITICS

Jeffrey Weeks

The label 'LGBT' (Lesbian, Gay, Bisexual, Transgender) emerged in the early 1990s, frequently with additional initials – most commonly Q (Queer), and I (Intersex) – suggesting an alliance of dissident sexualities and genders embracing both diversity and a sense of common cause and adversary. Language, words, categorization and self-description have been critical elements in the development of a consciousness of same-sex and what have come to be known as trans identities in America and Europe since the late nineteenth century. Terms such as homosexual, invert, third-sexer, intermediates, eonists, transvestites and transsexuals were all early efforts to break with the harsh language of perversion, abnormality or 'queerness' historically deployed to shame and outlaw same-sex desire and gender nonconformity. Some of the words subsequently changed their meanings, most notably homosexual which became virtually a medicalized term rather than a positive self-description. The widespread deployment of the word gay to describe a new personal and collective identification from the late 1960s (alongside the new affirmative use of the word lesbian) was a crucial step in the articulation of a new positive sense of self and political project. Similarly, twenty years later, the old term of abuse, queer, was resurrected within the gay world as a reversal of the discourse, now suggesting a self-adopted critical distancing form the norms and values of the heterosexual world. Words are magic, as Sigmund Freud suggested, and the words denoting dissident sexual and gender meanings, subjectivities, identities and belongings have had their own magical influence, creating as much as describing new forms of politics and cultural positionings.

Shifts in language are shaped by, and help shape, social change and political practice. The symbolic starting point for modern LGBT politics was the Stonewall riot in the early hours of 28 June 1969, in New York's Christopher Street. The riot was, in subsequent mythology, the day the queers fought back against the police, and the queers included drag-queens and transsexuals as well as respectable homosexuals and street gays. In this beginning was a common enemy, and an emerging common identity. The New York Gay Liberation Front (GLF) was established shortly afterwards, with the word gay representing this embryonic new identity. The gay liberation movement rapidly spread across the US, and within a year had crossed the Atlantic: the London GLF was founded in October 1970, and within a couple of years similar movements had spread rapidly in Europe and Australasia (Adam 1995). There had been a number of homophile reform movements in Western societies beginning in the late nineteenth century, and with notable new groupings after World War II in Scandinavia, Netherlands, France, Great Britain and the USA, but they were not necessarily or overtly movements of self-declared homosexuals, let alone of tranvestites or transsexuals, and they were certainly not mass movements. The new movement sought to transform that by creating a new type of mass mobilization.

Gay liberation was first and foremost an assertion of a new collective identity. At first gay was used as an all-embracing term, uniting men and women, young and old, black and white, homosexuals, transvestites and transsexuals. That soon changed, but it should not hide the sense of a mass emergence, and the significance of finding a new self-description. For over a hundred years homosexually inclined individual men and women lived in the shadows or closet, in large part shaped by the rigidities of gender. Gay liberation offered a new form of visibility, with 'coming out', openly declaring your homosexuality or gender dissidence, a central strategy. Coming out was a mark of pride and self-confidence, and a challenge to the status quo.

A sense of closely intertwined sexual and gender oppression initially held people together, though tensions were evident from the start. Especially for gay men the new politics was in the first place about sexual freedom. In the years that followed an explosion of sexual possibilities opened up. But it was soon apparent that the new movement was more than simply about sex, or about men. Lesbians from the start were reluctant to subordinate their own struggles to the sexualized needs and passions of gay men. A whole gamut of other identity positions soon spun off, around bisexuality, transvestism and transsexuality, sado-masochism, butch-femme relationships between women, and most controversially of all, inter-generational sex, often in sharp conflict with one another. Lesbian feminists were often vehemently hostile both to gay men and to transsexuals. Other voices were heard, from minority lesbians and gay men, arguing that the definitions of sexual freedom were too white, male, middle class. Each national experience proved to be subtly different from the dominant American norm (Tremblay et al. 2011). Other political, cultural and religious influences shaped different identity patterns: gay Marxists were balanced by gay Coservatives, even gay fascists;

gay Christians, gay Jews, gay Muslims, struggled to assert their own subjectivities. And from a wider perspective it soon became clear that however powerful the new gay consciousness was it was inevitably refracted through the limits of global circuits of power, the post-colonial experience, and the difficulties of local and regional struggles over sexuality (Adam et al. 1999).

It was soon apparent that the sexuality-gender nexus was an infinitely complex set of relations, locked into different regimes and matrices of power, giving rise to a variety of different sets of structures, histories and subjectivities. And LGBT identities could not easily be seen as the simple expression of a hitherto hidden essence. The new LGBT theorists spoke of the 'social construction' of sexualities, arguing that sexual and gender identities were historical inventions. There was no such thing as *the* homosexual, but instead there were many homosexualities (and indeed many hetero-sexualities) and many possible gender patterns, giving rise to many different ways of life. Identities were 'fictions', products of particular social situations and struggles (Weeks 1995); and were performative, acting out subject positions, sustained by constant repetition (Butler 1990). Identities were troubling, and they caused trouble, they disrupted things. People need them to give a sense of narrative continuity and ontological security. They locate us in a world of varying possibilities. They help to get things done. But identities were limiting, they fixed you, and potentially trapped you, even the new identities that emerged in the wake of gay and women's liberation.

From the early 1970s there was a huge expansion of LGBT community expressions in most Western countries, and wider – neighbourhoods, clubs, bars, self-help groups, campaigning groups, phone lines, newspapers, magazines, political caucuses, faith networks, mobilization around health issues, especially around HIV/AIDS from the early 1980s, sexual subcultures, shops, restaurants, trade union factions, legal campaigns, parenting support groups, campaigns against violence, student groupings, teachers' groups, business organizations, etc. The list was potentially enormous, reflecting the dynamism and ever increasing diversity of the LGBT world. The movement had morphed into a sometimes warring, but closely interlinked, loosely organized but emotionally and sexually intertwined civil society, in a continuous conversation about the meanings and possibilities, hopes and desires, of an every growing LGBT counter-public. But this powerful presence in most Western countries posed new questions about the implication of what was happening. Two different sorts of directions emerged.

On the one hand there was the consolidation of what was in effect akin to a gay ethnic identity. This was especially true in the USA, where the idea of a gay minority fitted readily into the pre-existing models of social and political organization, and readily gave rise to claims to rights based on claimed minority status. Gay liberation had set out to liberate the gayness of everyone, to end the category of the homosexual, and of the heterosexual too. Now the gay world was apparently moving towards a much narrower identity politics, organized around a very specific type of orientation, and this represented a real potential loss in freeing sexuality from the narrowing and defining and restricting categorizations that had been so vital a part of the forms of power that had regulated sexual desire. The search for the gay gene or the gay brain was now seen by many as an essential part of the claim to minority rights. Many out gay people affirmed their own sense of self and respectability by distinguishing themselves from sexual dissidents, including bisexuals and transgender people.

On the other hand, the growing reality was of a diversification of identities, a pluralism of subjectivities, and of political and cultural projects: a multiplication of politics around the body and subjectivity. There was no natural unity based on a given orientation. For many, moreover, sexuality was a preference, not a given biologically based orientation, a choice rather than a destiny. Unity was a matter of political positioning, not of natural affinities. So increasingly there was a weakening of the idea of a single movement. People could come together in particular crises, liked the one developing around HIV/AIDS in the 1980s, or against generally repressive backlashes, or in campaigns for specific rights. But such campaigns had to be shaped and constructed, not assumed. The queer insurgency that emerged in the wake of AIDS, and the development of what became known as 'queer theory' were prime examples of this – in part seeking a revival of the radicalness of early gay liberation, in part responding to new challenges in the wake of AIDS. For some queer activists, the consolidation of a gay ethnicity was a trap, a new form of regulation and control. The emergence of the LGBT label signalled this new position. Lesbian, gay, bisexual, transgender, queer, querying, intersexed – what unified them was less a specific orientation and more a strategic positioning, a political alliance that was not pre-given but was always in process of construction.

Accompanying these developments on the gound there was an increasingly sophisticated theoretical analysis. A series of new concepts had been developed to explain the specifics of gay oppression. 'Homophobia' was perhaps the first and this has been enormously influential. Originally seen as a form of phobic hostility towards homosexuality, it broadened into a term for a generalized hostility towards homosexuality expressed in a variety of forms ranging from personalized violence and media prejudice to legislative and judicial practice (Weeks 2011). Related concepts such as biphobia and transphobia later emerged to describe entrenched hostility towards bisexuality and transgender. The early concept of heterosexism moved things further by positing that prejudice and discrimination against LGBT people were based on notions of innate heterosexual superiority. This was to become a central motif of LGBT and queer theory.

This has been discussed in various terms such as 'compulsory heterosexuality', the 'heterosexual matrix', the 'heterosexual panorama' and the 'heterosexual imperative' while queer theorists developed the concept of 'heteronormativity' (Warner 1991). All are attempts to explain the defining, normalizing power of the heterosexual assumption, embodied in historical and social structures, which marginalizes sexual and gender dissidence at best, and invalidates them at worse. At its heart is a binarism that enshrines and legitimizes the apparently exclusive definitions of heterosexuality and homosexuality, and encodes sexual and gender norms: homosexual desire and gender nonconformity are the Others, whose existence confirms the normality of the dominate term, heterosexuality.

There is another question lurking behind this theoretical position, and that is how this binary, hierarchically system intersects with other structures of power, because power is complex, positive and protean: it takes many forms. The interlocking, mutually reinforcing intersections of various forms of power and domination around sexuality was first identified by Black feminists in the 1980s as it became clear that white feminist analyses could not speak to the experience of all women. A vast amount of work has now been done on these issues, and LGBT or queer theory has become increasingly sophisticated in the ways in which it analyzes the social relations of sexuality, the specifics of heteronormativity, and the intersections of sexuality with other categories of difference (Taylor 2010). Individual identities are shaped by and at the juncture of a host of often conflicting dynamics: of class, gender, ethnicity and race, and a host of other influences including nationality, faith, geography, age and generation, ability and disability.

Early gay liberationists had taken for granted that gay freedom was incompatible with the existing sexual order. But since the 1990s there has been a remarkable, if uneven liberalization of social attitudes towards same-sex relations, especially in Western Europe, Australasia and North America. In the USA where LGBT rights are highly charged politically and fiercely contested, the LGBT community still remains the most vibrant and inventive in the world. In most of these countries formal equality has become the norm, laws enshrining unequal ages of consent and other inequalities have been repealed, the protection of the law has been extended to sexual minorities. Same-sex marriage or civil partnerships, and parenting rights have unexpectedly become central LGBT goals, and legislated for in many jurisdictions, reflecting a shift in emphasis in LGBT politics from a focus on identity towards one on relational rights. At the same time, transgender people have acquired new forms of recognition, such as the right to reassignment of gender in official documentation, though unevenly (Weeks 2011: 167–70, 217–18).

For many LGBT people themselves this is a move towards full and equal citizenship. For many queer critics, however, this is little more than an accommodation to, or assimilation within, the status quo. They point out the continuation of homophobic attacks, the reality of active discrimination in many areas of life, and the continuation of the hegemony of heteronormative values in cultural values and institutions. In many other parts of the world, homophobic and transphobic violence and discrimination is often linked to religious fundamentalism and a rejection of Western values. Across large parts of Africa and the Caribbean homosexuality has been denounced by post-colonial regimes as a Western import and imposition. LGBT people who have tried to form or join organizations have been violently persecuted in Uganda, Zambia, Zimbabwe, Jamaica and elsewhere. Transgender people have been murdered in the streets of some Latin American countries, such as Argentina, Brazil and Venezuela. But this is not simply a problem of the global South. In post-Soviet Russia and Eastern Europe the formal legalization of homosexuality has not changed the attitudes of conservative moral forces, and discrimination and persecution remain common (Kulpa and Mizielińska 2011).

Across the globe, declarations of conservative sexual morality are targeted particularly at women and sexual minorities, often to police the boundaries of nation or faith, and of gender and heterosexuality (Bhatt 1997). At the same time there is a new awareness of the importance of human rights discourses in developing social justice for sexual and gender minorities. A sense of common being has been encouraged by the growing awareness of various forms of discrimination against same sex and transgendered activities.

The promotion of positive LGBT identities has been taken up by a host of national and transnational NGOs and by international bodies such as the European Union, the Council of Europe, UNAIDS in the wake of the AIDS pandemic and even the United Nations (Altman 2001). The work of these international organizations has been crucial in shaping LGBT rights as human rights, and in putting them on the global agenda (Corrêa et al. 2008).

The danger, however, is that Western categories of identity do not necessarily map easily or at all on the complex gender and sexual maps of local cultures. The advocacy of gay rights per se may be inappropriate in societies that lack a categorical distinction between homosexuality and heterosexuality. Social anthropology has long known of the existence of long-established transgendered cultures in areas as wide apart as Latin America, India and the Philippines, but these cannot be read either as proto-gay cultures or as examples of contemporary trans identities. They exist in their own right, exemplars of the intricacies of sexual and gender subjectivities on a global scale. Both international bodies and NGOs in their enthusiasm for promoting human rights can impose culturally insensitive meanings on diverse cultures.

This poses an immense challenge to LGBT campaigners. In the end what they are supporting have to be more than particularist claims. They are in fact posing profound questions about what it means to be human in a globalized world, which in many parts still seeks to deny the humanity of non-heterosexual or gender challenging people (Butler 2005a). Sexuality and gender are more than simply attributes of an individual or the focus of identity. They define a relationship with the self and with others, they become central to one's very humanity. To assert the value of LGBT identities and ways of life is to challenge existing realities, and to show that there are many different ways of being both sexual and gendered – and of being human. This is the ultimate achievement of LGBT politics since the 1960s.

Further Reading: Aggleton, Boyce, Moore and Parker 2012; Moore 2007; Plummer 1995; Stryker and Whittle 2006; Weeks 2007.

THE MALE GAZE

Griselda Pollock

Rightly disowned as oversimplified, the concept of 'the male gaze' is the distorting shorthand for theoretical and aesthetic feminist work on power, desire and ethics in the visual field. Originating with Freud's revolutionary conceptualization of the eroticized looking and being looked at within infantile sexuality, itself theorized by Freud as being incited by dependency rather than an inborn essence, and then inflected by Lacanian structuralist positing of 'the gaze' as hauntingly lost psychic object 'a' that, signifying loss, incites desire, feminist theories of the gaze move from deconstruction of cinematic (and artistic) spectatorship to ethical encounters with the other and to modes of non-scopic gazing that are more associated with touching and connecting (Freud 1905; Lacan 1975; Ettinger 2006).

First, there is no such thing as 'the male gaze'; analyzing sexuality and spectatorship is radically short-changed by a tagline that links pleasure in looking at women to predatory masculine heterosexual eroticism. The gaze intersects with sexual difference where theorizing gender as a socio-cultural formation but more importantly as an asymmetrical relation of power (Scott 1986) meets cinema as a machine creating pleasure and meaning and ideologically replaying or reinforcing psycho-social formations of sexual difference (Metz 1977; Mulvey 1974/1988), and psychoanalysis as a theory of that formation of sexed subjectivities through the crises of loss and desire (Freud 1905; Lacan 1975).

What's wrong with the term *male gaze? Male* establishes both an opposition – its pair is female – positing gender as a binary of heteronormative difference (man/woman) in a term associated with zoology, assuming a given anatomy that pre-determines sex/gender. Drawn from psychology and more specifically from psychoanalysis, the term *masculine* at least posits a provisional psycho-linguistic, culturally determined *positioning*. Feminist theory, therefore, analyzes the *masculinization* of the privileged locus of seeing and associated fantasies of agency in the cinematic apparatus.

Shifting from the *gaze*, we move to the *scopic field. Skopein* is the Greek verb for watching with intent. Freud borrowed it to define one of the primary components of sexuality: *scopophilia,* using the sight of another erotically or pleasurably. Beyond perception, *scopic* field refers to a psychoanalytically conceived investigation into the ways in which humans psychically invest seeing, being seen, watching secretly, exhibitionism and anxiety about what we might see. The eye can be an erotic organ and vision a site of phantasy. Scopophilia, fetishism, voyeurism, exhibitionism, narcissism, and masquerade indicate how complex is 'sexuality in the field of vision' (Rose 1986).

Challenging *the* gaze, as if it were monolithic and singular, feminist theory deconstructs *the heterosexual masculinization of the spectator position* in cinema, the prime industrial apparatus creating a commoditized scopic field offering meaning and pleasure. Despite the hegemony of the *masculinized* viewing position, there are always resistant and transgressive counter-positions: queer, postcolonial, and gender-subversive gazes. There are non-phallic possibilities for subjectivities, desires and fantasy in an expanded scopic field (Ettinger 2006). Displacing misconceptions denouncing objectifying looking by 'men', the concept of a *masculinized* gaze becomes a prism to probe the pleasures and anxieties associated with seeing as a psycho-symbolic and psycho-sexual activity because it takes place in a historically specific *phallocentric* ordering of sexual difference (phallocentric means organizing s on a +/-binary: having/not having/ masculine/feminine). Psychoanalysis, however, insists that no subject position is ever fixed, no sexed subjectivity fully realized (Rose 1994). Thus recreated scenarios for watching and being seen offered by paintings, photographs or movies, offer to the spectator, irrespective of gender and sexuality, fluid possibilities for identifying in fantasy with various positions (Mulvey 1988). Hence pleasures of viewing can be contrary to sociologically assumed gender positioning even while narratives return us to dominant organizations of gender and sexuality. Recent theory has explored other kinds of gazing: curiosity (Mulvey 2006) and the 'pensive spectator' resulting from the effects of digitalization and home viewing of film on DVD (Mulvey 2006).

The classic theory of the gaze has two foundations. Freudian psychoanalysis identifies vision and the visual field as a component of the formation of sexuality and Lacanian psychoanalysis describes the drama of subjectivities sexed in relation to loss and desire itself generated by loss. For Freud seeing becomes erotic and hence violent, oscillating between a fantasy of mastery and a dread of a dangerous sight (Freud 1905). For Lacan scopic field is tragic, endlessly scanned for an unknown 'objet a' from which we imagine we have been severed when we assumed a sexed positionality (Lacan 1963/1997).

Second, structuralist film studies defined cinema as an apparatus (De Lauretis and Heath 1985). Industrialized cinema involves production and consumption: their intersection is 'the' spectator in relation to the screen. 'The' spectator is not an actual, embodied social viewer; it is an imaginary projection of the cinematic apparatus (shaped by film as text to organize a system of meaning in the specular situation in which film is consumed). It summons ordinary men and women with varied sexualities, ethnicities, class backgrounds, interests and competences into its dream world. Immobilized in darkness, we become regressed spectators, suspending our particularities to wander in the imaginary space unfolding on the screen that activates formative psychic mechanisms of identification with others who are at once like us, and ideal versions of what we narcissistically would like to be like (Metz 1977). The screen projects a fantasy world; we lend our own freewheeling fantasies to animate its anthropomorphic signifiers.

The concept of *the* spectator is not, therefore, generalizing or universalizing; the cinematic apparatus itself posits an ideal viewing position to which the socially determined cinematic world's ideological order is addressed, from which its stories make sense and into which we enter irrespective of class, gender or race, even while these realities can interrupt our pleasure and may damage us when finding only negative images of our sexualities, ethnicities or social origins on screen.

The projected spectatorial position is sewn into the movement of narrative, by edits, sequencing, suspense, framing, lighting, and by plots, characters, stars and endings. Hence cinema is a play of gazes: the camera's gaze that originally records the event often with a god-like omniscience or a capacity to see close up and in detail; the gazes that pass between and often form a hierarchy of looking/being-looked-at between characters in the narrative; the spectator's gaze at the screen, aligned with the originating camera's look, providing the spectator with the fantasy of omniscience (the world is offered to the viewer's visual mastery) and inviting identification, but selectively, with some of the privileged characters. This creates a gendered division of labour on screen, which supports the agency of looking for some characters and offers others to be gazed at, hence visually and narratively mastered, even while as actors and characters they have the power of sight as well.

How does this work?

In the most famous and consistently misread article about sexual difference and cinema (Mulvey 1974), Laura Mulvey identified a paradox at the heart of narrative cinema and its pleasures – for all its viewers, and particularly for those who watch cinema under the sign of 'woman'. Mulvey constructed a three-part argument whose architecture must be carefully plotted to grasp the inherent contradictions in the masculinization of the spectatorial position in cinema and the violence of the gender hierarchy it creates.

In Freud's theory of sexuality, the impotent infant masters the world initially through sight, investing its eyes with its earliest pleasures and fantasies of control. Active visual control of the other is matched by the pleasure in being embraced by the (maternal) gaze. Thus *active* scopophilia – pleasure in looking – oscillates in all infants with equally delightful *passive* exhibitionism, irrespective of any future gender identifications. With the formation of the ego, however, a conflict emerges. The ego narcissistically invests in its own body, self and even image, as well as aligning this emerging self with ideal others through identification, others already marked by cultural definitions of gender, i.e. differences of and power. They represent gendered oppositions of power/powerlessness back to the subject-to-be. Under a phallocentric organization of culture, the narcissism that dictates ego identification with agency comes into conflict with the earlier oscillations between active/passive looking. Solution: a split along gendered lines so that active looking is constructed as *masculine* and exhibitionism as *feminine*; masculine/feminine being merely terms for phallic binary of active/passive.

Then comes the sexualizing Oedipal crisis through which we are traumatically subjected to a phallocentric ordering of sexual difference based on threat and loss. Each subject must take up one position, giving up the mobility between active and passive pleasures typical of infancy. Why is it a crisis and how does it impact on the gaze in culture? If the cultural resolution of active/passive oscillation is to create a dichotomy in which the masculine is identified as the agent of a mastering and controlling gaze and the feminine is cast as the exhibitionist, coded as 'to-be-looked-at', and post-Oedipally as the erotic spectacle for the heterosexual masculine, it is the Oedipal situation that renders this very gendered and gendering division traumatic for the now masculinized position of visual agency.

The masculine is simply that position which is not the feminine, the latter appearing to lack the privileged signifier of power, the phallus. 'She'(-) is cast as castrated and hence her *image* threatens castration to anyone looking at the image of woman as a potential source of erotic pleasure: the masculine. If 'woman', the signifier of the desirable and the beautiful to look at is, in fact, the fatally deceptive screen for a bleeding wound and hence the bearer of a threat of mutilation that would disempower and destroy masculinity (defined by being the one who has it (+)), how can she(-) be good to look at?

Thus Mulvey's argument was never a simple one merely asserting that men liked to look at women's bodies erotically or objectified women sexually. *She was exposing its opposite.* She thus explained the doubled violence involved in the manufactured 'image of woman' in a phallocentric visual culture. What characterizes phallocentric cinema and visual culture by extension are the defensive manoeuvres formed to negotiate the contradictions inherent in creating a spectacular apparatus that masculinizes gazing. To defend the masculine subject as agent of the gaze from the threat posed by 'seeing' the castrated feminine, cinema performs two operations, sometimes together.

First, *fetishistic scopophilia* builds up the aesthetic beauty of the spectacle to distract and hence to displace the anxiety aroused by the image of woman. Fetishism is a theory by which two incompatible beliefs are held as a result of deadly anxiety. Thus, the fetishist *knows* that the woman does not have the phallus but *believes* she does by creating a fetish as stand-in for the missing phallus that simultaneously displaces the knowledge of castration and memorializes the site of perpetual threat. Extreme costuming and cosmeticized glamour makes the woman-image distractingly and impossibly beautiful while also often cruelly binding her body into extraordinarily fetishistic clothes that unnaturally redraw or exaggerate its contours (Mulvey 1988).

Second, *sadistic voyeurism* occurs more through narratives of investigation, which lead to punishment or death of an often transgressively active woman, the *femme fatale*, the gangster's moll, the feminist, or narratives of conquest that lead to her domestication and marriage.

Laura Mulvey exposed the knotting of several different levels of psychic formations, symbolic systems and the central drama of phallocentric ordering of sexual difference in visual representation through the identification of the feminine with castration, the negative position (-), producing fears of mutilation and dispossession threatening the narcissistic and paternally identified subject position: masculine (+). This structure equally signifies other relations of power and can be enacted between men to mark racial or social dominance. To grasp how dominant cinema and other visual regimes organize seeing and being seen as both gendered active/passive, masculine/feminine and as subject to the violent anxieties of phallocentric masculinity and its castration anxiety is to have both a means of analyzing the visual habits of cinema and its dominant narratives and a way to begin to imagine how else we might configure the cinematic field of vision, the forms of gazing in visual culture from art to our own photographic practices.

Often misreading the potential of her argument, some critiqued Mulvey for overlooking the social experiences of a viewer, a man or a woman, white or black, straight or queer, rich with their own complexities of lived social identities. This produced ethnographic and phenomenological explorations of how women and gay or minority men actually watch the movies and renegotiate dominant viewing positions and narratives that replay, at the level of story and character as well as textual structure, a privileged white, hetero-normative order (Stacey 1987). African-American bell hooks narrated her own anxious experience as a black child constantly searching the screen for anyone like her with whom to identify as a full subject as opposed to the limited figures of mammy, slave or seductress, and finding momentary gratification in the character of Paola Johnson (Freddi Washington) in *Imitation of Life* (John Stahl 1934), who resists her subordination as a black woman in a racist society and claims agency momentarily (hooks 1992). Jane Gaines indicted Mulvey for stressing gender at the expense of social and material determinants such as race and class, although the example she used, *Mahogany*, starring Diana Ross, the story of a Chicago working-class woman wanting to be a designer who becomes a fashion model, supports both Gaines's social and Mulvey's psychoanalytical readings: a key scene is between the black political activist Brian and the fashion photographer Sean, which reveals that the gendered hierarchy Mulvey structurally identified operates between men to reproduce power and emasculation (Gaines 1988).

In this scenario could there be a feminized spectator to counter this structure? In films addressed to women, like melodrama and the women's film where stories and characters aim to appeal to a specifically female audience, Mary Ann Doane 1987, using Freud's work on masochism (inverted sadism) has shown that such films structure a solely masochistic position for their leading feminine character who functions as an internal spectator. Her gaze is de-eroticized and the woman as spectator as a result disembodied (Doane 1982, Kaplan 1983).

As a filmmaker, Mulvey's purpose was polemical. She aimed to incite counter-cultural or avant-garde film practices that could create a 'new language of desire' in cinema. Filmmakers such as Mulvey, Chantal Akerman, Sally Potter, Sheila McLaughlin, Julie Dash, therefore, experimentally generated feminist cinematic techniques offering visual pleasures while not reinscribing racist, classist, and heteronormative and phallocentric effects. Not merely changing plotlines, counter-cinema has to alter the imaginary of spectatorship, creating critical, disenchanted viewers, with formally innovative reshaping of narratives about the psycho-social complexities of the feminine position and gendered experience across race, class and sexuality. They played with time and duration rather than quick cutting, use of uncut or long shots that refuse voyeurism, 360-degree pans so as to avoid suspense and voyeuristic expectation, and non-fetishistic framing of the women's bodies.

Feminist film theories and practices displace gender as identity to stress the formal and technical resources of the moving image that do not replay dramas of mastery and domination, do not fearfully enact violent humiliation and punishment, do not eroticize others while denying space for their desire and subjectivity.

More recent feminist cinema studies explore other dimensions of affect and meaning associated with the voice, colour and fluidity in women's directors like Jane Campion (Watkins 2009), the haptic (touching rather than vision) in diaspora cinema (Marks 1999) and the potential of Irigaray's aesthetics of sexual difference for analyzing cinema by men directors (Bainbridge 2008).

Painting and photography have also been critical sites of feminist deconstruction (Pollock 1988). Drawing on Lacan's radical retheorization of the gaze (Lacan 1963/1977) as a structural lost object, that we seek to re-find, or be re-found by, hence which incites our desiring scanning of the visual field for both the other and ourselves being seen within it, Bracha Ettinger theorizes a *matrixial gaze*, not premised on castration-based concepts of subjectivity that produce a logic of plus/minus/masculine/feminine (Ettinger 2006). She posits a psychic organization of primordial severalty and co-emergence, using the metaphor of prenatal/prematernal relations-without-relating, which makes us long, not for Lacan's lost object to make us whole, but for the lost connectivity with which we might be differentially, but mutually transformed. This matrixial gaze yields *fascinance*: an aesthetic experience of prolonged, non-dominative and speculative gazing, not *at*, but *with*, the experience of the other, that opens up a shared border space for trans-subjective affects to happen, thus shifting the field of vision from the erotic and sadistic, to the ethical and the compassionate (Ettinger 2005, 2006).

Further Reading: de Lauretis 1984; Doane 1982; Gamann and Marshment 1987.

MEN, MASCULINITY AND MASCULINITIES

Jeff Hearn

Introduction

The concept of 'men', like that of 'man' or 'Man', is frequently taken for granted as adults of the male sex. Yet, 'men', like 'women', is a social category. While studies that are implicitly about men are as ancient as scholarship itself, thanks to feminist, gay and a variety of other critical gender scholarship, a sub-field of gendered studies on men and masculinities, in which there is a more explicit naming of men as men (Hanmer 1990) has been established. This sub-field is known under various labels, including uncritically and ambiguously as 'men's studies'. A more suitable label, at least for critical work located within Women's and Gender Studies is Critical Studies on Men and Masculinities. While it is still relatively unusual to see 'men' as a social category, the concepts of masculinity and the masculine are well established. The concept of masculinities is much more recent, dating from the late 1970s.

Masculinity

The word, masculinity, derives from the Middle English *masculin*, from Middle French and from Latin *masculinus* ('male, of masculine gender', 'male person, male') and *masculus* (male). Recorded uses of *masculine* date from the late fourteenth century: 'belonging to' or 'of the male sex'. The grammatical use of masculine is from the same period. More specific meanings of having the 'appropriate' qualities of the male sex, such as 'virility' and 'powerfulness', date from the early seventeenth century. These have been elaborated to refer to characteristics thought to be suitable for men; traits of behaving in ways considered typical for or characteristic of men; or properties characteristic of the male sex. The concept links closely with concepts of manhood and manliness.

Modern analysis of masculinity can be traced to the pioneering psychologies of Freud and Adler, demonstrating that adult character was not predetermined but constructed through emotional attachments to others in a turbulent growth process. Anthropologists such as Malinowski and Mead further emphasized cultural differences in such processes. By the mid-twentieth century, these ideas had crystallized into the concepts of masculinity and male sex role.

The concept of masculinity has been used to analyze literary, cultural and other texts.

In the 1960s and 1970s masculinity was understood mainly as an internalized role, identity or (social) psychological disposition, reflecting particular dominant (often meaning US or Western) cultural norms or values acquired by social learning from socialization agents. In masculinity–femininity (m–f) scales certain items were scored as 'masculine' (e.g. 'aggressive', 'ambitious', 'analytical', 'assertive', 'athletic') compared with other items scored as 'feminine' (e.g. 'affectionate', 'cheerful', 'childlike', 'compassionate', 'flatterable'). The best known are various formulations of the Bem Sex Role Inventory (BSRI), some initially framed as a continuum, some later versions stressing separate dimensions for masculinity and femininity. Such notions of masculinity were subject to criticism in the 1970s and 1980s, both substantively and conceptually. For example, measurable m–f scales have been critiqued for ethnocentrism (especially US-centrism), obscuring of differences between cultural ideals and practices, ignoring which gender assesses which gender, bias in using students in constructing scales, and lack of power perspective (Eichler 1980).

At the same time, in various theories of patriarchy, men as a gender class, and different sub-categories of men within that class, were analyzed societally, structurally and collectively. Different theories of patriarchy have emphasized men's structural social relations to women, in terms of biology, reproduction, politics and culture, family, state, sexuality, economic systems, and various combinations thereof. However, by the late 1970s, some feminist critics were suggesting the concept of 'patriarchy' was too monolithic, ahistorical, biologically determined, and dismissive of women's resistance and agency.

Masculinities

Masculinities theory developed from the late 1970s at the same time as feminist auto-critiques of the concept of patriarchy. The twin debates and critiques – around masculinity/male sex role and patriarchy – in many ways opened up the conceptual and political terrain for a more differentiated approach to masculinities. Building on both social psychological and social structural accounts, social constructionist perspectives of various kinds highlighting complexities of men's social power have been developed. Masculinities have been interrogated in the plural, not the singular, as, for example, with hegemonic, complicit, subordinated, marginalized or resistant masculinities. Such different masculinities have sometimes been understood as *types*, sometimes as *social processes*. Key features in such analyses include: critique of sex role theory; emphasis on masculinities as power-laden, in men's unequal relations both to women and between men; highlighting the implications of gay liberation/scholarship and sexual hierarchies; acknowledgement of social and historical transformations, contradictions, resistance, and interrelations of institutional/social, interpersonal and intra-psychic (psychodynamics) dimensions. The concept of masculinities has been extremely important in widening the social and societal analysis of men and gender relations (Brod 1987; Carrigan et al. 1985; Brod and Kaufman 1993; Connell 1995). The construction of masculinities has been explored in many different arenas, including: global and regional; institutional; interactional; and individual men's gendered performance and identity constructions. Masculinities vary and change across historical time and cultural space, within societies, and through life courses and biographies.

The first substantial discussion of the idea of 'hegemonic masculinity' was in the paper, 'Men's bodies', written by Raewyn Connell in 1979 (Connell 1983). Its background was debates on patriarchy, and the hegemony in question was that involved in patriarchal gender relations. The paper examined the social construction of the body in boys' and men's practices. In discussing 'the physical sense of maleness', the social importance of sport as 'the central experience of the school years for many boys' was emphasized – taking and occupying of space, holding the body tense, skill, size, power, force, strength, physical development and sexuality. In addressing adult men's bodies, physicality within work, sexuality and fatherhood are highlighted. Connell stressed 'the embedding of masculinity in the body is very much a social process, full of tensions and contradiction; ... physical masculinity is historical, rather than a biological fact, ... constantly in process, constantly being constituted in actions and relations, constantly implicated in historical change' (p. 30).

The notion of hegemonic masculinity was elaborated in the early 1980s, in the light of gay activism and scholarship. It was argued that it is not men in general who are oppressed in patriarchal relations, but particular groups, such as gay men, whose situations relate differentially to the 'logic' of women's subordination to men (Carrigan et al. 1985: 586). In *Masculinities*, Connell (1995) discussed hegemonic masculinity in more depth, reaffirming the link with

Gramsci's analysis of economic class relations through cultural dynamics, and noting that hegemonic masculinity is open to challenge and change. Hegemonic masculinity is now defined as: 'the configuration of gender practice which embodies the currently accepted answer to the problem of legitimacy of patriarchy, which guarantees (or is taken to guarantee) the dominant position of men and the subordination of women' (p. 77).

Though stable, hegemonic masculinity is seen as contested and subject to struggle and change. The most powerful bearers of the cultural ideal of hegemonic masculinity are not necessarily the most powerful individuals. Indeed individual holders of power may be very different to those who represent hegemonic masculinity as a cultural ideal. Even so there is often some degree of correspondence between the cultural ideal and institutional power, such as state and corporate power. There are also complex interplays of hegemonic, subordinated, complicit and marginalized forms of masculinity, as when some black men or gay men adopt or accept aspects of hegemonic masculinity but remain marginalized. In 2005 Connell and Messerschmidt re-evaluated the concept of hegemonic masculinity. They suggested rejection of the continued use of psychological trait theory and of too simple a model of global gender dominance. Some ways forward are presented, including more holistic understanding of gender hierarchy; importance of geographies of masculinities; emphasis on social embodiment; and dynamics of masculinities, including contestation and democratization.

Development and critique

The reformulation of masculinity to masculinities is not, however, without problems. The term, 'masculinities', has been used in very different, sometimes confusing and even circular, ways (Clatterbaugh 1998). It can be unclear if we are talking about cultural representations, everyday practices or institutional structures. How exactly the various dominating ways of men – tough/aggressive/violent; respectable/corporate; controlling of resources; controlling of images; and so on – connect with each other is not resolved. The concept of hegemonic masculinity may fail to demonstrate the autonomy of the gender system from class and other social systems. In particular, we may ask: why is it necessary to hang on to the glossing concept of masculinity, rather than being more specific by referring to, say, men's practices, men's identities, men's psychodynamics or men's collective actions (Hearn 1996)?

One way of proceeding in the light of these critiques is to conceptualize masculinities as discursive positionings. Many detailed discursive and ethnographic researches have provided close-grained descriptions of multiple, internally complex masculinities, for example, in how men talk about themselves. Margaret Wetherell and Nigel Edley (1999) identified three specific 'imaginary positions and psycho-discursive practices' in negotiating hegemonic masculinity and identifications with the masculine: heroic positions, 'ordinary' positions, and rebellious positions. The first conforms more closely to the notion of complicit masculinity: '... it could be read as an attempt to actually *instantiate* hegemonic masculinity since, here, men align themselves strongly with conventional ideals' (emphasis in original) (p. 340). The second seeks distance from certain conventional or ideal notions of the masculine; instead the 'ordinariness of the self; the self as normal, moderate or average' (p. 343) is emphasized. The third is characterized by its unconventionality, with the imaginary position involving flouting social expectations (p. 347). With all these positionings, especially the last two, ambiguity and subtlety are present in (self-)constructions of masculinity, hegemonic or not. Indeed one feature of the hegemonic may be its very elusiveness: the difficulty of reducing it to a set of fixed positions and practices. Other approaches see masculinity as specific meanings maintained in local language use analyzed through conversation analysis or as comprising signs and practices obscuring contradictions.

In identifying forms of domination by men, of both women and other men, the concept of hegemonic masculinity has been notably successful, even surprisingly so. One reason why the concepts of masculinities and hegemonic masculinity have been so well used is their heuristic and pedagogical strength. On the other hand, the very vagueness of hegemonic masculinity and associated masculinities, and the different ways in which the concepts can be employed, sometimes talking past each other within contrasting political, disciplinary and epistemological positions, can be part of the reason for its relatively strong take-up. Moreover the broad frame of masculinities theory has developed from a wide range of influences, from Gramscian Marxism and critique of categoricalism to pluralism, intersectionality, practice theory, structuration theory, and psychodynamics, so that different adherents can emphasize different theoretical bases. It has even been adapted via discourse theory and poststructuralism, as well as in literary studies, visual studies and the humanities more generally. Hegemonic masculinity has acted as a way of talking about men and gender relations, even though there are major disagreements in how the concept is to be used. It has been a key theme around which research and policy debates have been conducted, and used in quite different, even opposing, ways in specific national and regional contexts. Yet notably, focused analysis of hegemony and legitimacy are typically absent from many applications of hegemonic masculinity (*pace* Hearn 2004; Howson 2006; Aboim 2010).

Much recent work has emphasized multiple or composite masculinities, multiple ways of being men and multiple forms of men's structural, collective and individual practices, interrelations between them, and complex intersections of masculinities, powers, other social statuses and indeed violences. There has been a strong emphasis on the interconnections of gender with other social divisions, such as age, class, disability, ethnicity, nationality, religion and sexuality. Analysis of relations of gender and class can demonstrate how different classes exhibit different forms of masculinities and the ways in which these both challenge and reproduce gender relations among men and between women and men. Masculinities are placed in cooperative and conflictual relations with each other – in organizational, occupational and class relations – and in terms defined more explicitly in relation to gender, such as family, kinship, sexuality. Such relations are beset by contradictions, ambiguities and paradoxes, intrapersonally, interpersonally, collectively and structurally. Debates on masculinities can also be conceptualized as debates on intersectionality that stress relations between gender, class and other categories. Intersectional perspectives link with research on comparative, global, (neo-)imperialist, postcolonial and transnational relations (Ouzgane and Coleman 1998; Hearn and Pringle 2006; Ouzgane 2006; Parpart and Zalewski 2008), and such approaches are likely to become even more important in future research and theorizing.

There is growing debate and fundamental critique on the very concepts of masculinities and hegemonic masculinity from various methodological positions, including historical, materialist and post-structuralist (Whitehead 2002; Hearn 2004; Howson 2006; Aboim 2010). The range of conceptual and empirical debates points to more fundamental problematics and an increasing range of critiques. Masculinity and masculinities have been used in a wide variety of ways, often rather imprecisely; they have served as shorthand for a wide range of social phenomena. Sometimes their use may reinforce a psychological model of gender relations located in the individual, or represent masculinity/ies as a primary or underlying cause of other social effects. The concepts can thus lead to an anti-materialist orientation, that may not reflect historical, cultural, (post) colonial and transnational differences. It may be argued that to talk of masculinity/ies can reproduce heterosexual dichotomies. On the other hand, a rapidly growing area of scholarship is the separation of masculinity/ies from men, as within some queer studies and critical sexuality studies.

Back to men

Such critiques provide the ground for a turn to investigating the category of men in a more focused way. This can mean both the recognition of the profound importance of men as a social force in society, and the deconstruction, even abolition, of the social taken-for-grantedness of the category of 'men' and its own hegemony. Critique of the hegemony of men can bring together feminist materialist theory and cultural queer theory, as well as modernist theories of hegemony and poststructuralist discourse theory (Hearn 2004). One of the clearest statements of the possibility of abolishing men is Monique Wittig's (1992) analysis of the possibility of abolition of the categories of women and men:

> … it is our historical task, and only ours (feminists) to define what we call oppression in materialist terms, to make it evident that women are a class, which is to say that the category 'woman' as well as the category 'man' are political and economic categories not eternal ones. Our fight aims to suppress men as a class, not through genocidal, but a political struggle. Once the class 'men' disappears, 'women' as a class will disappear as well, for there are no slaves without masters.

In seeking to understand possible moves towards the abolition of men, there are many possibilities, with a variety of texts showing the limitations of viewing gender as overly dichotomized or in a fixed relation to sex. These include historical and cross-societal analyses of 'multiple gender ideologies' and 'third sex/third gender' approaches derived from dialectical processes of transformation of men as a gender class, as well as, diversely, those from gender queer, undoing gender, gender ambiguity, gender pluralism, overlapping gender, refusing to be a man, effeminism and queer heterosexualities. Indeed women and men, including transmen, can exhibit female masculinity (Halberstam 1998).

End comments

The considerable and important critical work on men and masculinities that has already appeared has opened up many new areas of scholarship. At times, this has meant an attempt to establish a 'new' and discrete disciplinary area. Increasingly, contemporary work on men and masculinities is not constructed as separate in that way, but links with and is part of a wide range of feminist and critical gender theories, including those that engage with animal studies, studies of ageing, 'crip' theory and disability studies, cyberstudies, medical and natural sciences, science and technology studies, transgender studies and transnational studies. These new approaches promise further insights.

Further Reading: Cornwall et al. 2011; Flood et al. 2007; Gardiner 2002; Kimmel et al. 2005; Reeser 2010; Ruspini et al. 2011.

NEW REPRODUCTIVE TECHNOLOGIES

Sarah Franklin

Technology and reproduction are both important topics to feminist theory and the analysis of gender. From conception to birth, the reproductive process has long been the subject of various kinds of assistance, from medicinal aids to religious rites (Jordan 1980). Birth itself is likely always to have involved assistance due to the challenges of bipedal parturition. Similarly, reproduction is highly organized through social technologies such as kinship and marriage, and is the object of much early human artistic activity. New reproductive technologies such as in vitro fertilization have both deepened the relationship between reproduction and technology to the level of reproductive substance itself, and have, at the same time, made the technological organization of reproduction more explicit. As a consequence, the feminist debate concerning the effects of NRTs on women has also concerned the nature of gender itself, and in particular has reinforced the analysis of gender *as* a technology.

Since the eighteenth century in Europe, pregnancy and childbirth have been increasingly medicalized, through what has frequently been described by feminist historians as a struggle between the male-dominated medical profession and the traditionally female occupation of midwifery (Donnison 1977). Sex and sexuality come to be similarly medicalized in this same period, leading to more acutely polarized definitions of gender difference, and the emergence of a modern biological model of human reproduction (Schiebinger 2004). Over the past two centuries, in addition to being medicalized, pregnancy has become increasingly subject to technological surveillance, intervention and management. Feminists have been strongly critical of the extent to which new technologies such as foetal monitoring and prenatal diagnosis have weakened women's control over pregnancy and childbirth (Duden 1993). While improvements in reproductive health have been welcomed by reproductive rights activists and scholars, the extent to which women increasingly experience reproduction, in the words of anthropologist Rayna Rapp, as 'a crucible of tough decision-making' (1999: 17) underscores the double-edged influence of new technology on the process of 'making babies'.

The ability to fertilize a human egg outside the body, under carefully controlled laboratory conditions, was first achieved at the University of Cambridge in 1969 by Robert Edwards, and it is particular to the emergence of new forms of technologically assisted conception that the term 'new reproductive technologies' refers. The birth of Louise Brown in 1978 introduced controversial new possibilities to assume technological control over the very earliest stages of human reproduction. A substantial feminist literature emerged to address the increasing technologization of reproduction by a still largely male medical and scientific community, eventually comprising one of the most important feminist debates of the 1980s. For some, such as the investigative journalist Gena Corea, whose 1985 monograph *The Mother Machine* offered the first comprehensive feminist analysis of 'reproductive technologies from artificial insemination to artificial wombs', technological assistance to conception merely extended male medical control over women's reproductive capacity to a new and dangerous degree. By contrast, New York sociologist Barbara Katz Rothman argued in her pioneering 1986 study of amniocentesis that new reproductive technologies could offer women greater reproductive choice and control, while also enabling a transformation of parenthood and the family.

The feminist debate over reproductive technology also has roots in both feminist theory and feminist science fiction. Writing in the 1960s, Naomi Mitchison explored alternative parenting possibilities in *Memoirs of a Spacewoman* (1962), based on the work of developmental biologist Anne McLaren. Similarly, Joanna Russ explored both reproductive technologies and cryopreservation in *The Female Man* (1975), as did Marge Piercy in *Woman on the Edge of*

Time (1976). The emphasis on the radical potential of reproductive technology to bring about social change in these novels has its parallel in feminist theory in the works of both Donna Haraway (1997) and Shulamith Firestone (1970), both of whom argue that radical new technological possibilities comprise an essential resource for feminist politics, and in particular for challenging the rigid binarisms of biological sex difference.

Following Rothman's influential sociological study of amniocentesis and Emily Martin's (1987) cultural account of reproduction, *The Woman in the Body*, published the following year, empirical studies of women's experiences of new reproductive technologies became an increasingly important subfield of both gender and kinship studies in the 1990s. In the first volume of its kind, Margarete Sandelowski's (1993) comprehensive study of IVF and other conceptive technologies, entitled *With Child in Mind*, presented a detailed empirical portrait of the experience of undergoing infertility treatment. Based on interviews with women and couples with fertility impairments, Sandelowski, who trained as a nurse before becoming a medical ethnographer, sympathetically documented both the pressures to undergo new treatments, and the challenges these (largely unsuccessful) treatments presented to patients. Her findings that women and couples felt 'compelled to try' such technologies, that they fragmented the reproductive experience, and that NRTs imposed high costs while most often resulting in disappointment have been widely repeated in many studies since (Becker 2000; Franklin 1997; Throsby 2004). These studies have similarly confirmed the 'never enough' quality of NRTs first identified and named by Sandelowski (1991) and the difficulty of returning to 'normal life' – even in the wake of successful treatment (Sandelowski 1993).

Paradoxically, while many of the most worrying feminist predictions from the earliest studies concerning NRTs have since been confirmed (that they would extend ever further into the process of conception, that practices such as surrogacy would create a new reproductive division of labour, and that the indications for NRTs would become ever more encompassing of more aspects of conception and pregnancy), feminist opposition to IVF, prenatal screening, and other reproductive technologies has diminished over time, giving way to a position better characterized as critical accommodation. This pragmatically equivocal stance, initially articulated in the early 1980s by feminist political theorist and reproductive rights activist Rosalind Petchesky in the context of abortion, acknowledges both the empowering and disempowering aspects of NRTs simultaneously: they 'may be an occasion of sorrow at the same time [offering] a condition of expanded human freedom and consciousness' (Petchesky 1984: 349).

A similar position has emerged from the study of IVF and NRTs in cross-cultural perspective, by feminist anthropologists such as Marcia Inhorn, whose 1994 study of 'the quest for conception' in Egypt strongly emphasizes the parallels between infertility treatment and religious pilgrimages. The sense of women making do as best they can under circumstances not of their own choosing strongly dominates this literature. Inhorn's Egyptian study, like that of anthropologist Susan Kahn in Israel (2000), also foregrounds the stigmatization of infertile women that results in their decisions to undergo IVF becoming, in Judith Lorber's words, a 'no-choice choice' (1994: 156). As Faye Ginsburg and Rayna Rapp argue in their overview of reproduction in the 'new world order', reproductive practices and procedures, including NRTs, are deeply enmeshed in transnational inequalities, as well as local ones. It is for this reason, they argue, that reproduction should be placed 'at the centre of social theory' and as the 'entry point' to the study of cultural and political life (1995: 1).

The rapid expansion of a new reproductive service industry in the late twentieth century, in which various techniques are increasingly combined (such as surrogacy with IVF, IVF with egg donation, or transnational egg donation with both IVF and surrogacy), has given rise to what feminist scholar Debora Spar has termed 'the baby business', a modern fertility trade that is subject to minimal regulation or monitoring either nationally or internationally. Still a public sector health service in a minority of countries, including the UK, Israel, France and Sweden, assisted conception has become an increasingly privatized, and profitable, global industry. In both India and China, for example, which have two of the world's largest assisted conception markets, nearly all treatment is privately funded. As Spar argues, the rise of the reproductive 'broker' as well as the rapidly expanding market in reproductive services and materials worldwide requires a commitment to enacting innovative regulation that is at present lacking in the majority of the countries where such markets are socially, commercially and legally supported (Spar 2006).

At the same time that feminists have identified the risks and costs associated with the rapid rise of NRTs, some evidence also points to the ways in which these technologies have begun to alter normative gender and kinship roles, as well as parenting strategies and mechanisms of family formation. In much the same way that the more optimistic, and even utopian, accounts from feminist science fiction writers envisaged an overthrow of conventional gender roles through NRTs, an increasing amount of social scientific research has documented significant changes in the definition of parenthood in the context of assisted conception. Among the first of these was the anthropologist Marilyn Strathern, who argued in a pair of 1992 studies that technological assistance to conception would have a 'displacing effect' on normative kinship values, by producing a substitute for 'natural' conception (1992a, 1992b) in the form of IVF. The introduction of an explicitly artificial form of producing 'natural kinship' would not only affect ideas about reproduction, she argued, but would trouble the assumption that either reproduction or sex are originally 'based on' natural facts. To the extent that reproductive technology enables the production of 'artificial life' it challenges the foundational presumption that kinship is rooted in nature – or that nature is prior to culture, she argued. 'Culturing' human oocytes to facilitate their fertilization in glass, and their surgical transfer to the uterus using sterilized microtools, reverses this order – producing a biological offspring whose coming into being is entirely dependent upon specialized technical skills performed by an expert in a laboratory. This high-tech process of 'culturing nature' confirms not only the scientific ability to successfully manipulate human reproductive cells in vitro, but also the underlying logic of artificial reproduction, which does not so much depend upon nature as bypass its 'blockages' with technology.

One reason, therefore, that feminist science studies scholar Charis Thompson (2005) has argued that NRTs comprise the 'perfect text' for feminism is the extent to which they replicate the same process by which feminists such as Judith Butler (1990) have argued that gender is itself 'technological'. Drawing on the work of feminist anthropologists such as Strathern (1980, 1988), who argued throughout the 1980s against the presumption that sex is to nature what gender is to culture on the basis that the nature-culture dichotomy is itself an artificial one, Butler argues that it is not only gender but sex that is culturally constructed, historically specific, and thus arbitrary. Like Michel Foucault, she argued that subjects are produced by the very same systems that name and govern them, and that consequently the sex/gender distinction cannot logically be 'based on' a pre-existing natural order. 'Gender is neither the causal result of sex nor as seemingly fixed as sex' and 'sex is as culturally constructed as gender', Butler argues (1990: 7). As Thompson points out, NRTs such as IVF ironically confirm the logic of Butler's argument, since assisted conception procedures employ technology to replace, or repair, the natural function of sex – thus literally constructing biology. As she also argues, the ubiquitous effort to naturalize assisted conception – to represent it as what nature would have done by itself 'anyway' – confirms the extent to which normative gender roles are also imagined to be 'based on' an underlying set of natural reproductive facts of life (Thompson 2005: 117–119).

NRTs have thus become increasingly important to the study of gender as well as kinship, reproduction and parenting. The feminist analysis of NRTs has strongly confirmed the extent to which women who are unable to conceive 'naturally' feel pressured to seek out NRTs in order to fulfil normative expectations about marriage, kinship, family, gender and sex, confirming how strongly these domains are linked (while also showing the links cannot be defined as 'natural'). Feminist research has also documented the high cost of such treatments not only to women who undergo procedures such as IVF, but to the often economically disadvantaged women who provide reproductive services such as surrogacy and egg donation (Nahman 2008). The lack of adequate regulation of the reproductive service industry has been criticized by feminists who argue women bear the burden of policy-paralysis and dilatory monitoring in this sector (Spar 2006).

At the same time as documenting their high costs to women, feminists have also pointed to the ways in which NRTs open up alternative routes to parenthood and non-traditional family-formation (Thompson 2005). The role of NRTs in de-naturalizing reproduction, and its putative foundation in a pre-existing natural sex binarism (Strathern 1992a & b), is but one example of the double-edged nature of these technologies. Thus, although they are associated with normalized and naturalized family forms, and the goal of their use is often linked to the (conventional) achievement of conjugal unity in the form of biological offspring, NRTs are also associated with a major disruption to the social and legal definition of family and parenthood, and the advent of alternative family and kinship structures.

Following the lead of feminist science fiction writers, feminist theorist Donna Haraway (1997) has argued that technologically assisted reproduction offers both actual and imaginative possibilities to leave behind the tyranny of the blood-based, bilateral kinship systems in favour of a more open-ended definition of both intimacy and politics. Haraway sees in the 'cyborg articulations' (1997: 269) of new relationships to technology a means of redefining the politics of reproduction to include what versions of the future will become generative of new worlds. Like Shulamith Firestone before her, who argued that new technologies of 'cybernetic reproduction' would be necessary in order to transform women's social position, Haraway argues that reshaping the agendas of science and technology should be foremost among feminist concerns. To a limited extent, the capacity of NRTs to loosen the normative constraints of gender and kinship roles has become visible, alongside their ability to strengthen these very same institutional structures, leaving women and couples vulnerable to feeling that they 'have to try' everything that is available. By imitating technologies of gender, NRTs have also made more explicit the instability of natural facts as the 'prediscursive' origin of either reproduction or sex. By making reproduction more explicitly artificial, they have provided a parallel in social practice for the challenge to the naturalization of the categories 'gender' and 'sex' in feminist theory.

Further Reading: Haraway 1997; Rothman 1986; Thompson 2005.

PERFORMATIVITY

Claire Blencowe

The theory of performativity, especially in the context of gender studies, is associated with US philosopher Judith Butler. In her 1990 book *Gender Trouble,* Butler introduced the idea that gender is 'performative' – that gender is produced as reality in and through its repeated performance (Butler 1990: esp. 171–190). We experience gender as a concrete reality, as an indisputable fact, not because gender difference is inscribed in nature, divine law or physical necessity, but because gender roles are *performed* and copied and repeated (iterated), and have been repeated so many times and with such daily frequency that we come to experience gender as a hard, inescapable, reality. Moreover, gender is a major part of how we play all manner of social roles and this means that we are forced to perform a gender whenever we participate in social life. Crucially (and more controversially) Butler added that 'sex', the supposedly 'pre-cultural' physical difference between men and women, is the *effect* – not the underlying cause – of gender. Butler originally developed the theory of performativity as part of her (ongoing) work to understand and undermine homophobia and the immense violence that it inflicts – which Butler refers to as the 'regime of compulsory heterosexuality'. By talking about gender as performative she aims not only to describe the production of gender but also to identify practices through which the rules and violence governing gender identity can be *subverted*. Over the past two decades she and others have extended this theory to address a broader range of norms (rules of acceptable, or 'normal', identity and behaviour) and sites of violence – including racism, the regulation of citizenship (including in Israel/Palestine), the 'war on terror', and international war.

The theory of performativity maintains that gender (and any aspect of identity) is not the outcome, expression or performance of an inner-core or deep reality, but is rather something that is constituted at the surface level, in the very moment of its performance; gender comes into being as, is nothing *before*, its performance. The internal reality – the supposed 'true self', 'authentic nature' or 'biological determination' – is not the cause of surface level performances and visible signs, but is rather the *effect* of the performance and the signs; the real inside is the effect of the superficial visible activity. In line with this Butler contests the distinction that has long been drawn in feminist theory, between a (supposedly universal) biological sex-difference between men and women and a cultural interpretation of that difference as 'gender' (seen as contextual, artificial and thus transformable). Butler argues that gender is not the cultural *expression* of a biological, pre-cultural sex. Rather the whole idea and experienced reality of biological sex-difference is an *effect* of gender performance (1990: 47–48; 177–178). This is not to say that sex-difference is not real, but that it is a reality that has been created through the enormous, perpetual, long-historical work of people playing their gender roles well, performing *as if* there was such a thing as a fixed biological sex-difference dividing all the living bodies in the world into just two categories (man and woman). Crucially, this suggests that the idea of sex-difference (as a universal, fixed, dualistic category of biological difference and cause of identity) is as vulnerable to transformation, contestation and disruption as is gender.

It would be a mistake, however, to think of the performance of gender in terms of self-conscious actors choosing their role, learning their lines and then stepping out onto the social stage to perform their part. Rather the conscious actor, the doer (that does the performing) is constituted *in* the act of performance. Performativity is not a theory about what conscious actors (subjects) do; rather it is a theory about how actors come to *be* in the first place. In this Butler is influenced by psychoanalytic theory concerning the unconscious formation of conscious desires and identities (as phantasm) and poststructuralist arguments concerning the need to reject the idea of a self-determining conscious will or 'subject'. It is, then, important to distinguish between *performance*, which assumes a subject (a preexistent agent consciously doing the performance) and *performativity*, which contests the very notion of the subject (Butler 1994).

Performativity has an 'iterative structure' (Butler 1990: 178–180; 1997: 147–159). This means that all performances of gender *repeat* and imitate previous performances. Our capacity to perform a gender derives from our experience of other performances of gender, performances that we imitate. This means that how we do gender is not a matter of free choice; we can only iterate, imitate, what we have experienced before. Most importantly we cannot choose *not* to perform a gender, because all the available scripts for the performance of social life (performing human, performing citizen, performing student, solider, technician, parent, paramedic …) are gendered. To participate in social life, to be able to perform at all, we are forced to perform a gender.

The experienced reality and strength of ideas about gender derives from this perpetual repetition of gender performance. However imitation can take many forms, and the repetition of a performance might disrupt and challenge, rather than reinforce, the fixedness of ideas about gender (Butler 1990: 178–190). Because gender has to be repeatedly performed to go on existing, it is vulnerable to transformation by the performers. Gender (and any other attribute of identity for that matter) can be 'misperformed'; we can perform our gender in ways that break the rules of gender. Not only does this mean breaking the rules on a particular occasion; misperformance of gender can also upset the whole spectacle through which we have come to experience particular gender rules as inescapable, authentic reality, or 'biological fact', creating powerful symbolic challenges. Performances of gender that parody gender norms could shatter the illusion that there are only two genders – man and woman – and lead to a proliferation of genders; or rather to a recognition of, and ability to speak about, the already existing great diversity of genders, sexualities, bodies and pleasures.

The idea that there is a distinction between sex, as a hard determining concrete reality that is before and outside of culture, and gender, as the cultural expression of that distinction, is a powerful component in the regime of compulsory heterosexuality

(Butler 1990: 47). The belief that sex is the cause (rather than the effect) of gender has the powerful effect of *naturalizing* gender roles and 'foreclosing' (rendering unthinkable, unimaginable, unspeakable) the existence of bodies that do not fall into the categories of man and woman. To reveal the performed nature of sex-difference – for example, through cross-dressing performances that parody 'real' gender performance – is to radically undermine the force of the gender norm, showing that gender (and equally sex) is a matter of performance, not of fixed nature.

In addition to theorists such as Jacques Derrida (1988) and Pierre Bourdieu (1991), Butler's theory of performativity draws upon Michel Foucault's (1977) critique of the subject and his account of the productive nature of power. For example, she draws upon Foucault's account of the production of soul of the prisoner through the disciplinary practices of the prison. Foucault argues that the internal conscious, or soul, of the prisoner is produced through the gaze of the prison guard and the performance *as if* one had a conscious that that gaze provokes (Butler 1990: 171–172). This is part of a Nietzschian general critique of values, or 'genealogy', which aims to show that all values and norms are constructed in history (and have dubious origins).

Feminist politics and the question of agency

Butler developed the concept of performativity as part of an effort to rethink and rework the character and basis of feminist politics, continuing in the tradition of lesbian feminists, such as Monique Wittig, that questioned mainstream 'second wave' feminism (Butler 1990). Butler rejects the idea of feminism as 'identity politics'. Instead of defending and liberating women as an identity group, Butler argues that feminism should be engaged in the *subversion* of identity itself. As such Butler's theory of performativity is part of the broader project of 'poststructuralist' feminism.

'Identity politics' refers to political movements that have developed in opposition to practices and perceptions that discriminate against, and subordinate, a group of people on the basis of a particular identity trait (such as being black, being a woman, being gay, being Muslim, being disabled), and which seek to overcome and redress that subordination: by challenging the perception of the identity trait as something negative (including changing the perceptions held by members of the group itself); by demanding recognition and respect for that identity; by developing solidarity and support amongst the members of the identity group; and by defending the social, economic and political interests of the members of this group against a power structure or against those that have benefited from the discriminatory practices. In the case of feminist identity politics, this means celebrating 'women' and things that are traditionally seen as 'feminine'; seeking to develop solidarity between women; working towards and on behalf of a 'global sisterhood'; and acting to defend and advance the social, economic and political interests of women against structures of domination and exploitation, or against men.

The ideal of feminist politics as women's identity politics (a politics for and on behalf of all women, or a 'global sisterhood') has been repeatedly challenged throughout the history of feminism, particularly by black and 'Third World' feminists such as by Sojourner Truth, bell hooks and Chandra Mohanty. Black and 'Third World' feminists (alongside working-class feminists, lesbian and bisexual feminists, religious feminists and others) have argued that whilst feminist identity politics presents itself as being of and for *all* women it has in fact been led and shaped by a very particular group of women – that is, white, Western, middle-class, straight, secular women. In some instances this has meant that the movement has overlooked or misunderstood problems faced by other specific groups of women. In others the ideal of a universal feminist project has been used *against* the interests, empowerment and recognition of specific groups of women. For example, early twentieth century American feminist, Charlotte Perkins Gilman, sought to promote the full and equal entry of 'women' into the workplace by transferring the undesirable tasks of domestic labour from 'women' to specific groups of people (implicitly black and lower-class men and women) deemed 'more suited' to this work (Scharnhorst 2000). In the contemporary era a narrowly defined 'universal' ideal of women's emancipation is frequently used to justify a structure of global power wherein it is seen as legitimate for Western governments and NGOs to interfere with the ways of life of people in 'developing' countries (Mohanty 1991). In the worst instances 'feminist' arguments concerning women's empowerment and liberation have been appropriated to justify the dismantling of welfare services in non-Western countries (Petchesky 2003), or military occupation of non-Western countries (Power 2009; Butler 2009) – such as when then US President George W. Bush (partially) justified military occupation of Afghanistan in terms of the liberation of Afghan women from patriarchy. Of course few feminists would support such uses of 'feminist' arguments, but the fact that feminist arguments can be appropriated for such uses points to a general problem with the conceptualization of feminism as a universal project.

One approach to this problem has been to fragment and pluralize feminist identity politics, such that we have black-feminist identity politics, working-class-feminist identity politics, lesbian-feminist identity politics, Islamic-feminist identity politics and so on. Another approach – which is called 'poststructuralist feminism' – has argued for the abandonment of identity politics altogether and for a re-thinking of feminist politics in terms of resistance to gender norms and the destabilization of categories, including the category of 'woman' itself.

Butler's theory of performativity can be understood in the context of this poststructuralist feminism. A fundamental problem that is posed by the rejection of identity politics is that of where *agency* comes from if it is not from the solidarity and 'subjecthood' (that is to say consciousness and self-determining will) of the identity group. Indeed, many have argued that the rejection of feminist identity politics means giving up on the possibility of feminist agency and politics altogether. The theory of performativity can be seen as an attempt to address this issue – to identify sites and sources of feminist agency that do not refer to women's identity, a universal subject of emancipation, or a pre-contextual self-determining will or soul. What Butler does, in effect, is to say that *all* agency exists at the level of surface performance. Agency, she argues, does not derive from universal truths or the depths of the soul, nature or a true self (or true womanhood), but rather from the effects of repetition – iterated performance – and this goes for both the imposition of norms (domination) and the resistance to, subversion of, such norms (feminist politics).

Butler maintains that the power of norms is generated and maintained through the everyday repetition of gender performance (1990: 181–190). Not only does this mean that those norms are unstable, changeable, temporal and vulnerable to challenge. It also means that the power of the norm (being constituted in the everyday and everywhere act of its repeated performance) is readily *available*. The power of the norm is accessible to all those people that are engaged in its performance. Moreover, and crucially, the iterative power of the norm might be directed at the *subversion* rather than the consolidation of that norm. For example, a term of derision can be taken up as a term of affirmation and turned back against the regime of discrimination from which it arose (Butler 1997: esp. 40–41). This has been the case with the term 'queer' as attached to homosexuality. 'Queer' has been transformed from a term of derision (designating gay people as unnatural, strange, abnormal) to a term of positive affirmation in the celebration of 'queer politics' and of 'queering' as a progressive, critical and creative act. Not only is the formerly derided 'queer' celebrated in this move, but also the entire logic of heterosexist thinking is challenged as the very presumption that normality (being normal, conforming to the norm) is desirable is called into dispute. Similarly, segregationist rules governing what people of different races can do, not only enforce the repeated performance of and naturalization of racist norms, they also create new capacities to resist and undermine racism. Laws and customs in Montgomery (southern USA) in the first six decades of the twentieth century sought to segregate black and white people whilst travelling on buses and to give white people a privileged access to seats where there was a shortage. The rules created the repeated performance and thus consolidation of the racist norm (producing a perceived 'real', 'natural', 'internal' difference between black and white people as its effect). But it also created the capacity for Rosa Parks to not only 'misbehave' by refusing to give up her seat to a white passenger, but through this act to call the whole regime of racial segregation (and the racism it naturalized) into question – creating an enormously powerful, resonant, symbolic act that augmented the black civil rights movement (Butler 1997: 147). The agency of resisting racist oppression is contained within the tools of its perpetuation. Norms contain within themselves the power to subvert and challenge the norm.

Critical questions and new directions

Recent controversies within the broadly 'performative perspective' point towards the development of a more varied and complex picture of the performative production of norms and of feminist agency. A number of feminists have highlighted the way that Butler's concept of performativity seems to imply that all creativity, politics and agency rests in a cultural or discursive world, to the exclusion of the material and embodied. These feminists suggest either that we should replace the concept of performativity with a more materialist conception of creative processes, or that performativity should be thought of as incorporating the liveliness and creativity of material and non-human things that do not speak or interpret symbols (e.g. Grosz 1995; Barad 2007). These concerns point towards a development of a more complex theory of performativity, that would embrace more deeply the co-constituted or 'ecological' character of being, and adopt a greater humility with respect to our ability to know how things are created, or how we are involved in creative processes (Bell 2012).

Others have argued that the dualistic model of agency assumed in Butler's work, whereby agency appears as either the consolidation or the subversion of norms, is too narrow. Saba Mahmood (2005) explored the performative production of patriarchal norms and women's agency in the context of the women's piety movement in Egypt. Here women *self-consciously* engaged in the inscription of norms upon their 'inner soul' through performative acts; performing *as if* one were modest is a deliberate strategy through which to cultivate the real, internal, virtue of modesty. In this context the whole drama of subverting norms through the demonstration that they are performatively created makes no sense. Moreover, these women engage norms and agency in complex ways, sometimes using patriarchial norms of Islamic teaching in order to wield power over men, to whom the set of norms positions them as subservient (such that it is not at all obvious that the feminist thing to do is to subvert the existing norms). Again this suggests the need for greater complexity and humility with respect to our understanding of the creation of both norms and feminist agency.

Further Reading: Bell 1999, 2007; Butler 1993; Butler and Scott 1993; Parker and Sedgwick 1995.

POSTCOLONIALISM

Suki Ali

Like 'feminism', or 'postmodernism', the term 'postcolonialism' has no singular and fixed meaning, nor does it inevitably help with a critical interrogation of issues of gender. It is a complex 'umbrella' term that aims to capture the way in which utilizing 'postcolonial thinking', 'postcolonial theory' or a 'postcolonial perspective' may help us to understand the social world. For feminist postcolonialists the centrality of gender to all of these endeavours, and the unevenness of gender relations, are both explicit and fore-grounded. Despite its disparate forms, a concern with 'postcoloniality' inevitably requires an attention to a situated politics of knowledge, which is informed by and relates to political and social action and change. This means attending to the specific and local alongside the transnational in both lived experience and ways of thinking. Given this rather vague and wide-ranging way to approach 'the postcolonial' it is no wonder that there are numerous articles and collections which tend to cover four key areas: the what, when, where and who of postcoloniality. Of course, no such divisions are possible, but including all of these 'parts' may help illuminate a much greater 'whole'.

Stuart Hall (1996c) suggests that postcolonial analyses decentre 'the Western frame of West and the Rest'. This is, of course, something of a simplification and should not obscure the heterogeneity of these terms themselves. However, 'decentring' engages a set of key problems: spatial relations of power, critiques of linear time, and a reconfiguration of 'the subject'. Not limited to acts of criticism, investigating these problems requires challenges to Eurocentric discourses of modernity, and strands of European Enlightenment thinking that privilege ideas of progress and civilization in contrast to the pre-modern, traditional and uncivilized. European Enlightenment thinking was also diffuse and varied, contradictory and contested, yet ideas about 'Man' as a moral and political being underpinned and justified colonial expansion. Much of this thinking classified human difference and organized people into categories such as race, gender, ethnicity and religion that were hierarchically ordered. Postcolonial studies interrogate these concerns through a multi- and trans-disciplinary field of enquiry which includes area studies, literary criticism, anthropology, sociology, economics and history to name but a few. Many claim its contemporary form has its origins in literature studies and the development of colonial discourse analysis. Although centrally concerned with art, culture and literature, critics use these forms to make a much broader critique of Eurocentric views of the world and particularly claim about the transformations of modernity. Cultural approaches to postcolonial studies, which draw upon poststructural and psychoanalytic theory, have been seen as responses to and extensions of Marxist analyses that focused on political and economic features of counter-colonial and anti-imperial struggle. This (neo-) Marxist, materialist vs. cultural, literary split is, as ever, not representative of the wide variety of work that is now invoking the postcolonial; many authors combine cultural criticism with structural and material analyses.

The 'when' of postcolonialism is particularly hard to separate from the 'where' – the spatial relations of power and the question of time. Colonialism has always been a feature of human history.

European imperialism and colonialism began in earnest in the fifteenth century, culminating with a period of domination in the nineteenth and early twentieth centuries. By World War I imperial powers controlled nine-tenths of the surface territory of the globe (Young 2001: 2). For many, the key difference between European and prior forms of colonization is that they went hand in hand with the development of capitalism, and involved the restructuring of local economies, tying them into complex and enduring relationships of dependency (Loomba 1998). One could simply position 'the postcolonial' being 'after colonialism', but this oversimplifies the differences between colonial powers and the particularities of colonial 'contact zones' (Pratt 1992). Some argue that the term postcolonialism problematically privileges of the model of linear time which flows from the past to the present, with an eye to the future, suggesting progression from the pre-colonial to colonial, into a postcolonial present (McClintock 1993). Such accounts are not value free, and hidden within the language of the 'march of progress' is a discourse of 'development'. While this may be seen more overtly in work on material, economic, political and technical development, it is also present in some literary criticism. Within so-called Third World literary criticism there is often a narrative that invokes 'progress' from protest literature to resistance literature through to national literature (ibid.). But the relationship between time and space is problematic in other ways.

A key feature of philosophical thinking which helped inform and sustain colonialism was the fixing of geographic spaces and the people who occupied them in the past, yet also paradoxically, as being people without history (e.g. Eze 1997). These spatio-temporal relations between the forward-facing, modernizing European, and backward-facing, anachronistic barbarian formed the basis for differing modes of colonial governmentality. The 'civilizing mission' of the colonizers was to bring the ahistorical 'savage' into the modern era, by force or cooption. Colonialism became the defining feature for entire nations and peoples, who were situated relationally to it, in both space and time. Invoking 'the postcolonial' does not *inevitably* challenge the hidden relations of power in discourses that entangle time and place. The varieties of spaces and places that have experienced colonization and independence cannot easily be collapsed under the term postcolonial. We can see some of the limitations when we consider these examples: British control of Hong Kong and its return of the territory to China took markedly different forms than that of the colonial and imperial control of India and its struggles for independence; the continuation of unequal relations of power within global capitalism might be seen as continuities of colonialism or forms of neo-colonialism; some former colonies have become colonial powers themselves, e.g. the United States; and finally, is it useful to think of a former colony like Australia through the same framing as that of, say, Algeria?

Despite the difficulties and dissent with terminologies and approaches, attempts have been made to collectivize some features of postcolonial thinking. Rattansi argues that postcolonial studies are centrally concerned with exposing the mutually constituent nature of colonizers and colonized (Rattansi 1997: 481); an approach exemplified in Edward Said's *Orientalism* (1985). This multi-disciplinary work demonstrates the way in which knowledge (both academic and popular) was a form of power integral to the shaping of colonial rule. Using discourse analysis Said argued that the idea and representation of the 'Orient' simultaneously produced the Occident. Colonialism and its agents produced an *Other*, but simultaneously produced a 'self' and ordered them hierarchically. Thus the 'superior West' justified its control of the 'inferior East'. Rather than seeing European knowledge as simply exported one way, from the centre to the periphery, metropole to colony, knowledge flows both ways. Said used Marxism to explore material conditions of colonial control but was also interested in representation and 'styles of thought'. He drew upon Gramscian understandings of 'hegemony' arguing that the authority of the 'West' is maintained in part through local consent, and within institutions such as the army and schools. Said's work has been criticized on a number of levels, including a failure to fully engage with gender. He suggested that the Orient and the Oriental other is eroticized, feminized and feminine; the Occident is masculinized and masculine. However this framing is not sufficient to explain the ways in which colonialism and colonial knowledge have helped construct differing racialized masculinities and femininities, how these are imbricated within heteronormative sexual regulation, and how diverse groups of men and women were differentially positioned in colonial relations of power.

The masculinist nature of colonialism and imperialism are evident in discourse and practice. It has been argued that the then emergent sciences of human difference exemplified androcentric ways of thinking. The language of control, domination and penetration of nature is evident in much colonial writings. (Some) men are held up as reasoned and rational, women as irrational and emotional, with the former valued over the latter. Female bodies symbolized conquered land, but the characteristics of the woman of the colonies varied according to location. For example, naked American and African woman were contrasted to the clothed and exotic Asian woman. Non-European women were not solely positioned as 'passive'; they were also seen as 'Amazonian' savages, and in some cases hyper-sexualized (Loomba 1998: 151–72). This kind of variation can also be seen in discussion of colonial masculinities. For example, British colonialism relied upon a 'cult of masculinity' that was imagined and enacted in a variety of ways (Sinha 1999). However, it is not adequate to, for example, contrast 'British' and 'Indian' masculinities any more than it is to consider masculinity in simple binary relationship with feminine. Indian scholars show multiple axes of difference upon which gradations of masculinity were organized. These changed over time as the need for more soldiers took priority. For example, 'manly' Punjabi men were contrasted to the 'effeminate' Bengalis. Ashis Nandy argues that the rigid gender binaries introduced by the British re-shaped more fluid gender identities in Indian tradition (Sinha 1999). This illustrates how interactions between the colonialists and local knowledges and resistances informed each other in complex ways. The production of racialized gender norms was imbricated with the production and regulation of sexualities and we cannot consider the one without the other.

The examples above show the importance of historical work that challenges dominant, sanctioned accounts of history, the importance of subaltern histories, and 'recovering' marginal voices. Gayatri Spivak challenged the Subaltern Studies Group through her analysis of British attempts to reform the practice of sati (widow immolation) in India. Women were absent from discussions, and the combination of colonialism and patriarchy made it impossible for the subaltern woman to 'speak'. Spivak inserts 'the brown woman' as a category oppressed by both colonizers and colonized. While elite native men found a way to speak, the subaltern woman could not represent herself therefore her voice cannot be recovered. Spivak (1988: 297) suggests the colonial discourse in India was 'white men are saving brown women from brown men'. Her work demonstrates how the treatment of women by men is used to measure civilization and modernity. Contemporary postcolonial studies show the continuation of this theme. Similar ideas are evident in the so-called clash of civilizations discourse, and in the justification of the 'war on terror' based in part on concerns about the excessively patriarchal treatment of women, and increasingly, sexual and gender minorities (Butler 2008). Spivak's work also informs transnational and 'Third

World feminism' which challenges contemporary 'colonial feminism' (Alexander and Mohanty 1997).

Postcolonial critique should be 'activist writing' that takes inspiration from the past but is responsive to political priorities of the moment, centralizing history's 'new subjects' (Young 2001: 10). Therefore, postcolonial theory has an important role to play in contemporary work on national and cultural formations, questions of belonging in national and transnational frames, and the formation of contemporary gendered, racialized identities and subjectivities. Franz Fanon's work has been influential here. Fanon wrote on a wide range of subjects including colonial subjectivity, the making of national consciousness, and the place of violence in revolutionary struggles. While working as a psychiatrist in Algeria, his clinical experience led him to question the psychic structuring of race, processes of racialization and 'the depersonalisation of colonial man'. Fanon suggested that the Black man exists as other to the white man by which he meant that minority and oppressed subjectivities are made in relation to those of the dominant culture (Fanon 1991). Importantly he noted how the loss of one's own culture and the imposition of the culture of another (e.g. language) is a form of cultural, epistemic and psychic violence. Again, Fanon's work has been critiqued for a limited engagement with gender and sexuality, but has been widely used, adapted and extended to explore contemporary racial identification in differing sites. Fanon, like others who followed, argued that identities are not simply imposed by colonizers upon the colonized but complex and ambivalent relationships develop in which knowledges, politics and subjectivities of both are shaped and contested. Postcolonial societies, if we can call them that, require us to think about transcultural and intercultural exchange. The fear of racial and cultural mixing under-scored the need to control gender and (hetero)sexual relations. For postcolonial studies, cross-cultural exchanges have meant a particular focus on questions of cultural hybridity and syncretism. Contemporary work often considers the marginal and 'interstitial' spaces of the nation where new forms of identity and politics are negotiated. This has proven particularly important for work on diaspora, and for understanding multiculturalism societies. Of course, these concerns must remain firmly grounded in analyses of the material and economic conditions shaped by global capitalism in which gender is a key feature.

One of the major criticisms of postcolonial theory is that it is dominated by intellectual elites who reside within Northern academic sites. Arif Dirlik goes so far as to suggest that 'Postcoloniality is the condition of the intellegentsia of global capitalism' (cited in Loomba 1998: 247) and that the writers emanating from Africa, the Middle East and South Asia are 'Western trained' retaining Eurocentric ways of working. Latin American writers argue that the 'modernity' that is being challenged excludes the knowledge that comes from the 'first' modernity of the Spanish and Portuguese colonialism in the sixteenth century. It is possible to see some of this Northwestern postcolonial theory as perpetuating intellectual hegemonies and failing to consider the specificities of coloniality in the Americas which would challenge knowledge of racial, spatial and temporal hierarchies (see e.g. Moraña et al. 2008). Similarly, understanding Asian colonialism is still a project limited by processes of translation. Scholars from Central and Eastern Europe have debated the usefulness of Northern Euro-American postcolonial theory given the different social and political histories of the region. But Korek (2009: 1) argues that similar approaches can be used to consider imperialist discourses of the 'West' on the subject of the European 'East', as well as challenging Slavonic and Soviet Studies produced during the Cold War.

It is clear that we cannot pin down a term like 'postcolonialism' – nor should we. Invoking the postcolonial has become 'fashionable' in some academic circles. However, its mainstreaming may indicate an evacuation of the politics that informed the earliest postcolonial writing. Simply by stating one works from a postcolonial perspective is inadequate. There is no one-size-fits-all theory or concept. The term requires sustained engagement with the complex ways in which racial, gendered, sexualized relations of power are shaped – culturally, materially and politically – under conditions of globalizing capital and late modernity.

Further Reading: Cooper 2005; McClintock et al. 1997; Lewis and Mills 2003; Loomba et al. 2005; Schwarz 2005.

POSTFEMINISM

Stéphanie Genz

Postfeminism is a fundamental, yet contested concept in the lexicon of cultural/media studies and, to a lesser degree, political and social sciences. Prevalent in North America and Western Europe, the term emerged as early as 1919 (after the vote for women had been won by the suffrage movement) but only gained prominence in the 1980s, first in the popular press and then in wider cultural and academic circles (see Cott 1987; Bolotin 1982). Here, the term depicts a reaction to – and, some critics argue, against – earlier, in particular 1970s forms of feminist activism and politics, often condensed under the heading of 'second wave' feminism. Since then, the term has acquired a number of different meanings and discursive connotations: in popular culture, it is used as a descriptive marker for a number of female characters, from Helen Fielding's chick heroine Bridget Jones, to the Spice Girls and cyber babe Lara Croft. In academic writings, it sits alongside other 'post-' discourses – including postmodernism – and refers to changing constructions of identity and gender categories (like 'woman', 'man' and 'feminist'). Likewise, in social and political writings, postfeminism has been read as symptomatic of a post-traditional era characterized by dramatic changes in social relationships, role stereotyping and conceptions of agency. More recently, postfeminism has been anchored within neoliberal society and consumer culture, where it resonates with ideas of the self-regulating and enterprising individual whose consumption patterns come to be seen as a source of power and choice.

A coherent definition of the term has thus proven elusive, spawning criticism that postfeminism might become 'more and more an empty signifier' that is 'infinitely adaptable' (Whelehan 2010: 159, 162). Postfeminism's non-exclusive signifying practices – the ways in which it claims and commands a number of different meanings – are apparent on a purely semantic level where confusion arises around what a 'post-ing' of feminism might imply. For some, postfeminism proclaims the passing of feminism – in Hawkesworth's words, feminism is 'gone, departed, dead' (2004: 969) – while for others, it should be read as 'post revolutionary' and 'boundary-crossing', opening up 'an array of relationships and connections within social, cultural, academic and political arenas' (Stacey 1987: 8; Genz and Brabon 2009: 7). What these debates centre on is exactly what does the prefix 'post-' accomplish (if anything) – what happens to feminist perspectives and goals in the process? And what does the strange hybrid of 'postfeminism' entail?

Early articulations of postfeminism invoke a narrative of progression that insists on a time 'after' feminism. This is the case in the numerous obituaries for feminism that keep appearing in media quarters, announcing if not the death then at least the redundancy of feminism. While *Harper's* magazine published a 'requiem for the women's movement' as early as 1976, *The Times* informed its readers that 'feminism went nuts' in 2007. In this context, postfeminism signals the 'past-ness' of feminism – or, at any rate the end of a particular stage in feminist history. One of the first critical examinations of this trend was provided by journalist Susan Faludi from the United States who describes postfeminism in terms of a 'backlash' – which also serves as the title of her 1992 bestseller – that devastating reaction against the ground gained by the feminist movement (Faludi 1992: 15). Other critics have been less convinced of the conceptual equivalence between postfeminism and backlash, arguing for a more nuanced understanding that takes into account the term's pluralistic structure and diverse entanglements with feminism. It has been suggested that postfeminism is 'neither a simple rebirth of feminism nor a straightforward abortion … but a complex re-signification that harbours within itself the threat of backlash as well as the potential for innovation' (Genz and Brabon 2009: 8).

In many ways, conceptions of the term are dependent on the critical positionings and background of commentators themselves: for feminist media scholars, postfeminism's relationship with feminism – as a critical and political paradigm – is paramount and they focus on how, to varying degrees, postfeminist culture incorporates, commodifies, depoliticizes and parodies feminist ideas and terminology, resulting in the worst case in an 'undoing' and 'othering' of feminism (McRobbie 2004; Tasker and Negra 2007: 4). Situating postfeminism within the theoretical frameworks of anti-essentialist and anti-foundationalist movements – like postmodernism and poststructuralism – underscores its formation as a cultural construct committed to pluralism and difference, whereas embedding it within contemporary politics and lifestyle reinforces its consumerist, individualist dimensions (see Brooks 1997; Gill 2007). Also, it is worth remembering, as Whittier reminds us, that the 'postfeminist generation is not a homogeneous, unified group' (1995: 228). In its present incarnation, postfeminism has matured and developed a critical history that spans the politically conservative 1980s, the more liberal 1990s and the uncertain, post-9/11 years of the new millennium. Consequently, critics have come to expect contradiction as a constitutive feature of postfeminism: in Projansky's words, 'postfeminism is by definition contradictory, simultaneously feminist and antifeminist, liberating and repressive, productive and obstructive of progressive social change' (2007: 68).

Notwithstanding interpretations of postfeminism as a journalistic buzzword, theoretical stance and/or a more generalized cultural climate or atmosphere, the term can successfully be circumscribed within a particular framework specific to a time, place and even class. It is widely acknowledged that 'postfeminism can … be located in a late twentieth- and early twenty-first-century context and period in Western Europe and the United States that emphasizes consumerist, middle-class values' (Genz 2009: 24). It appeals to a generation of women and men – although there is an undeniable gender bias as the wealth of critical literature on female/feminine representations demonstrates – who have been the beneficiaries of social and political gains of feminist activism (enfranchisement, equal pay, sexual liberation, etc.) and now treat these emancipatory ideals as quasi-commonsense. In effect, postfeminism distances itself from some feminist tenets that have proven problematic and/or evasive: for example, the communal idea of 'sisterhood' – central to many expressions of collective feminist politics – is now eschewed in favour of a self-governing individual who embraces (consumer) choice and self-rule as guiding principles. Aspects of postfeminism also re-evaluate the relationship between feminism and femininity and carve out a subjective space for women beyond feminism's critique of feminine appearance and behaviour – famously denounced by feminist veteran Betty Friedan as 'the problem that has no name' (1992: 54). In order to promote its mantra of individual choice and feminine agency, postfeminism often speaks through consumer and popular culture and advocates 'lifestyle' politics and ironic modes of critique that mock rather than condemn stereotypes and imagery that might be considered retrograde and/or sexist. Critics have taken issue with these consumerist, individualist and, to some extent, classist dimensions of postfeminism and mounted accusations of cooption of feminism's language of choice and empowerment that, they argue, is now distorted in the service of capitalist, middle-class and patriarchal ideology. As Tasker and Negra write, 'postfeminist culture works to incorporate, assume, or naturalise aspects of feminism; crucially, it also works to commodify feminism via the figure of women as empowered consumer … postfeminism is white and middle class by default, anchored in consumption as a strategy (and leisure as a site) for the production of the self' (2007: 2).

Popular culture in particular has proven a fertile ground for the examination of postfeminist subjects who pit sexual, feminine and consumer pleasures against political participation and engage in expressions – or fantasies, depending on your viewpoint – of self-management and choice. In this context, postfeminism has been linked with the publishing phenomenon of 'chick lit', a highly lucrative and female-oriented form of fiction that emerged in the 1990s. Frequently characterized by ubiquitous pastel-coloured, fashion-conscious covers, chick lit has simultaneously attracted the adoration of fans as well as the disdain of critics who have dismissed it as trashy fiction. In these scenarios, young urban women (also known as 'singletons' or 'chicks') re-address femininity – and its traditional, heterosexual trappings (beauty and body practices, sexiness, domesticity) – and balance private and public success. Epitomized by Bridget Jones – heroine of Helen Fielding's bestselling 1996 novel – and the main protagonists of the US television series *Sex and the City* (1998–2004), the female characters spend much of their time in pursuit of heterosexual enjoyment and designer commodities, while debating problems – mostly related to their single lives and dating habits – within their network of friends. Simultaneously presented as independent working women enjoying financial and sexual freedom and as body-conscious, at times neurotic romantic heroines, the 1990s chick has been seen as exemplary of the controversies and contradictions surrounding postfeminism. Unashamedly commercial – typified for example by Sophie Kinsella's series of *Shopaholic* novels – and endorsing an often nostalgic view of hetero-patriarchal femininity, chick lit/flick is taken to task for its supposed lack of feminist credentials (see Whelehan 2000). At the same time, the genre is also described as rife with 'possibilities and potential', addressing 'issues and questions about subjectivity, sexuality, race, class in women's texts for another generation of women to ponder' (Ferris and Young 2006: 12).

More recently, postfeminism's maxim of individual consumption as a means to empower the gendered body has been given emphasis in pop culture and music through the notoriously successful figure of Lady Gaga (aka Stefani Joanne Angelina Germanotta). Ever since Gaga grabbed the headlines at the MTV Video Music Awards in 2010 appearing in a controversial designer dress made entirely from cuts of raw meat, she has become the subject of popular and academic accounts that debate her use of sexuality/femininity as commodity and the critical capacity inherent in her mainstream otherness. Always eager to challenge her audience by celebrating the 'freak' and the 'monster', Lady Gaga's graphic use of sex and sexuality in her lyrics and music videos works in the contested field of postfeminism. While for some Lady Gaga can be seen as 'a gendered warrior allied with ongoing feminist struggles', she has also been denounced for contributing to 'the continued objectification and dehumanization of women' (Fogel and Quinlan 2011: 187). Pushing the boundaries of acceptable female sexual expression, Gaga's narrative of self-empowerment is inextricably tied to a hedonistic individualism linked to the consumption of fame and sexuality. In this sense, her invocation of 'monstrosity' – a self-defined ability to shock and criticize – works within the bounds of mainstream popular culture and designer femininity where the cultivation of difference – itself a key element of theoretical versions of postfeminism – has become a marketing tool.

In this sense, the impact of postfeminism for modern media, gender and social studies might lie in its ability to open up new lines of analysis and provide forays into unfamiliar and contradictory subject/agency positions. For example, in her examination of gender representations in the media, Rosalind Gill discusses postfeminism in terms of a 'shift from sexual objectification to sexual subjectification' to describe highly sexualized contemporary women who are not 'straightforwardly objectified but are presented as active, desiring sexual subjects' (2007: 258). Here, the long-standing opposition between subject and object – transferable to some extent to the categories of feminism and femininity – are re-examined to account for the fact that modern-day femininity is formed in relation to feminism, while not necessarily being identified or defined as 'feminist' (see also Genz 2009). Other critics want to complexify politicized conceptions of postfeminism by expanding the vocabulary of political actions to include instances of individual agency and consumer empowerment (see Genz 2006; Mann 1994). The notion of postfeminist 'micro-politics' is particularly useful in this regard in understanding consumer agency as a potential starting point for (political) activism. While none of these enactments are straightforward – postfeminist politics in particular has been conceived as an 'impure practice' (Genz 2006: 338) – they highlight the diverse and at times paradoxical identity positions that people adopt in contemporary society. In this context, postfeminism develops into a distinct mode of critique that accommodates the complicated entanglements that characterize gender, culture, theory and politics in late modernity. Importantly, these debates signal that more work needs to be done in relation to the sociological aspects of postfeminism to investigate how consumer agency and feminine/sexual empowerment might be experienced by some subjects as entirely legitimate and even authentic. As a twenty-first-century critical lens, postfeminism provides an opportunity to practise conflict constructively and re-articulate terms (like 'agency', 'consumption', 'choice' and 'authenticity') that we might take for granted but now demand new analytical frameworks.

Further Reading: Brooks 1997; Genz and Brabon 2009; Gill 2007; McRobbie 2009; Tasker and Negra 2007.

POWER

Carolyn Pedwell

Such is the diversity and richness of feminist theory that generalizations are often problematic. Yet, what has arguably propelled and given shape to a broad range of differently situated feminist interventions is a concern with 'thought's effective power' (Colebrook 2000: 5). As Claire Colebrook argues in her introduction to a collection exploring possible affinities between the work of French philosopher Gilles Deleuze and feminist theory, 'feminism at its most vibrant has taken the form of a demand not just to redress wrongs *within* thought, but to think differently' (original italics, 2000: 2). From Mary Wollstonecraft and liberalism, to Clara Zetkin and Marxism, to Simone de Beauvoir and existentialism, to Audre Lorde and the civil rights movement and second wave feminism, to Judith Butler and poststructuralism and psychoanalysis, feminist theorists and activists have grappled with the question of 'how can one speak in such a way as to address the current corpus of concepts while at the same time seeking to think differently' (Colebrook 2000: 9). To rephrase Lorde's (1984) potent formulation, feminism has always been compelled to use the master's tools to destroy his house; yet it has done so with critical awareness that mobilizing the master's structures and terms creates space to re-activate the concepts they offer – to explore how these concepts might work differently, how they might become otherwise. In this way, Colebrook suggests, feminism can be understood as a 'theoretical heritage where questions have always been voiced in terms of what thought might become (rather than the correctness of this or that model)' (2000: 10). Thus, if we can identify any shared and abiding concern with power within the diversity of feminist theory and practice, we might describe it as an interest in 'the power to become'.

If feminists have been interested in power as potentiality – the possibility inherent in reality to be different than it is – they have had to flesh out the ways in which existing social forms were impoverished, damaging or unliveable. As such, they have also explored how power works to mark, exclude, control, discipline and regulate. In this context, 'patriarchy' has figured as a central feminist concept. Writing in 1988, Lorraine Code defines patriarchy as a 'set of power structures, social practices and institutions that disadvantage and marginalize women' (1988: 1). Patriarchal societies are 'those in which men have more power than women and readier access than women to what is valued in the society or in any social sub-group'. Consequently, 'men in such societies or groups occupy positions that permit them to shape and control many, if not most, aspects of women's lives' (Code 1988–1993: 2). From the 1960s onwards, the concept of patriarchy was mobilized differently by feminists working from different theoretical and political perspectives. For example, in *The Feminine Mystique* (1963a), widely viewed as a liberal feminist text, Betty Friedan's reference to 'the problem that has no name' calls attention to the limiting effects of patriarchal gender roles that made white, middle-class, suburban housewives feel 'empty', 'frustrated' and 'not alive' despite (or indeed because of) their comfortable nuclear family lives. Friedan advocates education and meaningful work as essential in enabling women to transgress 'the feminine mystique'. By contrast, in *The Dialectic of Sex* (1970), which combines radical and Marxist feminist analysis, Shulamith Firestone argues that the problem of patriarchy runs much deeper than anything policy reform or women's integration into the labour force can remedy because sexual difference permeates 'culture, history, economics, nature itself' (1970: 2). From her perspective, women's oppression is rooted in biological differences and it will take nothing less than women's 'seizure of control of *reproduction*' (9) – through, for example, artificial reproduction and cybernetics – to overturn 'the discriminatory sex class system' (8). What these and other feminist articulations of patriarchy shared, however, was a desire to show how current social configurations that disadvantaged and devalued women and femininity were *not* natural or inevitable, but rather only *one* possible way of organizing social life and conceptualizing sexual difference and its implications.

The questions provoked by the concept for patriarchy, however, were not limited to concerns of gender or sexual difference. For Audre Lorde, feminist efforts to address patriarchy would only succeed in reinstalling social hierarchies unless they addressed the assumptions of whiteness and heterosexuality underlying ideals of women's liberation. To imply, she asserts in 'An open letter to Mary Daly' (1979/1984), 'that all women suffer the same oppression simply because they are women is to lose sight of the varied tools of patriarchy. It is to ignore how these tools are used by women without awareness on each other' (1984: 67). Given Black women's relationship to diasporas produced via histories of slavery, colonialism and imperialism, theorists such as Valerie Amos and Prathiba Parmar also stressed the importance of a feminist perspective that engaged international relations of power. A 'definition of patriarchal relations that looks only at the power of men over women without placing that in a wider political and economic framework', they asserted, 'has serious consequences for the way in which relationships within the Black community are viewed' (Amos and Parmar 1984: 9). White feminists' focus on the family as a source of women's oppression, for instance, ignored the fact that British state immigration legislation 'has done all it can do destroy the Asian family by separating husbands from wives, wives from husbands and parents from children' (1984: 15). Alongside other Black, lesbian and working-class feminist scholars and activists, these thinkers located patriarchal power in the context of imperialism, racism, classism and heteronormativity and argued for the need to analyze power as multifaceted and co-constituted through intersections of gender, race, class, nation and sexuality. Thus, while feminist analyses of patriarchy gave a powerful name and analytical coherence to a seemingly disparate range of acts, relations and norms that served to limit and control women whilst maintaining male privilege, the *force* of patriarchy as a concept was less to provide a 'correct picture' of the world, than it was to 'create possibilities for thinking beyond what is already known and assumed' (Colebrook 2001: 19).

If theories of patriarchy conceptualized power primarily as domination or repression, scholars working from postmodernist and poststructuralist frameworks argued for the need to expand feminist frameworks to address how power could be productive. In this respect, the work of the French philosopher Michel Foucault, most notably *Discipline and Punish* (1977) and the *The History of Sexuality Volume 1* (1978), has been a key resource. Through his examination of how power disciplines and regulates embodied subjects in a range of social institutions, from prisons and asylums to schools and the military, Foucault develops an understanding of modern power as distributed through complex social networks rather than possessed by any dominant group. Instead of relying on direct and violent shows of force, he argues, 'disciplinary' power operates through omnipresent surveillance that compels subjects to internalize, and hence perform, norms of social control. Disciplinary power is 'productive' because it achieves subservience through increasing 'the mastery of each individual over his [or her] own body' (1977/1984: 182).

Within Foucault's framework, power is thus not imposed from the top downwards but rather is made up of 'infinitesimal relations and tactics', which are 'produced from one moment to the next,' (1978: 93). As such, it creates 'docile bodies' whose 'forces' are habituated to external regulation, subjection, transformation, 'improvement' (Bordo 1989: 14). Feminist theorists such as Susan Bordo and Sandra Bartky drew explicitly on Foucault's analysis of disciplinary power to discuss the reproduction of femininity in the context of patriarchy. In doing so, they extended his framework but also called attention to its blind spots with respect to the ways in which disciplinary practices are gendered and how women's bodies are frequently rendered more docile than the bodies of men. Addressing the history of so-called 'feminine' disorders such as anorexia, for example, Bordo considers how 'the anorexic' is not repressed or made obedient through overt external violence or oppression, but rather through her own individual quest for self-mastery over her body. As a docile body, she thus 'becomes enmeshed, at times, into collusion with forces that sustain her own oppression' (1989: 15). For Bordo, this is linked to prevalent cultural and media imagery of ideal femininity that produces a sense of omnipresent surveillance, which leads to self-surveillance.

Although Bordo acknowledges that anorexia can be seen as a form of embodied protest, she underscores the self-defeating nature of such protest: feelings of strength, control and self-mastery are, for the anorexic, twinned with the reality of obedience in ways that maintain the patriarchal status quo. From this perspective, anorexia and other embodied 'pathologies' elucidate Foucault's central analytical claim that resistance emerges *within*, rather than outside of, social networks of power.

Yet if this is the case, feminist scholars asked, what possibilities exist for political action that dismantles rather than shores up dominant social hierarchies? This is a key question addressed by Butler in her analysis of gendered subject formation in *Gender Trouble* (1990) and *Bodies that Matter* (1993). For Butler, gender and sex are not pre-given or fixed, but are rather performative effects of power. From the moment we are born and the doctor announces 'It's a girl!' or 'It's a boy!', she argues, we are compelled over and over again to respond to gendered norms that are deeply ingrained in cultural, social, political and psychic life. These expectations simultaneously idealize patriarchal and heterosexual relations. That is, they are based on the assumption of 'gender coherence': the belief that there are two discrete and hierarchically ordered sexes (male and female) that correspond to two discrete and hierarchically ordered genders (masculinity and femininity) and, in turn, that persons of one sex/gender should desire (only) persons of the 'opposite' sex/gender. As such, Butler points out, our very understanding of 'what is possible in gendered life' is 'foreclosed by certain habitual and violent presumptions' (1990/1999: viii). It is through repeatedly (often unconsciously) responding to and performing these norms that sex, gender and sexuality congeal into identities that come to seem *as if* they were natural. In a similar manner to Foucault, she argues that there is no single agent wielding the power that produces gendered identities; rather this power circulates through regulative discourses in which we all participate. The possibility for *agency*, however, exists in practices of repeating gender norms *differently*. Through embodied practices that trouble expectations of gender coherence, and thus expose its fictive aspects, such as drag, Butler suggests, normative and limiting gender categories might be 'denaturalized' and 'resignified'. She is careful to emphasize, however, that the effects of subversive gender performances are both context-specific and unpredictable.

More recently, scholars have queried whether a feminist framework that analyzes power as working primarily through the consolidation or disruption of norms can account for the myriad ways that power circulates and shapes social and political ways of being and knowing. In *The Politics of Piety*, Saba Mahmood argues that an investment in the category of 'resistance' in feminist and post-structuralist theory often imposes 'a teleology of progressive politics onto the analytics of power' which makes it difficult to identify and conceptualize forms of agency 'that are not necessarily encapsulated by the narrative of subversion and reinscription of norms' (Mahmood 2005: 9). In her study of women active in the Islamic mosque movement in Egypt, she suggests that agential capacity for these subjects 'is entailed not only in those acts which resist the norms but also in multiple ways in which one inhabits norms' (2005: 15). Mahmood is thus most interested in 'the way in which gender norms are "performed, inhabited and experienced" differently in different contexts, with varying implications for women's agency' (22).

Coming from a different perspective in *Time Travels: Feminism, Nature and Power*, Elizabeth Grosz seeks to 'push even further the drive towards antihumanism that has been central to some post-Foucauldian developments in feminist theory' (2005: 185). Distinguishing her perspective from Butler's focus on performative processes of 'subject-constitution and consolidation', she advocates a feminist framework in which 'inhuman forces, forces that are both living and non-living, macroscopic and microscopic, above and below the level of the human are acknowledged and allowed to displace the centrality of both consciousness and the unconscious' (2005: 186). Such an approach, she suggests, might allow us to develop a feminist 'politics of acts, not identities' (186). This politics would think less through the notions of 'power from' or 'power over' associated with concepts of freedom, liberation or autonomy, and more in terms of an affirmative 'power to' become otherwise.

In exploring how power might be understood in more 'affirmative' terms feminist scholars have found the work of Gilles Deleuze pertinent. Like Foucault, Deleuze sees power as distributed through multiple and fluid networks; yet if Foucault focuses on the workings of power in discourse and social institutions, Deleuze is more interested in how power structures thought itself. One of his chief concerns in *Difference and Repetition* (1968/2004) and *What is Philosophy?* (1994) is how we might think 'difference' differently. He aims to create a new ontology of 'pure difference' that would enable understanding of power that exceeds binary forms of representation (i.e. male/female; white/black; heterosexual/homosexual; human/animal). From this perspective, power works not primarily through dualistic modes of differentiation, 'othering' or exclusion, but rather as a productive intensity: as the capacity to affect and be affected. Theorizing power as intensity, for Deleuze, dovetails with the recognition that reality is never fully captured by representation, but rather always in flux, always becoming (Grosz 2005). From Colebrook's perspective, drawing on Deleuze to conceptualize feminism itself as a becoming – a dynamic interweaving of acts and relations concerned with the possibility of being otherwise with no origin or end-point – enables a move away from teleological narratives of feminism's engagement with power. It allows us to interpret historically contextualized feminist interventions affirmatively with respect to how they thought 'from the present or actual world to a virtual world or future that [was] not yet given' (Colebrook 2001: 8). It also enables us to keep radically open the possible futures feminism might inhabit.

Further Reading: Allen 2011; Brown 1995; Fraser 2008; Pedwell 2010; Young 1990.

REFLEXIVITY

Sumi Madhok

In an important article, Kathy Davis (2008: 79) explores the attributes of a 'successful feminist theory' and concludes in favour of one that is engaged in advancing a 'reflexive, critical, and accountable feminist inquiry'. But of course, it can be argued that in its concern with the normative and ethical elements of research (Jamal 2011: 203), reflexivity, in fact, encompasses the dimensions of critical enquiry and responsibility too. As a conceptual, epistemological and a methodological device, reflexivity unsettles and destabilizes the power and politics of knowledge, and of 'theory'; it demystifies the research process, identifies and 'locates' the 'knower' in a specific discursive, historical, geopolitical and institutional dynamics of scholarly production. 'Doing reflexivity' is to engage in contextualizing all knowledge in a particular materiality while also implicating it in specific relationships of domination, hierarchy and inequality occurring as these do in and across 'uneven and dissimilar [transnational] circuits of culture and capital' (Grewal and Kaplan 2000). Reflexive research and writing helps bring into view some of the 'worldliness' (Said 1983/1985) of the text while also querying the author's own location in the world. Intrinsically tied to the worldly nature of texts are important questions of intellectual and political investments – of responsibility, accountability and the importance of engaging in politically committed scholarship. In short, reflexivity is linked to concerns of power and of representation; to the ethics of representing others as well as to the practices of representation; to objectivity/subjectivity in research and to researcher/researched relationships; to positionality and location and to questions of justice, political engagement and responsibility in theoretical and empirical research.

Reflexivity not only underpins feminist epistemological and methodological research thinking and practice, but is also a feature of feminist creative arts, and here, the intensely self-reflexive work of Louise Bourgeois is paradigmatic. Epistemic questions and forms of epistemological enquiries – of 'knowers, knowing and known' (Hawkesworth 1989) – their resultant knowledges and the forms of sociality these privilege are central to feminist thinking not only because of their power to define who gets to be a 'subject' within these but also due to their ability to determine which knowledges receive recognition and, thereby, intellectual and 'cultural' legitimacy.

Epistemological enquiries and processes uphold a particular view of the world, endorse certain forms of gender relations and assume a specific set of hierarchical social and political relations as standard. In insisting that knowledges are 'situated' (Haraway 1988) and produced by specific 'knowers' based in specific locations mean that knowledges are in themselves 'specific'. Reflexive practices help critically prise apart aspects of the research process in order to bring into view not only assumptions about gender, race, sexuality, disability and how these intersect and impact a specific project (Maynard 1994), but also enable recognition of the essentially relational nature of the research encounter (Rankin 2010). That knowledges have specific geographies and histories which tie them to particular kinds of politics is powerfully invoked by Adrienne Rich when she writes 'a place on the map is also a place in history within which as a woman, as a Jew, a lesbian, a feminist I am created and trying to create' (Rich 1986: 212). The important point about the idea of location is to acknowledge, explore and articulate the impact of the researcher's location or where it is that they are speaking from on the production of knowledge. It is important to note here that emphasizing location is not to speak of a direct correlation between experience and knowledge but to insist on the contextual nature, specificity and the 'struggling' that accompany knowledge production, or as feminist standpoint theorists point out, knowledges grounded in women's lived experience and of oppression or 'situated knowledges' are generated in and through the 'struggle' of the marginalized and the subjugated.

The processes and outcomes of knowledge production, feminist scholars have argued, are strongly linked not only to the location and institutional dynamics of those involved but also to their intellectual biographies and intersectional identities. Contrastive to positivist social science, the assumption here is not only that value free research is 'unachievable' but also that it is 'undesirable' (Harding and Norberg 2005). Feminist scholars have argued for taking 'subjectivity into account' (Code 1993) pointing out that researchers far from being neutral, detached and unaffected/ing observers have particular reasons for wanting to engage in research projects; their particular attachments having a bearing on the shape and outcome of the research. Methodologically, such an understanding of the researcher/researched relationship translates into a concern to document the 'subjective experiences of doing research' (Maynard 1994: 16) and can be viewed as an attempt to develop a method for evaluation of the role of the researcher in relation to the social world (including researched), and one that is now – as Kathy Davis writes in her article – a central part of feminist theories of knowledge and research practice. Kim England (1994: 244) refers to reflexivity as a 'self-critical sympathetic introspection and the self-conscious analytical scrutiny of the self as researcher … critical to the conduct of fieldwork; it induces self-discovery and can lead to insights and new hypotheses about the research questions'. Similarly, Finlay (2002: 532) defines reflexivity as 'thoughtful, conscious self-awareness', adding that 'reflexive analysis in research encompasses continual evaluation of subjective responses, inter-subjective dynamics, and the research process itself'. And Lather (1993: 675, 676) writes, reflexivity is 'seeing what frames our seeing … to establish and maintain dialogue with readers … and making decisions about which discursive policy to follow, which "regime of truth" to locate one's work within, which mask of methodology to assume'. Fonow and Cook (2005: 2219) look back to their understanding of reflexivity as articulated in their seminal publication *Beyond Methodology: Feminist Scholarship as Lived Research* (1991) and note, 'In *Beyond Methodology*, we defined reflexivity as the tendency of feminists to reflect on, examine critically, and explore analytically the nature of the research process … Today, in addition to the researchers' reflections on methods and the subjects' reflections on the meaning of experiences under investigation, reflexivity has also come to mean the way researchers consciously write themselves into the text, the audiences' reactions to and reflections on the meaning of the research, the social location of the researcher, and the analysis of disciplines as sites of knowledge production.'

Reflexivity is not just passive reflection, it requires one to be actively involved in the construction of knowledge; how to be reflexive, however, is a hard and at times confusing practice – there is little by way of reflexive guidelines on what constitutes reflexivity. Despite the difficulties in practising reflexivity, what is evident, nonetheless, is that there is no one way of being reflexive – there are many different approaches depending both on disciplinarity and methodology. In nearly all cases, though, reflexivity foregrounds subjectivities. Linda Finlay (2002) usefully 'maps' out the different ways in which reflexivity is used in various methodological settings. For instance, reflexivity in phenomenology, she writes, usually involves an evaluation of the researchers' own experience, historical background and specific understandings that they bring to the research. In other words, subjectivity is a starting point of phenomenological research, rather than something that is picked up during research. Similarly, she considers the use of reflexivity within social constructionism, whose central idea is one of seeing the self and human sociality, in general, as a 'construct', pointing out that in these accounts, reflexivity is not about taking an 'inward approach to subjectivity' (2002: 534) but involves instead focusing attention on the processes of subject formation occurring as these do in and through 'interaction, discourse and shared meanings' (534). Reflexivity in this context involves among other practices, thinking through and distinguishing between narratives and 'technologies' that impact and influence the dominant discourses shaping the self.

In discussing the 'challenges' to practising reflexivity, Finlay warns of the dangers of 'enhanced self awareness' and of 'navel gazing' and writes for an 'adequate balance between purposeful, as opposed to defensive or self indulgent, personal analysis' (2002: 542). Furthermore, and in this regard it must also be pointed out that 'doing reflexivity' does not mean that the researcher is somehow an 'all-seeing analyst' (Rose 1997: 305) able to map out an extensive or even comprehensive 'account' of the existing power relations between the researcher and the researched, where power is shown to only ever flow uni-directionally, i.e. from the researcher to the researched, nor does it imply that there is a stable 'conscious agent', always already present who is waiting to be 'reflected in a research project' (316). Instead, reflexivity should help track the movement of power between participants at different stages of the research process, and register the 'uncertainties' and lack of transparent ways of knowing both 'the self' and 'the context' with a view to not try and resolve and seek to 'know' these more completely, but to realize the limitations, both of knowledge and of knowing (Rose 1997). And finally, while an important effect of the concern with reflexivity is self-consciousness of one's location and positionality, this awareness must not translate into privileging one's experience of research as though it might be self-evident or in a position to speak for itself. Here, Joan Scott's caution (1992) against 'naturalising "experience" and of treating "experience" as if it were a "foundational concept"' (37) is instructive. In place of privileging and according an evidentiary status to 'experience', Scott advocates treating all 'categories of analysis as contextual, contingent and contested' (36) and of turning one's focus towards the 'discursive nature of "experience", including "on the politics of its construction"' (37).

If reflexivity heightens our awareness of the political nature of the research process; and, if in uncovering the identity of the 'knower' and the nature of 'knowing', feminist theory is committed to knowledge as not only imbricated in particular circuits of power but also as linked to a certain politics, then surely it only follows that researchers open themselves up to ethical scrutiny of not only their research process but also to the 'political and social consequences of their research' (Harding and Norberg 2005). And furthermore, if feminist scholarship must offer a 'politics of engaged, accountable positioning' (Haraway 1988: 590), then how does reflexivity enable such accountability and help practise this responsibility? As noted earlier, being reflexive does not imply that somehow both the self and the context are 'transparently understandable' (Rose 1997: 318), or that by incorporating reflexive modes of conducting research, we are somehow dealing with existing societal power relations effectively or indeed engaged in minimizing these (England 1994). While it is the case that reflexivity is notoriously difficult to practise, these anxieties must not mean a 'retreat' from either fieldwork or from engaging with difference.

It does however mean that we exercise constant vigilance over our research practices and explore ways of practising reflexivity that helps uncover power relations in a 'structurally unequal world' (Nagar 2007) while also engaging in devising ethical ways of reaching out across these 'in a more egalitarian language of alliances, coalitions, and solidarity' (Abu Lughod 2002: 789). Richa Nagar and Susan Geiger (2007: 268) aim to 'reframe' the discussion on reflexivity which, they write, must be underpinned by two 'key questions': of how to produce knowledge across 'multiple divides' without privileging the privileged, and how to anchor one's knowledge practices to 'material politics of social change in favour of less privileged communities and places'. Katharine Rankin reminds us that feminist research practice includes

> locating one's own experience, even at 'home', in relation to the histories of others, and … through contextually specific examinations of relational reflexivity, 'difference' can be understood, not as broad conceptual categories of 'self' and 'other', or as something to merely recognise and celebrate, but as indexing unequal access to resources and power.
>
> (Rankin 2010: 195)

In an insightful and skilful reading of Spivak's call for hyper-reflexivity or vigilance 'in relation to our own practice', Ilan Kapoor

(2008) distils a 'step-wise approach' from Spivak's writings to show how this might be attempted. He puts forward five 'Spivakian tests' for developing an 'ethical relationship with the Other' (Kapoor 2008: 57) that according to him includes: 'intimately "inhabiting" and "negotiating" discourse'; acknowledging both one's location in discourse, structures, institutions or 'worlding' as also one's complicity in it; 'unlearning one's privilege as loss' or 'reversing the gaze'; 'learning to learn from below' (57). Kapoor's fifth 'Spivakian test' is 'working "without guarantees"' which, he writes, involves learning to accept the unknowability of the other and 'accepting that it exceeds our understanding or expectations' (58).

This insistence on hyper-reflexivity can be read as a call towards entering into an ethical politics of responsibility through practising ethical research relations. The emphasis on reflexivity is, therefore, intertwined with and invoked alongside a set of ethical research practices – taking responsibility for one's location; acknowledging complicity and implication in the very structures and relations of inequality that one might be engaged in unmasking; admitting accountability for the consequences of research; and finally, exercising constant vigilance over our research practices.

Further Reading: Chow 2006; Fonow and Cook 1991; Jouve 1991; Kulick and Wilson 1995; Lorde 1979; McCorkel and Myers 2003.

REPRESENTATION

Sadie Wearing

Representation is a concept that describes a process as well as a cultural object, or a particular subject or set of subjects. The process is that of presenting (literally, making present) one thing in the shape or form of another, so representation describes the act of symbolically producing presence from absence. For example, portrait painting is a representation, which takes the form of an object (a likeness on a canvas) of a subject (the sitter) who does not need to be physically present in order to be 're-presented' in the picture. This simple enough idea is yet highly complex, in that the concept also carries with it the idea that to represent is to 'stand in for', and, in the political sense, to be accountable to the origin. In the cultural sphere this means that representations maintain a relation to the social world but the process of representation is also, and at the same time, one of accruing and acquiring meanings and therefore that relation is not one of 'mere' record – rather, the process itself produces a new range of possible understandings of the subject represented.

In terms of political representation, the concept carries with it the idea of representation as standing in for the larger group and making up for their lack of physical presence. So, broadly, representation as a concept nearly always holds an ambiguity or tension between these related senses: the sense of standing in for something else (re-presentation), the sense of representation as a dynamic process, a production with social effects and affects, and finally the sense of representation as related to accountability and ethics, entailing a responsibility to, for example, a group, a country or an institution.

Raymond Williams cites the term represent as having two overlapping but distinct meanings dating from the fourteenth century, both of which refer to 'making present', either in the sense of introducing or offering a person to another. And this sense still stands: on formal occasions we are still 'presented' to one another, and this sense of representing oneself in a specific (perhaps advantageous) light hints at the productive capacity for representation to confer or alter perception, and therefore to stage an effect in the world, to make meanings rather than simply reflecting them.

The second overlapping sense Williams notes is that of making present not the physical person but rather to 'call to mind' the person, idea or object (Williams 1988). An 'extension' of this he also traces back to the fourteenth century, which is the sense of representation as related to symbolization – the 'standing in' for something else. It was not until the seventeenth century that the extended associations with standing in for, representing others became more widespread.

Importantly, Williams notes an uncertainty at the root of the term representative which hinges on the difference between the 'symbolic' sense and the 'political'. This uncertainty is maintained in both the political and the 'artistic' or cultural realm – the uncertainty relates to the question of the relation between the source (the electors, say, or the model in the painting) and the representative or representation itself – the person representing supposed to be 'typical' of the electors, speak on their behalf (in any way they see fit), or speak *for* them – as in ventriloquize their views. These are key questions for representative democracy and they have a clear gendered dimension – does it matter whether women speak for women or on their behalf? Can an elected body be truly democratic if its representatives are dominated by only one gender? In the cultural realm too how does the work of representation relate to the sense of representative-ness – of taking responsibility for the relation between the social reality and its cultural embodiments?

For gender representation these ideas are also in tension, since it is in the sphere of representational practice that many of the meanings that circulate around gender (in the sense of masculinities and femininities) accrue, take shape and materialize. At the same time, they are often in the process naturalized, policed and/or contested (Butler 1999). Questions of representation are key not only to the analysis and understanding of gender but of class, 'race' and ethnicity, age, ability and sexuality, indeed it is hard to imagine analysis of any of these which would not take questions of representational practice or what are sometimes called 'regimes of representation' seriously. The term 'regime' is useful here in that it points directly to what is often considered central about representational practice, its relation to the dominant or the 'hegemonic', those understandings of the world which pass by unnoticed because they are held to be 'common sense'. However, representation is also understood as a possible arena for the disruption of such understandings and it is on the ground of representation that many significant battles for equality have been fought. This ambiguity around the politics of representation, the understanding that it has a role in the maintenance but also the possible disruption of the status quo means that there is a weight that attaches to gender representations, which can be related closely to the meanings attached to representation in its narrowly political sense. In this latter sense too the gendered question of representation is key so questions will frequently be asked about the gender make up of political representation. For feminist political theorists the question of who represents who is one that is frequently asked given the distinct imbalance of elected male and female political representatives in most national contexts (Phillips 1995). For feminist theory and epistemology the question of representation has also been posed in the related but distinct sense of who gets to speak for whom, which 'women' stand in for other women and what are the ethico-political dilemmas associated with such representational privilege? (Spivak 1988; Alcoff 1995). In relation to these epistemological questions are the specific dilemmas that this raises for feminist research practice and methodologies which has acknowledged the responsibility of the researcher who in speaking 'about' as well as 'for' their research subjects is inevitably involved in the 'construction of their subject position rather than simply discovering their true selves' (Alcoff 1995: 101). For feminist social research then, representing others requires a careful examination of the dynamics of representation and its enmeshment in the relations between power and knowledge (hooks 1984; Harding and Norberg 2005), which has in turn led to careful consideration of the complexity and fluidity of such relations (e.g. Reay 1996; Thapar-Björkertand Henry 2004; Grenz 2005).

Representation has a been a key concept for those working in cultural and media studies who have, again, been concerned to explore the question of representation in relation to power. Richard Dyer's account locates three main questions surrounding 'representation'. He suggests, 'The complexity of representation lies then in its embeddedness in cultural forms, its unequal but not monolithic relations of production and reception, its tense and unfinished, unfinishable relation to the reality to which it refers and which it affects' (Dyer 1993: 4). He notes the role of representation as 'presentation' 'always and necessarily entailing the use of codes and conventions of the available cultural forms of presentation' (1993: 2). Dyer argues that this means we need to be alert to the 'restrictions' and 'shapes' of cultural forms so questions of narrative or genre, which may enable and restrict images, work in particular ways and we need to pay attention to those restrictions and possibilities and understand how they work. Whilst these forms – for example, the musical or a novel – have particularities which help us to 'read' them in particular ways this doesn't mean that all meaning or 'reading' is determined in advance, rather, individuals may well 'make sense' of representations in different ways 'according to the cultural (including sub cultural) codes available to them' (2). This expressly complicates the widespread view that gender representation might be understood as 'positive' or 'negative' – or indeed, 'sexist' – and raises important issues for feminist study of media and culture since much of its political thrust is predicted on the assumption that a representation of, say, a scantily clad woman draped over a car to sell that car can be reliably critiqued as 'sexist'. Perhaps instead it will be read as 'ironic' or as a direct critique of the objectification and commodification of the female form? For some feminist media scholars, however, the point is that representation is emphatically culpable in reproducing not only myths about femininity and sexuality but also in the production of the female body as precisely (even primarily) an object of the male desiring gaze (Mulvey 1974; Berger 1972), thus even 'ironic' representations are caught in a web of meanings which preceded the particular image and the consumption of that image is therefore to engage not in a solitary act of 'decoding' (Hall 1980) but in a social engagement. The key point that Mulvey makes is that mainstream representation is implicated in reproducing and reinforcing a split between active looking and passive appearing, which divides along gender lines with an active male subject and a passive female object. This is not to say that representations cannot be read 'against the grain' but it is to highlight the limits of such 'polysemy' (multiplicity of meaning). Mulvey's argument has been widely contested, not least by Black feminist writer bell hooks, who argues that in the realm of representation looking and being looked at are not only gendered but also racialized and that both returning the gaze and developing oppositional forms of representation have a history and are powerful forms of resistance (hooks 2000); further, that the violence of looking relations is exacerbated by the failure of white feminists to acknowledge the whiteness of the construct 'woman' (see also, Young 1996). Again this points to the politics of representation in a double sense, both in terms of the matter under discussion, the relation of spectators to mainstream texts and the ways these are gendered and raced, but also the caustic effects of the representational strategies of feminism itself. Richard Dyer makes a related point arguing that whilst we view differently from different perspectives and with different histories this is not to negate the importance of considering power in relation to representation rather than, as hooks suggests, we need to be careful about how we conceptualize that power. He insists:

> We are all restricted by both the viewing and the reading codes to which we have access (by virtue of where we are situated in the world and the social order) and by what representations there are for us to view and read. The prestige of high culture, the centralization of mass cultural production, the literal poverty of marginal cultural production: these are aspects of the power relations of representations that put the weight of control over representation on the side of the rich, the white, the male, the heterosexual.
>
> (Dyer 1993: 2)

So in terms of class and race a range of questions related to representation are also crucial. The history of colonialism demonstrates how the representation of the colonized as profoundly, if contradictorily, 'other' was key to the processes of empire building (Said 1978/1985; McCintock 1995; Gilman 1985; Brantlinger 1985) and in the nineteenth century involved the dissemination of a set of representational strategies which, whilst various and sometimes contradictory, were nonetheless consistent in ensuring the 'flexible positional superiority' (Said 1978/1985) of the European who occupied a position of alterity to the, for example, primitive, degenerate, mysterious or inscrutable 'other'. Such representational strategies are, however, additionally complex, in that they refer not only to the singular dimension under consideration (say, 'race', 'class', 'gender') but also to these elements in *relation* to one another: for example, racialized representation is both classed and gendered.

The 'native' and the working class in Victorian England were both represented as 'childlike and dependent', but also as savage and amoral, and these 'attributes' are of course gendered. The battle over representation has been a key component of the questions raised by postcolonial theory (McCintock 1995; Spivak 1988; Said 1978/1985, 1983; Hall 1996c; Bhabha 1994). For some, one of the key points here is the relation of racialized, classed and gendered representations to the stereotype. Stereotyping is an ordering process which distils specific characteristics and generalizes these as pertaining to a group (women, lesbians, Italians) repeated across a range of contexts over time and texts, so Scots are careful with money, Africans have a superior sense of rhythm, women are caring and so on. Whilst not all stereotyping appears to be explicitly aggressive (what's wrong with a having a superior sense of rhythm or being caring?) the reproduction of stereotypes nonetheless performs a form of 'symbolic violence' (Hall 2007: 259), in its reducing or essentializing 'the other' to fixed and predictable figurations. Countering so-called 'negative' stereotypes with 'positive' ones cannot go very far in shifting the terms of dominant representations and their power relations. What is needed, it is argued, is an understanding of the roles of identification and desire in the representation of difference (Hall 2007; Bhabha 1994), and inequalities of access to the means of production to generate and regenerate popular stereotypes (Dyer 1993; Shohat and Stam 1994).

This is one reason why 'counter' narratives and representations are crucial to progressive politics. For example: in the UK, in the wake of widespread so called 'race riots' of the early 1980s, it was through cultural production and the workshops funded by the Greater London Council and Channel 4 television, that the Black British experience was re-imagined and re-evaluated. Examples include the Black Audio Film collective, Sankofa film and video and Ceddo film/video workshop.

These were sites of resistance to negative stereotypes and the mainstream dominant forms of representation; but they were also – at times – formally experimental (Mercer 1994; Pines 1996; Hill 1999; Hall 1996a). This reflects another dimension of the question of representation since it counters the idea that representation in the cultural sphere has to be about 'typicality'. This point can be related both to the question of the 'burden' of representation and also the problem Shohat and Stam (1994) have identified in relation to the analysis of stereotypes – that such analysis inevitably runs the danger of reproducing the terms of engagement rather than adequately deconstructing those terms.

For class as well as race representation is a key arena for the reproduction of ideas, attitudes and understandings of difference and despite much rhetoric over the demise of class in the UK context sociologists such as Beverley Skeggs have noted the narrow range of representations of the 'working class' in the UK as an important aspect of the 'symbolic evaluation' (Skeggs 2004) of what it means to have personhood or a 'self'. Skeggs and others have noted the ways in which, for example, white working-class women are targeted by the media as 'pramface' (McRobbie 2009) or 'chav mum' (Tyler 2008) in representations that corresponds to long-standing imagery of the 'deserving and undeserving poor'.

So representation then is a concept that has a range of related meanings; it is a significant concept for gender because of the ways that the process of representation is understood as productive, generative and dynamic. Representation is understood as both having an effect in the world, acknowledging its power to shape the meanings attached to gender, and as a responsibility, owing to its root in the creation of a presence out of an absence.

Further Reading: Dyer 1993; Hall 2007; hooks 1996; McClintock 1995; Shot and Stam 1994.

THE SEXUAL DIVISION OF LABOUR

Clare Lyonette

Definition of concept

The sexual division of labour refers to the way in which men and women (in couple households) divide and share both paid and unpaid work in order to maintain a home and family. Paid work refers to work carried out, usually for an employer outside the home, in exchange for a wage, while unpaid work includes household work and the care and maintenance of other family members.

The major focus of discussions about the sexual division of labour, particularly within feminist circles, relates to the unequal distribution of tasks between women and men, specifically domestic work and childcare, which continue to be primarily undertaken by women, in spite of their increased participation in the labour market. Other terms often used in critical debates are the 'gendered' division of labour or, because of the primary focus on housework and caring, the domestic (or 'household') division of labour.

Background and history of the term or concept

Patriarchy and male ownership of household resources have a long history, and were common even in pre-industrial societies when women typically contributed to the household wage by participating in paid employment. During the second part of the nineteenth century in the UK, however, the rise among the middle classes of the 'male breadwinner' model (the notion that a man's wage should be able to support his family without a wife or children having to work for pay), and the corresponding notion that women's efforts should be channelled within the home, led to the increasing segregation of men's (paid) and women's (unpaid) work. This ideology of 'separate spheres' for men and women is described by Davidoff and Hall (1987), where 'men were to be active in the world as citizens and entrepreneurs' and 'women were to be dependent as wives and mothers' (1987: 450). The male breadwinner model continued well into the twentieth century (women were drafted into traditional male jobs such as engineering during the Second World War, but only on condition that they would leave when the war was over). Indeed, post-war UK government policy explicitly endorsed the 'proper' roles for men as paid work and for women as household and childcare duties, and in so doing, further embedded a set of social 'norms' (or accepted behaviours).

For women who wanted to engage in paid work or who had to work for financial reasons, government legislation and organizational restrictions meant that they were barred from entering many occupations and professions, could not progress into managerial or higher-level positions, or were paid at a lower rate than men for the same work. In spite of the rise of 'second wave' feminism in the 1960s and 1970s, and government legislation that banned inequalities in the workplace, there continue to be persisting beliefs about what men and women should and should not do. Gender differences in both paid and unpaid work remain firmly in place in the UK and in many other countries, although it should be noted that couples in Scandinavian countries demonstrate a more equal distribution of domestic labour and childcare, partly as a result of family policies which have been directed both at mothers *and* fathers. High levels of state support for dual-earner families in these countries have been accompanied by efforts to encourage men to undertake more domestic work, and in particular more childcare.

There are various explanations for the continuing disparities between men and women. Feminist sociologists such as West and Zimmerman (1987) argue that the prevailing sexual division of domestic and caring work is a central element in 'doing gender' (whereby behaviours are organized in such a way that 'gender' is done or produced in everyday activities such as household work and childcare). Feminist arguments highlight that the normative assignment of housework and childcare to women is so firmly entrenched that women will continue to do more, even if they are working as many hours as their male partners.

On the other hand, 'rational' economistic arguments (see e.g. Becker 1991) stress the importance of both 'time availability' and 'relative resources' within couple households: time availability explanations suggest that carrying out domestic tasks is based on the time available to both partners. As fathers tend to spend more hours in paid work than mothers (especially if women are working part-time or not at all), mothers have more time to carry out domestic work. Closely linked to this is the relative resource hypothesis, which argues that the partner with greater resources will retain the power to get the other partner to do more housework. If these arguments are valid, as women engage in paid work and earn more, their male partners should do more domestic work and childcare.

In recent decades, there has also been more discussion and research relating to men's desire for greater involvement in the home (terms such as the 'new man' and 'involved fathering' are common) and that men do not undertake more domestic tasks because of the constraints of paid employment (long working hours and perceived commitment, etc.) and, in some cases, because of the choices made by women. Catherine Hakim has argued that mothers' employment patterns reflect the choices or 'preferences' made by different types of women. In other words, those women who work part-time or not at all are more home-centred and those who work full-time are more work-centred. Feminist authors have fiercely opposed the argument that women 'choose' to retain the major responsibility for housework and childcare, however. Lewis and Giullari (2005) argue that the normative assignment of caring and domestic work to women means that women do not have the same capacity to 'choose' between care and paid employment as men do. Thus women's 'agency freedom' is restricted and they are unable to compete on a similar level with men in the workplace.

How the concept is used in practice/study

Rosemary Crompton (2006) examined British Social Attitudes survey data over time to show that attitudes to gender roles have changed significantly, but they also vary by gender, age and class. For example, in 1989, 32 per cent of men agreed that 'a man's job is to earn money; a woman's job is to look after the home and family', compared with 26 per cent of women. In 2002, only 20 per cent of men and 17 per cent of women agreed with the statement. In addition, 67 per cent of men in 1989 believed that a woman should stay at home when there is a child under school age, compared with 61 per cent of women, and these figures reduced to 51 per cent for men and 48 per cent for women in 2002. Later work showed that attitudes became even less 'traditional' in 2006 for both men and women. In general, older people report a more traditional domestic division of labour than younger people, and those in higher occupational classes report a less traditional division of domestic labour than those from lower occupational classes (although more recently, men from lower occupational classes have been changing their attitudes in line with men from higher occupational groups).

In order to examine the validity of the relative resource hypothesis, some researchers have studied households in which women earn more than men (as girls continue to out-perform boys at school and increasingly in higher education, this may be a growing phenomenon). In Australia, for example, Bittman et al. (2003) found that men's levels of domestic labour were not significantly affected by their female partners' relative contribution to the household. In fact, women's hours of housework appeared to increase once they reached a similar level of household income as their partners. Bittman explained this finding as an attempt by women to protect their men from a deviation of typical gender norms by neutralizing their gender 'deviance.' Men and women in such households accordingly 'display' their gender (see Brines 1994) by increasing or decreasing their levels of domestic work. In this way, gender overrides resources or money, providing support for the feminist sociological perspective.

Other researchers have cast some doubt on the concept of 'gender deviance neutralization' (for a recent review, see Sullivan 2011). For example, Gupta (2007) argues that women's absolute earnings are more important in men's undertaking of household work than their relative earnings. Kan (2008) also finds a linear relationship between working hours and housework (i.e., longer paid working hours are associated with less hours of housework for both men and women), although women with more traditional attitudes still do more.

Although men's share of domestic work has risen since the 1960s, this increase reached a plateau during the 1990s (Coltrane 2000) and men are still less likely than women to do mundane household chores such as washing and cleaning. Indeed, a more recent study by Kan et al. (2011) shows that in the UK, men's contribution has in fact steadily risen into the twenty-first century, but that their efforts are concentrated more in non-routine domestic work than in caring and routine tasks.

Significance and impact of the concept today in modern practice/study

The debate about the sexual division of labour is still widely discussed and argued in academic, political and popular literature. In fact, over recent decades there has been an ongoing criticism of feminism, with suggestions that many social problems are a consequence of women's employment. Some argue that women should therefore rediscover their 'innate' nurturing abilities and devote themselves to the care of children, rather than seek success in paid work (Kristol 1998). There has been also a rise in popular works such as *Men are from Mars, Women are from Venus* (Gray 1992) which highlight the 'essential' differences between men and women (for example, caring women and competitive men). Others emphasize the positive outcomes of a return to traditional gender roles, although these continue to be contested by many feminist authors.

As researchers have shown, men do appear to be responding to women's increasing participation in the workforce, albeit slowly. This 'lagged adaptation' (Gershuny et al. 1994) to women's increasing participation in paid work is argued to be a major factor contributing to persisting gender inequality. In 1990, Joan Acker described contemporary employment as constructed on a full-time 'adult worker' model in which organizations require an 'abstract, bodiless worker who occupies the abstract, gender-neutral job' and 'does not procreate' (1990: 151). Domestic responsibilities undoubtedly make it difficult to meet these 'adult worker' requirements. Part-time and flexible employment, and strategies such as 'scaling down' individual employment intensity, are not compatible with career success. However, more than 20 years after Acker's influential work, women make up 74 per cent of all part-time workers, and, while the gender pay gap persists for all working women, part-time women are particularly badly affected, being paid significantly less than equivalent full-time men. In other words, women's continued responsibility for domestic work and caring has long-term implications for both career success and financial independence.

Further Reading: Crompton 2006; Hakim 2000; Sullivan 2011; West and Zimmerman 1987.

SUBJECTIVITY

Henrietta L. Moore

All humans are born into worlds not of their making, and for theorists of gender this raises two intractable issues. The first is how we become gendered as opposed to merely sexed and the second is how we become individuals within specific social and cultural formations. If we simply assume that processes of socialization or internalization solve these difficulties we make recourse to the untrammelled workings of power and the perfect reproduction of the social, a move that immediately negates individual agency and raises issues of freedom. Subjectivity is the term we use to refer both to the process and the form of the relation of the individual to the social, and it remains a contested term by virtue of the fact that there is no possible resolution to the debate as to how the two definitively interrelate.

If subjectivity is both the process and the result of the relationships the subject forms to discourses, norms and power relations then analysis must focus on the social conditions that enable the subject's emergence. Yet, this is still inadequate for an account of subjectivity because it takes no account of fantasy or desire, or of the particular ways in which the psychic does not repeat the social. At the heart of this discussion with regard to gendered subjectivity has been a series of disagreements between psychoanalysis and feminism. Psychoanalytic theories are diverse, but they do all focus on the fact that the entrance of any human subject/self into existing social relations and cultural discourses always involves negotiating relations with parents and significant others. Thus sexual difference resides at the base of both psyche and culture, and one cannot become a social being without taking up a position in relation to the male and the female. For psychoanalytic theorists, sexual difference is distinct from gender, it is not socially contingent, but operates at the level of the symbolic, functioning as an historically and culturally invariant psychosexual structure. Yet, if these structures are invariant, if women are constantly reinscribed as the sex that marks the difference from the norm, then what hope is there for a feminist politics? A further difficulty is that the binary character of sexual difference does not provide much purchase when confronted with the multiple models of gender, gender identifications, and gender practices in any particular historical context. Whatever a gendered subjectivity may be, it is clearly not arrived at by acquiescing to a single model of gender nor by being marked by sexual difference understood as the binary difference between the male and the female. The picture is much more complex, and recent psychoanalytic writing has acknowledged that there is always a tension between gender ideals and the experience of being a gendered individual, and that gender identities in any given historical context are not singular or fixed, but are made up of a series of subject positions based on gender (e.g. Dimen and Goldner 2002; Fairfield et al. 2002).

This shift in perspective was driven both by feminist theorizing and by postmodern and deconstructive theories of knowledge that sought to critique received notions of power, truth, self and language (Flax 1990). Key to this theoretical turn was the deconstruction of the unitary subject of humanism (e.g. Soper 1990), and the move away from the notion of a self-identified and self-identificatory subject to ideas about multiply constituted subjects, and their multiple, contradictory, and conflicting forms of subjectification. In terms of the genealogy of feminist thought, this can be broadly sketched as a move from the analysis of the differences between women and men to a focus on the differences among women, to a concern with the differences within each woman. The basic premise was that discourses and discursive practices provide subject positions, and individuals take up a variety of subject positions within different discourses. The result is that a single subject can no longer be equated with a single individual. Individuals are multiply constituted subjects who exist and develop a sense of self through multiple and potentially contradictory positioning and subjectivities. Multiple forms of difference, such as race, class, gender, ethnicity and sexuality were initially analyzed as additive, then as serial and ultimately as mutually constitutive. Identity is constituted through the intersection of multiple discourses on difference, and does not result from a straightforward process of cultural socialization. The result was a shift away from the binary models of gender difference to an emphasis on difference as the condition for the possibility of subjectivity, its constitutive limit (Moore 1994).

There were two further theoretical trends underpinning theorizing through the 1980s and 1990s. The first had its roots in feminist standpoint theory, and in the idea that how we are located in the world makes a difference to our experience of it (Harding 2004). This was a material 'politics of location' that also incorporated an analysis of the self-ascribed location of the theorist/feminist/activist (e.g. Grewal and Kaplan 1994). The second drew directly on postmodernist philosophy and in particular the work of Foucault to emphasize that the subject is constituted in language and cannot be the sole author of their experience or desire. Many inspired by Foucauldian analysis also drew on Lacanian psychoanalysis with its constitution of the subject in language and the ceaseless disruption of self-identity by the workings of fantasy and the unconscious. Lacan, like Freud, emphasizes the materiality of consciousness, and the fact that we develop an internal world and the capacity to relate to others and the wider social world through representations. It is the formation of the unconscious that provides the condition for subjectivity and consciousness, but it is also the guarantee that the psychic cannot be wholly determined by the social. The different formulations of the subject and of subjectivity through the last decades of the twentieth century were both varied and contentious, and very often depended on the specific theorist's preferences for either social or psychoanalytic determinations or some combination of both. However, running like a fault line through all these debates was a three-way tension – sometimes faltering, at others strongly expressed – between power, language and embodiment.

Becoming a subject is never a finished or closed process. Power and ideology certainly work to produce subject positions, but they cannot determine how individuals will identify with and take up different subject positions at different times, nor can they determine exactly how individuals will be involved in the transformation of discourses of power and difference over time. Particular social and cultural circumstances produce historically situated modes of being, particular ways of thinking about the world and about ourselves as subjects and agents in history. Social and political change alter ways of feeling, acting and understanding, and new forms of knowledge revise our relation to things, to others and to ourselves. Processes of subjectification involve aspects of identification and recognition, and in many contexts distributions of power are overt. For example, in his discussion of masculinity in Colombia, Viveros Vigoya (2012) demonstrates that with regard to gendered subjectivities relations of class, gender and race not only co-exist, but also co-produce and reproduce each other. Drawing on his research, he shows that several conflicting forms of masculinity co-exist and that rather than being constructed exclusively in relation to femininity, according to a binary model of differentiation, these masculinities are constituted in and formed in conjunction with racial and class subject positions. The result is a series of racialized hierarchies that frame the masculinity of dominant classes and ethnic groups through ideals such as 'responsible providers' and 'present fathers', in contrast to other groups who are labelled 'unfaithful spouses', 'absent fathers' and 'irresponsible providers'. Such labelling may make certain forms of masculinity unliveable or rather provide points of identification and/or subject positions that undermine black and lower class men's ability to assert and promote the value of their intimate/loving relationships in the context of other hegemonic, more culturally valued forms of masculinity.

What makes such analyses valuable is the dynamic intersection of recognition and identification, the way that a complexly constituted self identifies with and/or resists and transforms the various gendered subject positions available within a particular social, cultural, economic and political context. But, it also demonstrates that gendered subjectivities are not comprehensible outside their constitution within active matrices of difference, and allows researchers to focus on processes of failure, resistance and change in the acquisition of gendered subjectivities, as well as on compliance, acceptance and investment. This provides a means to emphasize the dual character of subjectification, accounting both for workings of power and difference, and for self-determination, creativity and projects of self-making. Globalization, capitalism and other large-scale processes of socio-economic change have had a major impact on understandings of gender and sexuality, and on intimate relations and self-understandings around the globe. In contemporary societies, sites of subjectification are heterogeneous, and in addition to intimate spaces and relations, the media, education, fashion and consumerism, as well as citizenship, health care and policy are creating new conditions for the possibility of new gendered subjectivities. New spaces, new practices, new forms of knowledge are opening up possibilities both for new identifications, and for more satisfying forms of attachment with older established values and subject positions. Projects of modernity, as well as nationalist projects, frequently involve new ideas about gender categories and intimate relations that in their turn underpin new eroticisms and forms of self-realization, casting new light on received ideas about personal autonomy and freedom.

Gendered subjectivities are historically specific and consequently they are open to change. However, this continues to raise questions about the relationship between subjectification and agency. In recent years, a number of critiques of the discursive construction of the subject have emerged. Taken together, they can be read as a return to 'materiality', as an invitation to refigure the social as something more than discourse, as something that is not necessarily confined within the terms or limits of language (e.g. Braidotti 2002a; Alaimo and Hekman 2008). Bodies carry their own signs; their own signifiers in ways that are often unconscious, and processes of identification can be reformulated through modes of bodily knowledge and the tactile nature of diverse bodily practices. Saba Mahmood describes a women's mosque movement in Egypt where women focus on the social practices and bodily comportment required for the cultivation of piety and an ideal virtuous self. Mahmood argues that we need to attend to how specific kinds of bodily practice 'come to articulate different conceptions of the ethical subject, and how bodily form does not simply express social structures but also endows the self with particular capacities through which the subject comes to act in the world' (Mahmood 2005: 138–39). For the women in the mosque movement what is at stake is a particular conceptualization of the role the body plays in the making of the self, one in which the outward behaviour and practices of the body constitute both the affective potential and the means through which the interior self is realized (Mahmood 2005: 159). Consequently, models of agency based on language – as are all feminist poststructuralist theories of subjectivity – are problematic here because they give insufficient attention to somatic and affective potentialities, and to how they engage with agency and emergent forms of sociality.

Recent critiques of the poststructuralist subject begin with discussions of intersubjectivity and its affective and political consequences. Intersubjectivity in this context involves not just affective relations between individuals, but also between humans and non-humans, including animals and machines. At the core of these ideas is the notion of the co-dependence of self and other, a radical rethinking of intersubjectivity that takes account of embodied, affective relationships, and thus considers human subjectivity within the frame of human environmental relationships in the broadest sense. From this perspective, subjectivity and agency are no longer confined to the human nor theorized from the perspective of the human alone (e.g. Braidotti 2006). The focus is not on the individual subject but rather on human and non-human actors in hybrid networks located in space and time. The politics being pursued here is not one based on empowerment of the liberal subject, nor on the self-making of the discursively constructed poststructuralist subject, but a politics of inclusion in which enhanced or expanded relations with others – specifically those excluded by power, and including the non-human – operate according to logics of reciprocity and co-dependence. The ethical good and the goal of such a politics is a radical relationality, an ability to enter into relationships with multiple others, including the non-human and the post-human.

Further Reading: Benjamin 1998; Biehl, Good and Kleinman 2007; Butler 2005b; Gill and Scharff 2011; Grosz 1994; McLaren 2002; Mansfield 2000; Moore 2007; Rose 2006.

TRANSNATIONAL FEMINISMS

Sunila Abeysekera

Linkages of women's movements and women's activism for emancipation and rights across national borders have a long and complex history. From international solidarity among women from different parts of the world in the 1920s onwards, the process evolved to a focus on 'global' feminism in the 1970s and 1980s and, most recently, to the articulation of transnational feminism as the conceptual framework that responds most effectively to the needs of women's movements around the world. In the contemporary world, women's movements in every part of the globe confront a range of political, economic, social and ideological challenges wrought by the processes of globalization, neoliberal capitalism, militarization and a growth in all forms of fundamentalisms and nationalist extremisms. Transnational feminism emerges as a collective and collaborative response of feminist scholars and activists to these challenges.

Women who were a part of the anti-colonial and nationalist movements of the global South in the first half of the twentieth century developed links across national and political borders and within broader social movements with a focus on international solidarity. The Votes for Women campaigns that linked women in Britain with women from the British Empire, especially in South Asia were one example. Broad alliances of women across the globe were also linked through faith and belief, such as through the Young Women's Christian Association, and through commitment to a cause, such as the Women's International League for Peace and Freedom (WILPF). In the 1960s women from left political parties and trade unions were a part of the internationalist movements emerging from the Soviet bloc, such as the World Federation of Democratic Women (WFDW).

In the 1980s, aid and development policies began to focus more on the situation of women in the southern hemisphere. With the growth of multinational corporations, women's engagement in the labour market began to take on a cross-national character. Advances in travel and in communication technologies also made linkages between women across continents much easier. In this context, women's organizations and networks began to question the division of the world into north and south, into the centre and the periphery. This line of questioning emerged not only in the developed nations of the 'Western world' but also in postcolonial states. The impact of the nexus of race and class on the organizing principles of women's movements around the world became as important a discussion as that of sex and gender. Angela Davis' book *Women Race and Class* (1982) raised some challenging issues regarding the erasure of black women's experiences within the women's movements of the USA. In contrast, Robin Morgan's anthology *Sisterhood is Global* (1984) looked outwards, documenting experiences of women from 70 countries within a framework that reflected an un-differentiated commonality of experience among women. Kumari Jayawardena (1986) challenged the idea that feminism was a concept and practice that developed in the 'West' and that was essentially Eurocentric, and defined feminism as a more inclusive phenomenon; her definition of feminism as 'an awareness of women's oppression and exploitation within the family, at work and in society, and conscious action by women (and men) to change this situation' (1986: 2) enabled the activism of many women in nationalist and anti-colonial struggles to be recognized as a part of global feminist movements.

The United Nations Conference on Women in Nairobi in 1985 provided a platform for these various strands of feminist thinking from around the world to interact, collaborate, dialogue and differ. Several international networks of women had emerged around specific issues, such as trafficking and sex tourism, or specific sectors, such as women workers in export-oriented industries, which crossed national borders in terms of implications and consequences for women. The Nairobi Conference witnessed the launch of the transnational women's organization Development Alternatives for Women in a New Era (DAWN). A panel on Women Law and Development paved the way for the formation of three cross-regional women's organizations focusing on the use of law to bring about change in women's lives: the Asia Pacific Forum on Women, Law and Development (APWLD), Women in Law and Development Africa (WILDAF) and the Latin American and Caribbean Committee for the Defense of Women's Rights (CLADEM). The articulation of transnational feminisms is rooted in all these diverse histories and narratives.

Many feminist scholars have explored the evolution of the concept of 'transnational feminisms' through the framework provided by a range of UN Conferences, including the series of Conferences on Women (Mexico 1975; Nairobi 1985; Copenhagen 1990; Beijing 1995) and in particular, the World Conference on Human Rights (Vienna 1993) and the International Conference on Population and Development (Cairo 1994). Feminist engagement with the preparations for the Conferences was expansive (cf. Antrobus 2004; Bunch 1996). Regional and sub-regional preparatory meetings organized by the UN were accompanied by parallel civil society/NGO processes that allowed women from diverse geographic and sector-level locations to interact and engage with one another, discovering a common cause and collective purpose, and identifying the potential for cross-national solidarity. They played an active role at each of the Conferences, engaging in advocacy with states to ensure Outcomes Documents that were gender-sensitive and that reflected women's concerns. They were also very active within the NGO Forums that accompanied each of these Conferences, where there was space for discussing issues that were not on the intergovernmental agenda.

Feminist scholar Amrita Basu (1995) described the period pre-1985 as one in which 'the global was in the ascendant over the local in defining the character of feminism', and saw the post-1985 phase as being one in which 'a new relationship emerged in which the local and the global became more interconnected in more complicated ways'.[1] As feminists confronted a world that was going through concurrent processes of globalization and fragmentation, they began to interrogate their cross-border and transnational connections and relationships more deeply. The terminology they used reflected the diverse political and ideological perspectives they represented.

The term 'global feminism' as defined by Robin Morgan and others (Morgan 1984) was viewed as a 'universalizing' project and one that did not adequately reflect the complexity of contemporary challenges to feminisms around the world. Feminists from post-colonial contexts developed terms such as 'Third World feminism' (Narayan 1997), feminism without borders (Mohanty 1992), post-colonial feminism (Ahmed 2000), and multicultural feminism (Shohat 1998) in order to challenge what they saw as the exclusion of 'the unique gendered realities of non-Western and non-white women' (Ahmed 2000: 111). It is within this discursive framework that we see the emergence of the concept of 'transnational feminism'.

Among the feminist scholars who have explored the promise of transnational feminisms are Inderpal Grewal and Caren Kaplan (1994), who presented the case for collaborative work to build transnational feminist alliances on the basis that 'if the world is currently structured by transnational economic links and cultural asymmetries, locating feminist practices within these structures becomes imperative' (1994: 3). If such a practice and analysis that could highlight the 'historicized particularity of women's relationship to multiple patriarchies as well as to international economic hegemonies' were not developed, they argued, feminist movements 'would remain isolated and prone to reproducing the universalizing gestures of dominant Western cultures' (ibid.). In their more recent work, Grewal and Kaplan have continued their focus on transnational feminisms as forms of alliance and subversion that operate in a privileged in-between space where asymmetries and inequalities between women can be acknowledged, sustained and critically deconstructed (2002).

Uma Narayan (1997) described transnational feminism as having the potential to both liberate and to build an understanding of the links of women's subordination to colonialism, imperialism and racism. As such, she argued, it resisted utopian ideas about 'global sisterhood' and worked to lay the groundwork for more equitable social relations among women across national borders and diverse cultural contexts. In a similar vein, Alexander and Mohanty spoke of 'looking for a more sophisticated understanding of transnational postcolonial feminist practices' (1997: xvii) and of building a new political culture which they called a Feminist Democracy.

The three key features identified with building a feminist democracy were: 1) bringing sexual politics to the centre of processes and practices of governance; 2) transformation of relationships, selves, communities and the practices of daily life leading to self-determination and autonomy for all peoples; and 3) theorizing the concept of agency differently, in the understanding that 'women do not imagine themselves as *victims* or *dependents* of governing structures, but as agents of their own lives' (1997: xxviii). In 2003, Mohanty wrote about 'feminism without borders', stressing that the most expansive and inclusive visions of feminism need to be attentive to borders while learning to transcend them. Decolonization, anti-capitalist critique and solidarity were her preferred responses to her inquiry into how one could develop a just and inclusive feminist politics for the present. Minoo Moallem (1999) emphasized the need for feminists to rethink subjectivity, difference and political community, calling for 'transnational feminist theories and practices that are based on historicity, subjectivity and the linkage between a macro- and micro-political and relational articulation of nation, race, gender, class and sexuality' (1999: 341).

Valentine Moghadam (2005) has viewed transnational feminism from the perspective of transnational feminist networks that have arisen in the context of economic, political and cultural globalization, which she identifies as an effective type of organizational structure. She points out that transnational feminist networks have helped to transcend earlier political and ideological differences through the adoption of a broader feminist agenda that includes a critique of neoliberalism and structural adjustment policies as well as an insistence on women's reproductive rights, bodily integrity and autonomy.

More recently, Amanda Lock Swarr and Richa Nagar (2010) have presented transnational feminism

> as a conceptual framework that strives to liberate itself from the political and intellectual constraints of international feminism and global feminisms. Whereas international feminisms are seen as rigidly adhering to nation-state borders and paying inadequate attention to the forces of globalization, global feminisms have been subjected to critical scrutiny for prioritizing northern feminist agendas and perspective and for homogenizing women's struggles for socio-political justice, especially in colonial and neo-colonial contexts.
>
> (2010: 4)

According to Swarr and Nagar, transnational feminisms are

> an intersectional set of understandings, tools and practices that can a) attend to racialized, classed, masculinized and heteronormative logics and practices of globalization and capitalist patriarchies and the multiple ways in which they re-structure colonial and neo-colonial relations of domination and subordination; b) grapple with the complex and contradictory ways in which these processes both inform and are shaped by a range of subjectivities and understandings of individual and collective agency; and c) interweave critiques, actions and self-reflexivity so as to resist a priori predictions of what might constitute feminist politics in a given place and time.
>
> (2010: 5)

Their focus is on collaborative practice and on challenging three sets of dichotomies: academic/activist; theory/method; individual/collective processes of knowledge making. As they say, 'We work within a crisis of representation that relies on critical transnational feminism as an inherently unstable praxis whose survival and evolution hinge on a continuous commitment to produce a self-reflexive and dialogic critique of its own practices rather than a search for resolution or closures' (Swarr and Nagar 2010: 9).

Among the best examples of contemporary transnational feminist activism are the Network of Women living under Muslim Laws,[2] the Women Human Rights Defenders International Campaign,[3] ISIS-Women's International Cross-Cultural Exchange,[4] DAWN,[5] and Gender Equality Architecture Reform (GEAR).[6] Some members of these networks have actively contributed to the processes of theorizing on transnational feminisms by academic feminists. In addition, some of the issues raised within the academic feminist discourse, for example, on the need to develop a nuanced understanding of inclusivity, of multiple subjectivities and of intersectional identities have influenced and shaped the nature and structure of some of these networks and organizations. The UN continues to provide spaces for convening and interaction, especially through the annual meeting of the Commission on the Status of Women and the regular sessions of the UN Human Rights Council, with continuing contestation of women's rights to choice and autonomy, especially rights relating to sexuality and reproduction. Transnational feminists also participate in the processes of the World Social Forum (WSF) and regional Social Forums; key among them are the World March of Women,

Articulación Feminista Marcosur and *La Via Campesina*. Janet Conway (2007) comments that 'feminist encounters in, over and around the WSF involve contestations among major transnational feminist networks over the character of feminism itself' (2007: 50). In the period from 2002 to 2007, feminist groups associated with the WSF developed the Feminist Dialogues to incorporate a specifically transnational feminist focus into the global justice issues being debated and discussed at the Forum. This led to the greater involvement of feminists in the decision-making structures of the WSF and to broader articulation of transnational feminist perspectives within the WSF programme. The Feminist Encuentros in Latin America and the Caribbean,[7] the European Feminist Forum,[8] the African Feminist Forum[9] and the Asian Feminist Forum[10] are all spaces created by transnational feminists at the regional level; the South Asian Feminist Declaration,[11] for example, reflects ongoing feminist concerns. Working transnationally, feminists seek to ensure that the specificities of women's diverse social and political experiences are consistently foregrounded within transnational feminist theory and practice.

A discussion about transnational feminisms would not be complete without also addressing the fact that parallel to the evolution of transnational feminisms, we have seen a phenomenal and exponential growth of transnational networks of right-wing and conservative religious groups that challenge feminist ideas, activism and politics at every level and in every arena. At the same time, transnational feminists must engage in a relentless struggle from within, against the internal tensions and contradictions that emerge, as they demand sharing of power and resources. Johannah Brenner refers to the dilemmas of transnational feminist organizations that try to chart a course between 'patriarchal nationalism and colonizing feminism' (2007: 28). Brenner refers to the consequences of dependence on external funding, for example, citing the negative implications of bureaucratization and processes of stratification among women's groups on the basis of who has better access to funders. She also refers to existing tensions between women's organizations and trade unions, for example, and 'strategic silences on the issue of abortion and sexual orientation' (2007: 32).

These studies make it clear that 'transnational feminisms' has evolved into a conceptual framework that strengthens understanding of feminist theory and practice around the world, foregrounding the re-thinking and the re-ordering of social relations and power relations, including among and between women, based on diverse, complex, multiple subjectivities and intersectional identities in the contemporary world. It allows for respectful relationships, partnerships and solidarity between feminists across national and other borders. It also enables global advocacy on matters of immediate concern, as well as the building of long-term vision, networks and alliances among feminists on social justice and transformation. The demands of afro-descendant women of Latin America, of indigenous women around the globe, of lesbians, bisexual women and trans persons, for example, continually challenge these frameworks and expand the bases of understanding the depth and complexity of transnational feminisms.

Further Reading: Alvarez 2000; Brah 1991; Desai and Naples 2002; Mohanty 2003; Mendonza 2002; Ong 1999.

Notes

1 http://www3.amherst.edu/womencrossing/basu
2 www.wluml.org
3 www.defendingwomendefendingrights.org
4 www.isis.or.ug
5 www.dawnnet.org
6 www.gearcampaign.org
7 http://awid.org/News-Analysis/Friday-Files/The-Relevance-of-the-Feminist-Encuentro-for-Latin-American-Feminist-Movements
8 www.europeanfeministforum.org
9 http://www.gearcampaign.org/news_events/wp-content/uploads/2010/12/December-2010-Statement-from-AFF-ENG.doc-Eng.pdf
10 www.apwld.org
11 www.sangatsouthasia.org

WOMEN'S STUDIES/GENDER STUDIES

Maria do Mar Pereira

Women's and gender studies (WGS) is an interdisciplinary field of research and education that analyzes all dimensions and institutions of social life in order to understand how gender is produced and reproduced across time and in different societies, how it shapes the subjectivity, experiences and opportunities of individuals, and how it intersects (see intersectionality) with other axes of difference and inequality, such as race, ethnicity, sexuality, class or disability. Historically and in the present, research and teaching in WGS has focused particularly, though not exclusively, on the subordination of women in both the so-called 'private' and 'public' spheres (see feminist politics), and on different forms and effects of gender-based violence. However, WGS does not examine only gendered inequalities between women and men, but also processes of construction of differentiations and hierarchies between different women, and between different men, on the basis of the kinds of femininities and masculinities that they enact.

Initiatives to create spaces in universities for research and education on these themes were very often triggered by, and an important element of, broader feminist movements for social and political change (see feminist politics), and so one of the main aims of WGS has been to contribute to improving women's lives and transforming gendered norms and inequalities. Therefore, WGS scholars established, and continue to maintain, close links with feminist activism outside academia, with those links taking many different shapes across periods, institutions and countries. These links with activism have been a key feature of WGS since its emergence. Another of WGS's key features is its explicitly political understanding of knowledge (see feminist epistemology). Scholars seek not only to create more academic knowledge about women and gender (namely to counteract the long-standing tradition within the mainstream sciences, social sciences and humanities of ignoring or devaluing women's experiences as objects of study), but also to critically examine how knowledge is produced in academia. They have been especially interested in uncovering the gendered assumptions on which that production rests and the power dynamics which it generates or helps to legitimate (see feminist epistemology). These efforts to problematize knowledge production also extend to WGS itself, and thus a third key feature of WGS is its preoccupation with critically examining its own practices of knowledge production (see reflexivity). Indeed, since the field's emergence, WGS scholars have had ongoing and intense debates about the field's disciplinary status (is it inter-, trans-, post-disciplinary?) (see interdisciplinarity and Hark 2007; Lykke 2010), its position within academia, the nature and boundaries of its objects of study, its name, and how canons are created and what they might exclude, to give just a few examples. A fourth key feature of WGS is its commitment to using different research methods – generally qualitative, but also quantitative (see feminist economics) – and to drawing on concepts, theories and tools from a range of disciplines (see interdisciplinarity).

The institutionalization of women's and gender studies

Women's studies courses (and later, degrees) emerged in the United States in the late 1960s, and in some European countries (namely the United Kingdom and Sweden) in the 1970s, in the context of second wave feminist mobilizing (see feminist politics). The timing and conditions of their emergence in other regions is very variable, and depends on a number of factors. These include a country's particular social and political history, the characteristics of its feminist movements, the features of the higher education system,[1] and the intervention of external bodies – such as non-governmental organizations, or national and supra-national equal opportunities agencies – in providing funding for WGS research and education (Griffin 2005b). Scholars seeking to create WGS courses and degrees across the world have faced many obstacles, partly because in many academic sites WGS was, and often still is, considered to be a less valid and valuable area of inquiry and teaching, allegedly because it is too political or specific to be able to produce 'proper' academic knowledge (see feminist epistemology and Pereira 2012; Stanley 1997). Over the past four decades, feminist scholars have used diverse strategies to address these resistances and have succeeded in institutionalizing WGS research and education to some degree in several universities and disciplines throughout the world. At present, there are many WGS degrees (particularly at postgraduate level) and courses on offer – in the US, for example, one of the countries where WGS has a wider and more solid presence in institutions, there exist more than 900 WGS undergraduate and postgraduate degree programmes, offering over 10,000 courses (National Women's Studies Association: www.nwsa.org). In addition, hundreds of WGS conferences are organized every year across the world, there is a growing number of national and international WGS journals and book series covering an impressive range of subthemes in WGS, and there are many active national and regional WGS professional associations working on several levels (producing events and publications, giving grants and awards, designing subject benchmark statements, etc.) to support and promote WGS (see, for example, the Worldwide Organisation of Women's Studies: www.ww05.org/wows; the Asian Association of Women's Studies: www.aaws07.org; or ATGENDER, the European Association for Gender Research, Education and Documentation: www.atgender.eu).

This institutionalization of WGS is, however, profoundly uneven in many ways. First, it is uneven across space. Indeed, WGS is not present in the same degree and shape across all institutions and countries. In some universities, WGS has to be taught covertly – i.e. WGS themes are taught in courses with non WGS-related designations – because there is significant opposition to the field. In others, WGS education and research is explicitly offered, and appears integrated within traditional disciplines and departments. In a growing number of universities worldwide, WGS is also present as a relatively autonomous field, with its own centres, institutes or departments. Since the emergence of WGS, scholars have debated the advantages and disadvantages of these different modes of institutionalization, and many have in recent decades opted to invest in a dual approach, aiming both at mainstreaming feminist insights into the traditional disciplines and at establishing separate, dedicated spaces for WGS teaching, research and publication (Hemmings 2006). The institutionalization of WGS is uneven across space in yet another way: opposing trends may, and do, occur simultaneously in different contexts. In the past decade, the UK has seen the closure of several WGS courses and degrees, while in other European countries such as Spain and Portugal the number and range of opportunities for WGS education has increased in the same period.

Second, institutionalization is uneven across different dimensions of WGS, because each aspect of the field does not become institutionalized at the same pace. For example, in many sites it has been easier to develop WGS research and publications than to establish WGS undergraduate or postgraduate degrees, because institutional resistance or national regulations on the creation of degree programmes have generated major obstacles to this. It is also important to bear in mind that institutionalization is frequently a contingent and precarious process. Existing WGS courses, programmes or research centres may, and sometimes do, close as student demand fluctuates and funding conditions change (Hemmings 2006). In many institutions across the world, just one or two scholars maintain WGS and there are no dedicated WGS positions, which means that WGS may disappear from the institution if those scholars move or retire. Therefore, institutionalization is always a work in progress requiring constant attention and significant effort on the part of WGS scholars (Morley 1998).

Time, turns and generations in women's and gender studies

Because it is relatively recent, usually precarious and very reflexive, WGS has been a particularly dynamic field. It is always shifting, not just in terms of its size, shape and institutional location, but also in the objects and directions of its research and teaching. Therefore, to understand the past and present life of WGS it is important to see it as a field always on the move, and to pay close attention to the ways in which it moves across time and space. Descriptions of how WGS scholarship has changed since its emergence are very often framed by claims that there have been different 'generations' and 'turns' in WGS. One very common narrative is that early (i.e. 1970s) women's studies research was closely linked to second wave feminist politics and so was particularly focused on examining the structural character of the patriarchal oppression of women, namely in relation to the sexual division of labour, gender-based violence and reproduction (see new reproductive technologies). A major transformation in the terms and objects of WGS debates happened, according to this narrative, in the early 1990s, inspired by the emergence of third wave feminism (see feminist politics) and also by the broader 'linguistic turn' and 'cultural turn' that had expanded and intensified throughout the 1980s.[2] Due to this, WGS became more focused on the study of subjectivity, representation (especially in media and film), and the performativity of gender. More recently, it has been argued that we may now be witnessing an 'affective turn' (see affect) in WGS.

These narratives can be useful because they help to systematize trends in the field, and to draw attention to some key features and priorities of feminist theorizing and empirical work at different moments in time. However, several authors (for example Hemmings 2011; Henry 2004) have shown that such narratives have significant limitations and may produce problematic effects. They argue that it is therefore necessary to engage reflexively and critically with descriptions of turns or generational change in WGS. One problem with these narratives is that they are based on, and reinforce, an overly simplistic and oppositional account of knowledge production in WGS. The division of WGS into different generations or waves, or into two periods of 'before' and 'after' a particular turn, tends to exaggerate the differences between those generations or periods, and also to render invisible the commonalities between the two periods or generations, and the internal heterogeneity of each one. Another problem is that they often fail to acknowledge the diversity of the WGS community, a community composed of scholars whose very different ages, backgrounds and theoretical affinities rarely fit neatly in these typologies. Such narratives can also work to flatten the history of feminist scholarship, because they represent that history as a linear one following a single trajectory. Finally, they describe features of the development of WGS in a very specific set of contexts – notably the US and the UK – but the located and non-generalizable nature of these accounts is often not acknowledged, and so these narratives are implicitly presented as general descriptions of WGS. They do not, however, accurately represent the history of WGS in most of the world, because WGS changed in each country through different sets of debates, although these will sometimes have been very strongly influenced by the Anglo-American scholarship and 'generations' described above. When examining WGS it is, therefore, crucial to remember that even though it can be seen as an integrated field, it is a diverse, heterogeneous and transnational one. As a result, any description of its history will always be selective, partial, and produced from a particular location in space that has to be acknowledged.

Space and travel in women's and gender studies

One issue, which illustrates particularly well why it is useful and important to consider space when thinking about the history of WGS, is the question of the name of the field. When it initially emerged in the US and the UK, the field was named 'women's studies' but over time that was gradually replaced by the designation 'women's and gender studies' or 'gender studies'. The latter is at present the most widely used name for the field in several countries and arenas (including among international publishers and funders, for example). This change has been the object of vocal contestation and intense debate (Hemmings 2006). For some feminist scholars this change shows, and leads to, a weakening of the field's focus on women and of its links with feminist activism, and so it can be understood as a form of deradicalization of WGS. Other scholars see it as a valuable change, namely because they consider that 'gender studies' is a broader and more inclusive label, which can help open the field much more to important objects of study (such as masculinities and transgender experience) and also foster stronger links with other critical research about sexuality, heteronormativity and LGBT politics.

This account of the transformation of the field's name and of the meanings and value attached to each one does not, nevertheless, easily translate to many contexts outside the US and the UK. Because the terms sex/gender do not have the same meanings (or do not even exist as such) in other countries, and the institutionalization of WGS has very distinct national genealogies, choices and debates about names will unfold differently and have different implications. In Taiwan (Chen 2004) and Chile (Montecino and Obach 1999), for example, references to gender are understood in some institutions as more radical and threatening than references to women (namely because the name 'gender studies' is seen to be associated with feminist scholarship, queer studies and research on sexuality), and so some scholars may choose a designation like 'women's studies' because it is perceived to be less explicitly critical and politicized, and more compatible with mainstream paradigms.

When considering the role of space in WGS it is not enough, however, to compare and contrast the history of the field, its name or its level of institutionalization in different regions; it is crucial to also examine movements of travel between regions. Indeed, those movements have played an absolutely central role in shaping WGS. The travelling of people has been constitutive of the field since its emergence. Because its institutionalization was, and continues to be, uneven, students and scholars based in countries where WGS is less established have often had to travel to other regions in order to access WGS training or jobs (Griffin 2005a). These movements, which have grown significantly in recent years as international travel and communication becomes easier and the global profile of WGS rises, have helped strengthen and sustain WGS education (especially at postgraduate level) in countries which attract these 'educational migrants' (particularly the US and the UK). These movements have also contributed to support and foster the institutionalization of WGS in these students' and scholars' home countries (for examples of how this occurs, see Chen 2004). However, this travelling of people raises problems as well, because it can reinforce class inequalities and global asymmetries within WGS. Indeed, studying WGS in another country can be extremely costly, and so the experience will often only be accessible to a limited, and usually relatively privileged, group of individuals. This flow of people, usually from the global South to the global North is also understood to function partly as a form of brain drain that reinforces the centrality and academic hegemony of a limited number of countries.

But it is not just people who travel from region to region; concepts, theories and books are also always on the move within WGS. Through educational migration, international conferences and circulation of literature, terms and texts created in a particular site get adopted, adapted and translated into other languages, becoming part of WGS debates in a range of settings, and often gaining new or different meanings along the way (Davis 2007b; Davis and Evans 2011). The notion of sex/gender is one conceptual tool in WGS that has travelled especially widely and had profound, although very complex and often fiercely contested, impacts on the local production of WGS knowledge in a range of countries throughout the world (Braidotti 2002b). These travels of concepts and theories help to generate shared (although not identical) languages for WGS scholars in distinct locations, but here too there are global asymmetries in the degree to which scholars from different regions are able to shape, and contribute to, this shared culture in WGS. Due to the centrality of Western countries in the global academic system, the status of English as the dominant language of communication within that system, and the structure of the international publishing industry (which tends to prefer to invest in English language books drawing on Anglo-American debates, as these are seen to be more easily 'exportable' to a wider range of regions), concepts and theories produced in the global North are more likely to travel and become read and used outside the contexts in which they emerged. This means that although we can speak of a global community of WGS, some members of that community have more access to recognition and visibility than others, and this affects the content and directions of the knowledge we produce. Therefore, thinking about the life of WGS demands paying close attention to these, and other, hierarchies and inequalities within the field, and working to develop reflexive and inclusive ways of producing knowledge and promoting feminist change within and outside academia.

Further Reading: ATHENA 2000–2009; Boxer 1998; Coate 1999; Griffin 2005b; Hemmings 2005a.

Notes

1 It has generally been easier to institutionalize WGS in systems with a high degree of university autonomy in developing curricula, flexible and modular degree structures, and less rigid disciplinary demarcations.
2 These are names given to a set of shifts in the social sciences and humanities, which occurred as poststructuralist theories became more popular across a range of fields and an increasing emphasis was placed on the study of language and cultural practices, and on conceptualizations of social processes that highlight their discursive or symbolic nature.

BIBLIOGRAPHY

Aapola, S., Gonick, M. and Harris, A. (2005) *Young Femininity: Girlhood, Power and Social Change*, Basingstoke: Palgrave Macmillan.

Aaron, J. and Walby, S. (eds) (1991) *Out of the Margins: Women's Studies in the Nineties*, London: Taylor and Francis.

Aboim, S. (2010) *Plural Masculinities: The Remaking of the Self in Private Life*, Aldershot: Ashgate.

Abu-Lughod, L. (1986) *Veiled Sentiments: Honor and Poetry in a Bedouin Society*, Berkeley: University of California Press.

—— (2002) 'Do Muslim women really need saving? Anthropological reflections on cultural relativism and its Others', *American Anthropologist* 103(3): 783–90.

Acker, J. (1990) 'Hierarchies, jobs, bodies: a theory of gendered organisations', *Gender and Society* 4(2): 139–58.

Adam, A. (2002) 'Cyberstalking and Internet pornography: gender and the gaze', *Ethics and Information Technology* 4(2): 133–42.

Adam, B. D. (1995) *The Rise of a Lesbian and Gay Movement*, New York: Twayne.

Adam, B. D., Duyvendak, J. W. and Krouwel, A. (1999) *The Global Emergence of Gay and Lesbian Politics: National Imprints of a Worldwide Movement*, Philadelphia, PA: Temple University Press.

Adkins, L. and Skeggs, B. (eds) (2004) *Feminism after Bourdieu*, Oxford: Blackwell Publishing/The Sociological Review.

Agarwal, B. (1995) *A Field of One's Own: Gender and Land Rights in South Asia*, Delhi: Cambridge University Press.

Aggleton, P., Boyce, P., Moore, H. and Parker, R. (eds) (2012) *Understanding Global Sexualities: New Frontiers*, Abingdon and New York: Routledge.

Ahmed, S. (2000) *Transformations: Thinking through Feminism*, London: Routledge.

—— (2004) *The Cultural Politics of Emotion*, Edinburgh: Edinburgh University Press.

—— (2010) *The Promise of Happiness*, Durham: Duke University Press.

Alaimo, S. and Hekman, S. (eds) (2008) *Material Feminisms*, Bloomington: Indiana University Press.

Albelda, R., Drago, R. and Shulman, S. (2004) *Uneven Playing Fields: Understanding Wage Inequality and Discrimination*, Cambridge: Economic Affairs Bureau.

Alcoff, L. (1995) 'The problem of speaking for others', in Roof and Weigman (eds) *Who can Speak: Authority and Critical Identity,* Urbana: University of Illinois Press, 97–119.

Alcoff, L. and Potter, E. (eds) (1993) *Feminist Epistemologies*, New York and London: Routledge.

Alexander, M. J. (1994) 'Not just (any) body can be a citizen: the politics of law, sexuality and postcoloniality in Trinidad and Tobago and the Bahamas', *Feminist Review* 48: 5–23.

Alexander, M. J. and Mohanty, C. T. (eds) (1997) *Feminist Genealogies, Colonial Legacies, Democratic Futures*, New York: Routledge.

Allen, A. (2011) 'Feminist perspectives on power', in *Stanford Encyclopedia of Philosophy* (first published 19 Oct, 2005; substantive revision 9 Mar. 2011).

Altman, D. (2001) *Global Sex*, Chicago: University of Chicago Press.

Alvarez, S. (2000) 'Translating the global effects of transnational organizing on local feminist discourses and practices in Latin America', *Meridians: Feminism, Race, Transnationalism* 1(1): 29–67.

Amos, V. and Parmar, P. (1984) 'Challenging imperial feminism', *Feminist Review*, 17: 3–19.

Anderson, B. (2000) *Doing the Dirty Work?: The Global Politics of Domestic Labour*, London and New York: Zed Books.

Anderson, E. (2011) 'Feminist epistemology and philosophy of science', in Edward N. Zalta (ed.) *The Stanford Encyclopedia of Philosophy* (Spring 2011 edn).

Anon (2009) *International Feminist Journal of Politics* 11(4) special issue.

Anon (2012) *European Reports on Interdisciplinarity for the Project 'Research Integration'*, available at http://www.york.ac.uk/res/researchintegration/Reports_Year_02_on_Interdisciplinarity.htm, accessed 4 April 2012.

Anthias, F. (1998) 'Rethinking social divisions: some notes towards a theoretical framework', *Sociological Review* 46(3): 506–35.

—— (2001) 'New hybridities, old concepts: the limits of culture', *Ethnic and Racial Studies,* 24(4), 619–42.

—— (2002) 'Beyond feminism and multiculturalism: locating difference and the politics of location', *Women's Studies International Forum* 25(3), 275–394.

Anthias, F. and Yuval-Davis, N. (1992) *Racialised Boundaries – Race, Nation, Gender, Colour and Class and the Anti-Racist Struggle*, London: Routledge.

Antony, L. M. (1993) 'Quine as feminist: the radical import of naturalized epistemology', in Louise M. Antony and Charlotte Witt (eds) *A Mind of One's Own: Feminist Essays on Reason and Objectivity*, Boulder and Oxford: Westview Press, 185–225.

Antrobus, P. (2003) 'MDGs – the most distracting gimmick', *DAWN Informs*.

—— (2004) *The Global Women's Movement: Origins, Issues and Strategies*, London: Zed Books.

Anzaldúa, G. (2007) [1987, 1999] *La Frontera/Borderlands*, San Francisco: Aunt Lute Books.
Asch, A. and Geller, G. (1996) 'Feminism, bioethics and genetics', in S. M. Wolf (ed.), *Feminism, Bioethics: Beyond Reproduction*, Oxford, UK: Oxford University Press, 318–50.
ATHENA (ed.) (2000–2009) *The Making of European Women's Studies*, Vols I–IX, Utrecht: Universiteit Utrecht.
Bainbridge, C. (2008) *A Feminine Cinematics: Luce Irigaray, Women, and Film*, London and New York: Palgrave Macmillan.
Balsamo, A. (1999) 'Reading cyborgs and writing feminism', in J. Wolmark (ed.) *Cybersexualities: A Reader on Feminist Theory, Cyborgs and Cyberspace*, Edinburgh: University of Edinburgh Press.
Barad, K. (2007) *Meeting the Universe Halfway: Quantum Physics and the Entanglement of Matter and Meaning*, Durham: Duke University Press.
Barnes, M. (2011) 'Abandoning care? A critical perspective on personalisation from an ethic of care', *Ethics and Social Welfare* 5(2): 153–67.
Barnett–Donaghy, T. (2004a) Applications of mainstreaming in Australia and Northern Ireland, *International Political Science Review* 25(4): 393–410.
—— (2004b) 'Mainstreaming: Northern Ireland's participative–democratic approach', *Policy and Politics* 32(1): 49–62.
Barrett, M. and M. McIntosh (1980) 'The "family wage": some problems for socialists and feminists', *Capital and Class* 4(2): 51–72.
Barth, F. (1969) *Ethnic Groups and Boundaries*, New York: Little, Brown.
Basu, A. (1995) *The Challenge of Local Feminisms: Women's Movements in Global Perspective*, Boulder: Westview Press.
Basu, A. (ed.) (2010) *Women's Movements in a Global Era: The Power of Local Feminisms*, Boulder: Westview Press.
Baumgardner, J. and Richards, A. (2000) *Manifesta: Young Women, Feminism and the Future*, New York: Farrar, Straus & Giroux.
Becker, G. (1991) *A Treatise on the Family*, Cambridge, MA: Harvard University Press.
—— (2000) *The Elusive Embryo: How Women and Men Approach New Reproductive Technologies,* Berkeley: University of California Press.
Bedford, K. (2007) 'The imperative of male inclusion: how institutional context influences world bank gender policy', *International Feminist Journal of Politics* 9(3): 289–311.
Begikhani, N., Gill, A., Hague, G. and Ibrahiim, K. (2010) *Honour based Violence and Honour based Killings in Iraqi Kurdistan and in the Kurdish Diaspora in the UK*, Final Report, Centre for Gender and Violence Research, Bristol University.
Behning, U. and Serrano, A. (2001) *Gender Mainstreaming in the European Employment Strategy*, Brussels: ETUI.
Bell, D., Loader, B. D., Pleace, N. and Schuler, D. (2004) *Cyberculture: The Key Concepts*, London and New York: Routledge.
Bell, V. (2007) *Culture and Performance: The Challenge of Ethics, Politics and Feminist Theory*, Oxford: Berg.
—— (2012) 'Declining performativity: Butler, Whitehead and ecologies of concern', *Theory, Culture & Society* 29(2): 107–23.

Bell, V. (ed). (1999) *Performativity & Belonging,* London: Sage (also published in *Theory, Culture & Society* 16(2)).
Beneria, L. and Sen, G. (1981) 'Accumulation, reproduction and women's role in economic development: Boserup revisited', *Signs* 7(2): 279–98.
Benhabib, S. (ed.) (1995) *Feminist Contentions: A Philosophical Exchange,* London: Routledge.
Benjamin, J. (1995) *Like Subjects, Like Objects: Essays on Recognition and Sexual Difference*, New Haven: Yale University Press.
—— (1998) *Shadow of the Other: Intersubjectivity and Gender in Psychoanalysis,* London: Routledge.
Benschop, Y. and Mieke, V. (2006) 'Sisyphus' sisters: can gender mainstreaming escape the genderedness of organizations?' *Journal of Gender Studies* 15(1): 19–33.
Berger, J. (1972) *Ways of Seeing,* Harmondsworth: British Broadcasting Corporation and Penguin.
Berlant, L. (1997) *The Queen of America Goes to Washington City: Essays on Sex and Citizenship*, Durham: Duke University Press.
Berlant, L. and Warner, M. (1998) 'Sex in public', *Critical Inquiry* 24(2): 547–66.
—— (2000) 'Sex in public', in L. Berlant (ed.) *Intimacy*, Chicago: University of Chicago Press, 311–51.
Best, M. and Humphries, J. (2003) 'Edith Penrose: a feminist economist?', *Feminist Economics* 9(1): 47–74.
Beveridge, F. and Nott, S. (2002) 'Mainstreaming: a case for optimism and cynicism', *Feminist Legal Studies* 10: 299–311.
Beveridge, F., Nott, S. and Stephen, K. (2000) 'Mainstreaming and engendering of policy-making: a means to an end?' *Journal of European Public Policy* 7(3): 385–405.
Bhabha, H. (1994) *The Location of Culture*, New York: Routledge.
Bhatt, C. (1997) *Liberation and Purity: Race, New Religious Movements and the Ethics of Postmodernity*, London: UCL Press.
Bianchi, S. M. (1999) 'Feminization and juvenilization of poverty: trends, relative risks, causes, and consequences', *Annual Review of Sociology* 25: 307–33.
Biehl, J., Good, B. and Kleinman, A. (eds) (2007) *Subjectivity: Ethnographic Investigations*, Berkeley: University of California Press.
Bittman, M., England, P., Folbre, N., Sayer, L. and Matheson, G. (2003) 'When does gender trump money? Bargaining and time in household work', *American Journal of Sociology* 109: 186–214.
Blackwood, E. (1998) 'Tombois in West Sumatra: constructing masculinity and erotic desire', *Cultural Anthropology* 13(4): 491–521.
Blakeley, G. and Bryson, V. (eds) (2007) *The Impact of Feminism on Political Concepts and Debates*, Manchester: Manchester University Press.
Boellstorff, Tom (2008) *Coming of Age in Second Life: An Anthropologist Explores the Virtually Human*, Rutgers, NJ: Princeton University Press.
Bolotin, S. (1982) 'Voices from the post-feminist generation', *New York Times Magazine*, 17 Oct.: 31.

Bordo, S. (1987) *The Flight to Objectivity: Essays on Cartesianism and Culture*, Albany: SUNY Press.

—— (1989) 'The body and the reproduction of femininity: a feminist appropriation of Foucault', in A. Jaggar and S. Bordo (eds) *Gender/Body/Knowledge: Feminist Reconstructions of Being and Knowing*, New Brunswick: Rutgers University Press.

—— (1993) *Unbearable Weight. Feminism, Western Culture, and the Body*, Berkeley: California University Press.

—— (1999) *The Male Body: A New Look at Men in Public and Private*, New York: Farrar, Straus and Giroux.

Boserup, E. (1970) *Women's Role in Economic Development*, London: Earthscan.

Bourdieu, P. (1973) 'Cultural reproduction and social reproduction', in R. Brown (ed.) *Knowledge, Education and Cultural Change.* Papers in the Sociology of Education, London: Tavistock.

Bourdieu, P. (1984) *Distinction: A Social Critique of the Judgement of Taste*, Cambridge, MA: Harvard University Press.

—— (1990) *The Logic of Practice*, Oxford: Polity.

—— (1991) *Language and Symbolic Power*, Cambridge, MA: Harvard University Press.

Bowles, G. and Duelli Klein, R. (eds) (1983) *Theories of Women's Studies*, London: Routledge and Kegan Paul.

Boxer, M. J. (1998) *When Women Ask the Questions: Creating Women's Studies in America*, Baltimore: Johns Hopkins University Press.

Brady, D. and Kall, D. (2008) 'Nearly universal, but somewhat distinct: the feminization of poverty in affluent Western democracies, 1969–2000', *Social Science Research* 37(3): 976–1007.

Brah, A. (1991) 'Questions of difference and international feminism', in J. Aaron and S. Walby (eds) *Out of the Margins*, London: Falmer Press.

—— (1996) *Cartographies of Diaspora*, London/New York: Routledge.

Brah, A. and Phoenix, A. (2004) 'Ain't I a woman? Revisiting intersectionality', *Journal of International Women's Studies* 5(3): 75–86.

Braidotti, R. (1994) *Nomadic Subjects: Embodiment and Sexual Difference in Contemporary Feminist Thought*, New York: Columbia University Press.

—— (2002a) 'The uses and abuses of the sex/gender distinction in European feminist practices', in G. Griffin and R. Braidotti (eds) *Thinking Differently: A Reader in European Women's Studies*, London and New York: Zed Books.

—— (2002b) *Metamorphoses: Towards a Materialist Theory of Becoming*, Cambridge: Polity Press.

—— (2006) *Transpositions: On Nomadic Ethics*, Cambridge: Polity Press.

Brantlinger, P. (1985) 'Victorians and Africans: the genealogy of the myth of the dark continent', in H. L. Gates, Jr (ed.) *'Race', Writing and Difference*, Chicago: University of Chicago Press.

Braziel, J. E. and Mannur, A. (2003) *Theorizing Diaspora: A Reader*, Malden: Blackwell.

Brennan, T. (2004) *The Transmission of Affect*, Ithaca: Cornell University Press.

Brenner, J. (2007) 'Transnational Feminism and the Struggle for Global Justice' in P. Waterman and J. Sen (eds) *The World Social Forum: Challenging Empires*, Montreal, New York, London: Black Rose Books.

Brewer, R. M., Conrad, C. A. and King, M. C. (2002) 'The complexities and potential of theorizing gender, caste, race, and class', *Feminist Economics* 8(2): 3–17.

Brines, J. (1994) 'Economic dependency, gender, and the division of labor at home', *American Journal of Sociology* 100: 652–88.

Brod, H. (ed.) (1987) *The Making of Masculinities*, London: Unwin Hyman.

Brod, H. and Kaufman, M. (eds) (1993) *Theorizing Masculinities*, Newbury Park, CA: Sage.

Brooks, A. (1997) *Postfeminisms: Feminism, Cultural Theory and Cultural Forms*, London and New York: Routledge.

Brown, I. and Misra, J. (2003) 'The intersection of race and gender in the labor market', *Annual Review of Sociology* 29: 487–513.

Brown, W. (1995) *States of Injury: Power and Freedom in Late Modernity*, Princeton: Princeton University Press.

Brownmiller, S. (1977) *Against Our Will: Men, Women and Rape*, Harmondsworth: Penguin.

Budlender, D., Sharp, R. and Allen, K. (1998) *How to do a Gender-Sensitive Budget Analysis: Contemporary Research and Practice*, London: Commonwealth Secretariat.

Bumiller, K. (2008) *In an Abusive State: How Neoliberalism Appropriated the Feminist Movement Against Sexual Violence*, New York: Duke University Press.

Bunch, C. with Fried, S. (1996) 'Beijing '95: moving women's human rights from margin to center', *Signs: Journal of Women in Culture and Society* 22(1): 200–204.

Butler, J. (1990) *Gender Trouble: Feminism and the Subversion of Identity*, London and New York: Routledge.

—— (1993) *Bodies that Matter: On the Discursive Limits of 'Sex'*, London: Routledge.

—— (1994) 'Gender as performance: an interview with Judith Butler', Peter Osborne and Lynne Segal, *Radical Philosophy* 67.

—— (1997a) *Excitable Speech: A Politics of the Performative*, London, Routledge.

—— (1997b) *The Psychic Life of Power: Theories in Subjection*, Stanford: Stanford University Press.

—— (2005a) 'On being besides oneself: on the limits of sexual autonomy', in N. Bamforth, *Sex Rights*, Oxford Amnesty Lectures, Oxford and New York: Oxford University Press, 2006, 48–78.

—— (2005b) *Giving an Account of Oneself*, New York: Fordham Press.

—— (2008) 'Sexual politics, torture and secular time', *British Journal of Sociology* 59(1): 1–25.

—— (2009) *Frames of War: When is Life Grievable?* London: Verso.

Butler, J. and Scott, J. (eds) (1993) *Feminists Theorise the Political*, London: Routledge.

Caple James, E. (2010) *Democratic Insecurities: Violence, Trauma, and Intervention in Haiti*, Berkeley: University of California Press.

Carrigan, T., Connell, R. and Lee, J. (1985) 'Toward a new sociology of masculinity', *Theory and Society* 14(5): 551–604.

Case, S. E. (1999) *The Domain Matrix: Performing Lesbian at the End of Print Culture*, Bloomington: Indiana University Press.

Casper, L. M., McLanahan, S. S. and Garfinkel, I. (1994) 'The gender–poverty gap: what we can learn from other countries', *American Sociological Review* 59(4): 594–605.

Cassell, J. and Jenkins, H. (2010) *From Barbie to Mortal Kombat: Gender and Computer Games*, Cambridge, MA: MIT Press.

Chambers, S. A. (2007) 'An incalculable effect: subversions of hetero-normativity', *Political Studies* 55: 656–79.

Chambers, S. A. and Carver, T. (2008) *Judith Butler and Political Theory: Troubling Politics*, Abingdon: Routledge.

Chant, S. (2007) *Gender, Generation and Poverty: Exploring the 'Feminization of Poverty' in Africa, Asia and Latin America*, Cheltenham: Edward Elgar.

—— (2008) 'The "feminization of poverty" and the "feminization" of anti–poverty programmes: room for revision?' *Journal of Development Studies* 44(2): 165–97.

—— (2009) 'The "feminization of poverty" in Costa Rica: to what extent a conundrum?' *Bulletin of Latin American Research* 28(1): 19–43.

Chant, S. H. (ed.) (2010) *The International Handbook of Gender and Poverty: Concepts Research, Policy*, Cheltenham: Edward Elgar.

Charusheela, S and Zein–Elabdin, E. (2003) 'Feminism, postcolonial thought and economics', in Marianne Ferber and Julie A. Nelson (eds) *Feminist Economics Today: Beyond Economic Man*, Chicago and London: University of Chicago Press, 175–92.

Charusheela, S and Zein–Elabdin, E. (eds) (2003) *Post-Colonialism Meets Economics*, London: Routledge.

Chen, P. (2004) *Acting 'Otherwise': The Institutionalization of Women's/Gender Studies in Taiwan Universities*, London: Routledge Falmer.

Chodorow, N. J. (1999) *The Power of Feelings: Personal Meaning in Psychoanalysis, Gender, and Culture*, New Haven, CT: Yale University Press.

Chow, R. (1993) *Writing Diaspora. Tactics of Intervention in Contemporary Cultural Studies*, Bloomington & Indianapolis: Indiana University Press.

—— (2006) *The Age of the World Target: Self–Referentiality in War, Theory and Comparative Work*, Durham and London: Duke University Press.

Choy, C. C. (2003) *Empire of Care: Nursing and Migration in Filipino American History*, Durham: Duke University Press.

Christopher, K., England, P., Smeeding, T. M. and Ross, K. (2002) 'The gender gap in poverty in modern nations: single motherhood, the market, and the state', *Sociological Perspectives* 45(3): 219–42.

Cicitira, K. (2004) 'Pornography, women and feminism: between pleasure and politics', *Sexualities* 7: 281–301.

Cixous, H. (1975) *Le Pie de la Méduse, L'Arc, pp. 39–54.* Trans. Keith Cohen and Paula Cohen, 'The Laugh of the Medusa', *Signs* 1(4) (1976): 875–93.

Clatterbaugh, K. (1998) 'What is problematic about "masculinities"?', *Men and Masculinities* 1(1): 24–45.
Clough, P. T. (ed.) (2007) 'Introduction', in P.T. Clough (ed.) *The Affective Turn: Theorizing the Social*, with J. Haley, Durham: Duke University Press, 1–33.
Clough, P. T. with Willse, C. (2011) *Beyond Biopolitics: Essays on the Governance of Life and Death*, Durham: Duke University Press.
Coate, K. (1999) 'Feminist knowledge and the ivory tower: a case study', *Gender and Education* 11(2): 141–59.
Cockburn, C. (2004) 'The continuum of violence: a gender perspective on war and peace', in M. W. Giles and J. Hyndman (eds) *Sites of Violence: Gender and Conflict Zones*, Berkeley and Los Angeles: University of California Press, 22–44.
Code, L. (1988/1993) 'Chapter One – Feminist theory', in S. Burt, L. Code and L. Dorney (eds) *Changing Patterns: Women in Canada*, Toronto: McClelland & Stewart.
—— (1991) *What Can She Know? Feminist Theory and the Construction of Knowledge*, Ithaca: Cornell University Press.
—— (1993) 'Taking subjectivity into account', in Alcoff and Potter (eds) *Feminist Epistemologies*, New York: Routledge.
Cohen, R. (1997) *Global Diasporas: An Introduction*, London: Routledge.
Colebrook, C. (2000) 'Introduction', in I. Buchanan and C. Colebrook (eds) *Deleuze and Feminist Theory*, Edinburgh: Edinburgh University Press.
—— (2001) *Gilles Deleuze*, London: Routledge.
Collins, P. H. (1990) *Black Feminist Thought: Knowledge, Consciousness, and the Politics of Empowerment*, Routledge: New York and London.
—— (1999) 'Moving beyond gender: intersectionality and scientific knowledge', in M. M. Ferree, J. Lorber and B. B. Hess (eds) *Revisioning Gender*, Thousand Oaks, CA: Sage, 261–84.
Coltrane, S. (2000) 'Research on household labor: modelling and measuring the social embeddedness of routine family work', *Journal of Marriage and the Family* 62: 1208–33.
Connell, R. (1983) *Which Way Is Up?* Boston: Allen & Unwin.
—— (1995) *Masculinities*, Cambridge: Polity.
Connell, R. and Messerschmidt, J. (2005) 'Hegemonic masculinity: rethinking the concept', *Gender & Society* 19(6): 829–59.
Conway, J. (2007) 'Transnational feminisms and the world social forum: encounters and transformations in anti–globalization spaces', *Journal of International Women's Studies* 8(3): 49–70.
Cook, R. J. (ed.) (1994) *Human Rights of Women: National and International Perspectives*, Philadelphia: University of Pennsylvania Press.
Cooper, F. (2005) *Colonialism in Question: Theory, Knowledge, History*, California: University of California Press.
Corea, G. (1985) *The Mother Machine: From Artificial Insemination to Artificial Wombs*, New York: Harper & Row.
Cornwall, A., Gideon, J. and Wilson, K. (eds) (2008) 'Reclaiming feminism: gender and neoliberalism', Special Issue, *IDS Bulletin* 39(6).

Cornwall, A., Edström, J. and Greig, A. (eds) (2011) *Masculinities and Development Reader*, London: Zed Books.

Cornwall, A., Harrison, E. and Whitehead, A. (eds) (2007) *Feminisms in Development: Contradictions, Contestations and Challenges*, London: Zed Books.

Corrêa, S., Petchesky, R. and Parker, R. (2008) *Sexuality, Health and Human Rights*, London and New York: Routledge.

Cott, N. F. (1987) *The Grounding of Modern Feminism*, New Haven and London: Yale University Press.

Council of Europe (1998) *Conceptual Framework, Methodology and Presentation of Good Practices: Final Report of Activities of the Group of Specialists on Mainstreaming. EG–S–MS*, Strasbourg: Council of Europe.

Cowen, M. and Shenton, R. (1995) 'The invention of development', in J. Crush (ed.) *Power of Development*, London: Routledge.

Craig, M. L. (2007) 'Race, beauty, and the tangled knot of a guilty pleasure', *Feminist Theory* 7(2): 159–77.

Crenshaw, K. (1989) 'Demarginalizing the intersection of race and sex: a black feminist critique of antidiscrimination doctrine, feminist theory, and antiracist politics', *University of Chicago Legal Forum*, Vol. 1989, 139–67.

—— (1991) 'Mapping the margins: intersectionality, identity politics, and violence against women of color', *Stanford Law Review* 43(6): 1241–99.

Crompton, R. (1998) *Class and Stratification: An Introduction to Current Debates*, 2nd edn, Polity Press: Cambridge.

—— (2006) *Employment and the Family: The Reconfiguration of Work and Family Life in Contemporary Societies*, Cambridge: Cambridge University Press.

Crutchfield, S. and Epstein, M. J. (2000) *Points of Contact: Disability, Art and Culture*, Ann Arbor: University of Michigan Press.

Currah, P. and Mulqueen, T. (2011) 'Securitizing gender: identity, biometrics and the transgender body at the airport', *Social Research* 78(2): 556–82.

Currie, D. H. (1999) Gender analysis from the standpoint of women: the radical potential of women's studies in development, *Asian Journal of Women's Studies* 5(3): 9–44.

Daly, M. and Rake, K. (2003) *Gender and the Welfare State: Care, Work and Welfare in Europe and the USA*, Cambridge: Polity, in association with Blackwell.

Damasio, A. (1994) *Descartes' Error: Emotions, Reasons and the Human Brain*, New York: Putnam Publishing.

Dash, J. (1993) *Daughters of the Dust and Daughters of the Dust: Making of an African-American Woman's Film*, New York: W. W. Norton.

Davidoff, L. and Hall, C. (1987) *Family Fortunes*, London: Hutchinson.

Davis, A. Y. (1982) *Women, Race and Class*, London: The Women's Press.

Davis, K. (1995) *Reshaping the Female Body. The Dilemma of Cosmetic Surgery*, London: Routledge.

—— (2007a) 'Reclaiming women's bodies: colonialist trope or critical epistemology?' *The Sociological Review* 55(s1): 50–64.

—— (2007b) *The Making of 'Our Bodies, Ourselves': How Feminism Travels across Borders*, Durham: Duke University Press.
—— (2008) 'Intersectionality as buzzword: a sociology of science perspective on what makes a feminist theory successful', *Feminist Theory* 9(1) 67–85.
Davis, K. (ed.) (1997) *Embodied Practices: Feminist Perspectives on the Body*, London: Sage.
Davis, K. and Evans, M. (eds) (2011) *Transatlantic Conversations: Feminism as Traveling Theory*, Farnham: Ashgate.
Davis, L. (2002) *Bending Over Backwards: Disability, Dismodernism, and Other Difficult Positions*, New York: New York University Press.
—— (2010) *The Disability Studies Reader*, New York and London: Routledge.
de Beauvoir, S. (1989 [1949]) 'The psychoanalytic point of view' in *The Second Sex*, trans. H. M. Parshley, New York: Vintage, 1989, 38–52.
—— (1989 [1949]) *The Second Sex*, New York: Vintage Books.
de Lauretis, T. (1984) *Alice Doesn't*, Bloomington: Indiana University Press.
de Lauretis, T. and Heath, S. (1985) *The Cinematic Apparatus*, New York: Palgrave.
Dean, J. (2010) *Rethinking Contemporary Feminist Politics*, Basingstoke: Palgrave Macmillan.
Deleuze, G. (1968 [2004]) *Difference and Repetition*, London: Continuum.
—— (1988) *Spinoza: Practical Philosophy*, trans. Robert Hurley, San Francisco: City Lights Books.
Deleuze, G. and Guatarri, F. (1994) *What is Philosophy?* London: Verso.
Derrida, J. (1982) '*Différance*'. *Margins of Philosophy*, trans. Alan Bass. Chicago: University of Chicago Press, 1–28.
—— (1988) 'Signature event context', in Webster and Mehlman (eds) *Limited Inc.*, Evanston: Northwestern University Press.
Desai, M. and Naples, N. (eds) (2002) *Women's Activism and Globalization: Linking Local Struggles and Transnational Politics*, New York: Routledge.
Deutsch, Helene (1944) *The Psychology of Women*, New York: Grune and Stratton.
Devine, F. (2008) 'Class reproduction and social networks in the USA', in L. Weis (ed.) *The Way Class Works*, London: Routledge.
Dietz, M. G. (2003) 'Current controversies in feminist theory', *Annual Review of Political Science* 6: 399–431.
Dimand, R. W, Dimand, M. A. and Forget, E. W. (2000) *A Biographical Dictionary of Women Economics*, Cheltenham: Edward Elgar.
Dimen, M. and Goldner, V. (eds) (2002) *Gender in Psychoanalytic Space: Between Clinic and Culture*, New York: Other Press.
Doane, Mary Ann (1982) 'Film and the masquerade: theorising the female spectator', *Screen* 23: 3–4, 74–88.
—— (1987) *The Desire to Desire: The Woman's Film of the 1940s*, Bloomington: Indiana University Press.
Dobash, R. P. and Dobash, R. E. (eds) (1998) *Rethinking Violence Against Women*, Thousand Oaks: Sage.
Donnison, J. (1977) *Midwives and Medical Men: A History of Inter-Professional Rivalries and Women's Rights*, New York: Schocken Books.

Duden, B. (1993) *Disembodying Women: Perspectives on Pregnancy and the Unborn*, Cambridge, MA: Harvard University Press.
Duffy, M. (2011) *Making Care Count: A Century of Gender, Race, and Paid Care Work*, New Brunswick, NJ: Rutgers University Press.
Duggan, L. (2003) *The Twilight of Equality? Neoliberalism, Cultural Politics and the Attack on Democracy*, Boston: Beacon Press.
Dyer, R. (1993) *The Matter of Images, Essays on Representation*, London and New York: Routledge.
Ehrenreich, B. and Hochschild, A. R. (eds) (2002) *Global Woman: Nannies, Maids, and Sex Workers in the New Economy*, New York: Metropolitan Books.
Eichler, M. (1980) *The Double Standard: A Feminist Critique of Feminist Social Science*, London: Croom Helm.
EJWS (2009) *European Journal of Women's Studies*, 16(3) *special issue.*
Elmelecha, Y. and Lu, H.-H. (2004) 'Race, ethnicity, and the gender poverty gap', *Social Science Research* 33(1): 158–82.
Elshtain, J. B. (1981) *Public Man, Private Woman: Women in Social and Political Thought*, Princeton, NJ: Princeton University Press.
Elson, D. (1991) 'Male bias in macro-economics: the case of structural adjustment', in D. Elson (ed.) *Male Bias in the Development Process*, Manchester: Manchester University Press.
—— (1999) *Gender-neutral, Gender-blind, or Gender-sensitive Budget?*, London: Commonwealth Secretariat.
Elson, D. and Pearson, R. (1981) '"Nimble fingers make cheap workers": an analysis of women's employment in Third World export manufacturing', *Feminist Review* 7: 87–107.
Engels, F. (2010) *The Origin of the Family, Private Property and the State*, London: Penguin Classics.
England, K. V. L. (1994) 'Getting personal: reflexivity, positionality and feminist research', *Professional Geographer* 46(1): 80–89.
Engster, D. (2007) *The Heart of Justice: Care Ethics and Political Theory*, New York: Oxford University Press.
Eriksen, T. H. (2006) 'Diversity versus difference: neo-liberalism in the minority debate', in R. Rottenburg, B. Schnepel and S. Shimada (eds) *The Making and Unmaking of Difference,* Bielefeld: Transaction, 13–36.
Eschle, C. and Maiguaschca, B. (2010) *Making Feminist Sense of the Global Justice Movement*, Lanham, Maryland: Rowman and Littlefield.
Ettinger, B. L. (2005) 'Fascinance and the girl–to–m/other matrixial feminine difference', in G. Pollock (ed.) *Psychoanalysis and the Image: Transdisciplinary Perspectives*, Boston and Oxford: Blackwells.
—— (2006) 'The matrixial gaze', in Brian Massumi (ed.) *The Matrixial Borderspace*, Minneapolis: University of Minnesota Press.
Evans, M. (1991) 'The problem of gender for women's studies', in J. Aaron and S. Walby (eds) *Out of the Margins: Women's Studies in the Nineties,* London: Taylor and Francis, 67–74.
—— (2002) 'Real bodies: introduction', in M. Evans and E. Lee (eds) *Real Bodies: A Sociological Introduction,* Basingstoke: Palgrave Macmillan.

Evans, M. and Lee, E. (eds) (2002) *Real Bodies: A Sociological Introduction*, Basingstoke: Palgrave Macmillan.

Eyben, R. (2010) 'Subversively accommodating: feminist bureaucrats and gender mainstreaming', *IDS Bulletin* 42(2): 54–61.

Eze, E. (ed.) (1997) *Race and Enlightenment – A Reader*, Oxford: Blackwell.

Fairfield, S., Layton, L. and Stack, C. (eds) (2002) *Bringing the Plague: Toward a Postmodern Psychoanalysis*, New York: Other Press.

Faludi, S. (1992) *Backlash: The Undeclared War against Women*, London: Vintage.

Fanon, F. (1952) *Black Skin, White Masks*, London: Penguin.

—— (1991) [1967] *Black Skins, White Masks*, London: Pluto Press.

Fausto-Sterling, A. (1985) *Myths of Gender: Biological Theories About Women and Men*, 2nd revd edn, New York: Basic Books.

Ferber, M. A. and Nelson, J. A. (eds) (2003) *Feminist Economics Today: Beyond Economic Man*, Chicago and London: University of Chicago Press.

—— (1993) *Beyond Economic Man: Feminist Theory and Economics*, Chicago and London: University of Chicago Press.

Ferriss, S. and Young, M. (eds) (2006) *Chick-Lit: The New Woman's Fiction*, New York and London: Routledge.

Fine, C. (2010) *Delusions of Gender: The Real Science Behind Sex Differences*. London: Icon.

Finlay, L. (2002) '"Outing" the researcher: the provenance, process and practice of reflexivity', *Qualitative Health Research* 12(4): 531–45.

Firestone, S. (1970) [1972] *The Dialectic of Sex: The Case for Feminist Revolution*, London: Jonathan Cape.

Fisher, B., and Tronto, J. (1990) 'Toward a feminist theory of caring', in E. K. Abel and M. K. Nelson (eds) *Circles of Care: Work and Identity in Women's Lives*, Albany, New York: State University of New York Press.

Flanagan, Mary (2002) 'Hyperbodies, hyperknowledge: women in games, women in cyberpunk, and strategies of resistance', in M. Flanagan and A. Booth (eds) *Reload: Re-thinking Women and Culture*, Cambridge, MA: MIT Press, 425–54.

Flax, F. (1990) *Thinking Fragments: Psychoanalysis, Feminism and Postmodernism in the Contemporary West*, Berkeley: University of California Press.

Flax, J. (1990) 'Postmodernism and gender relations in feminist theory', in L. J. Nicholson (ed.) *Feminism/Postmodernism*, New York and London: Routledge, 39–62.

Flood, M. et al. (eds) (2007) *International Encyclopedia of Men and Masculinities*, London: Routledge.

Fogel, C. A. and Quinlan, A. (2011) 'Lady Gaga and feminism: a critical debate', *Cross-Cultural Communication* 7(3): 184–88.

Folbre, N. (1993) 'Socialism, feminist and scientific', in M. A. Ferber and J. A. Nelson (eds) *Beyond Economic Man: Feminist Theory and Economics*, Chicago and London: University of Chicago Press, 94–110.

—— (1994) *Who Pays for the Kids? Gender and the Structures of Constraint*, London: Routledge.

Fonow, M. and Cook, J. (1991) *Beyond Methodology: Feminist Scholarship as Lived Research*, Bloomington: Indiana University Press.

—— (2005) 'Feminist methodology: new applications in the academy and public policy', in *Signs, Journal of Women in Culture and Society* 30(4): 2211–36.

Foucault, M. (1977) [1984] *Discipline and Punish*, London and New York: Penguin.

—— (1978) [1979] *The History of Sexuality Volume 1: The Will to Knowledge*, New York: Random House.

Franklin, S. (1997) *Embodied Progress: A Cultural Account of Reproduction*. London: Routledge.

Fraser, M. and Greco, M. (eds) (2004) *The Body: A Reader*, London: Routledge.

Fraser, N. (1989) *Unruly Practices: Power, Discourse and Gender in Contemporary Social Theory*, Cambridge: Polity Press.

—— (1995) 'From redistribution to recognition? Dilemmas of justice in a "post-socialist" age', *New Left Review* 212: 68–93; reprinted in Anne Phillips (ed.) (1998) *Feminism and Politics*, Oxford and New York: Oxford University Press, 430–60.

—— (1997) *Justice Interruptus: Critical Reflections on the 'Postsocialist' Condition*, New York: Routledge.

Fraser, N. (2008) *Unruly Practices: Power, Discourse and Gender in Contemporary Social Theory*, 2nd edn, Minneapolis: University of Minnesota Press.

Fraser, N. and Honneth, A. (2003) *Redistribution or Recognition? A Political–Philosophical Exchange*, London and New York: Verso.

Freud, S. (1905) [1953] *Three Essays on the Theory of Sexuality*, standard edn, London: Hogarth Press, 123–243.

Fricker, M. (2007) *Epistemic Injustice*, Oxford: Clarendon.

Friedan, B. (1963a) [1992] *The Feminine Mystique*, London: Penguin.

—— (1963b) [2001] 'The sexual solipsism of Sigmund Freud', in *The Feminine Mystique*, New York: Norton, 166–94.

Friedman, J. and Valenti, J. (eds) (2008) *Yes Means Yes! Visions of Female Sexual Power and a World Without Rap*, Berkeley: Seal Press.

Fukuda-Parr, S. (1999) 'What does feminization of poverty mean? It isn't just lack of income', *Feminist Economics* 5(2): 99–103.

Fuss, D. (1994) 'Interior colonies: Frantz Fanon and the politics of identification', *Diacritics* 24(2/3): 19–42.

Gabe, J., Bury, M. and Elston, M. A. (2004) *Key Concepts in Medical Sociology*, London: Sage.

Gaines, J. (1988) 'White privilege and looking relations: race and gender in feminist film theory', *Screen* 29(4): 12–27.

Gamble, S. (ed.) (2001) *The Routledge Companion to Feminism and Postfeminism*, London: Routledge.

Gamman, L. and Marshment, M. (eds) (1987) *The Female Gaze: Women as Viewers of Popular Culture*, London: Women's Press.

Garcia-Moreno, C., Jansen, H. A. F. M, Watts, C., Ellsberg, M. C. and Heise, L. (2005) *WHO Multi-country Study on Women's Health and*

Domestic Violence Against Women, Geneva, Switzerland: World Health Organization.

Garde-Hansen, J. and Gorton, K. (forthcoming) *Emotion Online: Theorising Affect on the Internet*, Basingstoke: Palgrave Macmillan.

Gardiner, J. K. (ed.) (2002) *Masculinity Studies and Feminist Theory*, New York: Columbia University Press.

Genz, S. (2006) 'Third way/ve: the politics of postfeminism', *Feminist Theory* 7(3): 333–53.

—— (2009) *Postfemininities in Popular Culture*, Basingstoke: Palgrave Macmillan.

Genz, S. and Brabon, B. (2009) *Postfeminism: Cultural Texts and Theories*, Edinburgh: Edinburgh University Press.

Gershuny, J., Godwin, M. and Jones, S. (1994) 'The domestic labour revolution: a process of lagged adaptation', in M. Anderson, F. Bechhofer and J. Gershuny (eds) *The Social and Political Economy of the Household*, Oxford: Oxford University Press.

Gibson, W. (1995) [1984] *Neuromancer*, London: HarperCollins.

Giles, W. and Hyndman, J. (eds) (2004) *Sites of Violence: Gender and Conflict Zones*, Berkeley: University of California Press.

Gill, R. (2007) *Gender and the Media*, Cambridge: Polity Press.

Gill, R. and Scharff, C. (eds) (2011) *New Femininities: Postfeminism, Neoliberalism and Subjectivity*, London and Basingstoke: Palgrave Macmillan.

Gilligan, C. (1982) *In a Different Voice: Psychological Theory and Women's Development*, Cambridge, MA: Harvard University Press.

Gilman, S. (1985) 'Black bodies, white bodies: toward an iconography of female sexuality in late nineteenth century art, medicine and literature', in H. L. Gates, Jr (ed.) *'Race', Writing and Difference,* Chicago: University of Chicago Press.

Gilroy, P. (1993) *The Black Atlantic: Modernity and Double Consciousness*, Cambridge: Harvard University Press.

Ginsburg, F. and Rapp, D. (eds) (1995) *Conceiving the New World Order: The Global Politics of Reproduction*, Berkeley, CA: University of California Press.

Ginzberg, R. (1987) 'Uncovering gynocentric science', *Hypatia* 2(3): 89–105.

Goldberg, G. S. (2010) *Poor Women in Rich Countries: The Feminization of Poverty over the Life Course*, Oxford, New York: Oxford University Press.

Goldthorpe, J. H. (1984) 'Women and class analysis: a reply to the replies', *Sociology* 18(4): 491–499.

Gonick, M. (2006) 'Between "girl power" and "reviving Ophelia": constituting the neoliberal girl subject', *Feminist Formations* 18(2): 1–23.

Gopinath, G. (2005) *Impossible Desires. Queer Diasporas and South Asian Public Cultures*, Durham: Duke University Press.

Gorton, K. (2007) 'Theorising emotion and affect: feminist engagements', *Feminist Theory* 8(3): 333–48.

—— (2009) *Media Audiences: Television, Emotion and Meaning*, Edinburgh: Edinburgh University Press.

Gray, J. (1992) *Men are from Mars, Women are from Venus: How To Get What You Want In Your Relationships*, London and New York: Harper Collins.

Greer, G. (1970) *The Female Eunuch*, New York: McGraw Hill.

Gregg, M. (2010) 'On Friday night drinks: workplace affects in the age of the cubicle', in M. Gregg and G. J. Seigworth (eds) *The Affect Theory Reader*, Durham: Duke University Press, 250–68.

Gregg, M. and Seigworth, G. J. (eds) (2010) *The Affect Theory Reader*, Durham: Duke University Press.

Grenz, S. (2005) 'Intersections of sex and power in research on prostitution: a female researcher interviewing male heterosexual clients', *Signs* 30(4): 2091–2113.

Grewal, I. and Kaplan, C. (1994) *Scattered Hegemonies: Postmodernity and Transnational Feminist Practices*, Minneapolis: University of Minnesota Press.

—— (2000) 'Postcolonial studies and transnational feminist practices', *Jouvert* 5(1) http://english.chass.ncsu.edu/jouvert/v5i1/grewal.htm, accessed January 2012.

Grewal, I. and Kaplan, C. (eds) (2002) *An Introduction to Women's Studies: Gender in a Transnational World*, Boston: McGraw-Hill.

Griffin, G. (2005a) 'The institutionalization of women's studies in Europe', in Gabriele Griffin (ed.) *Doing Women's Studies: Employment Opportunities, Personal Impacts and Social Consequences*, London: Zed Books.

Griffin, G. (ed.) (2005b) *Doing Women's Studies: Employment Opportunities, Personal Impacts and Social Consequences*, London: Zed Books.

Griffin, G. (ed.) (2006) '(Inter)disciplinarity and the Bologna process: walk on the wild side?' Special Issue of *Nora: Nordic Journal of Women's Studies* 14.

Griffin, G., Medhurst, P. and Green, T. (2006) *Interdisciplinarity in Interdisciplinary Research Programmes in the UK*. Report available at http://www.york.ac.uk/res/researchintegration/National_Report_UK.pdf, accessed 4th August 2011.

Grossberg, L. (1992) 'Is there a fan in the house? The affective sensibility of fandom', in L. A. Lewis (ed.) *Adoring Audience: Fan Culture and Popular Media*, London and New York: Routledge, 50–68.

—— (2010) 'Affect's Future: Rediscovering the Virtual in the Actual (Interviews by G. J. Seigworth and M. Gregg)', in M. Gregg and G. J. Seigworth (eds) *The Affect Theory Reader*, Durham: Duke University Press, 309–38.

Grosz, E. (1994) *Volatile Bodies: Towards a Corporeal Feminism*, Bloomington: Indiana University Press.

—— (2005) *Time Travels: Feminism, Nature and Power*, Durham and London: Duke University Press.

Guidroz, K. and Berger, M. T. (2009) 'A conversation with founding scholars of intersectionality: Kimberlé Crenshaw, Nira Yuval-Davis, and Michelle Fine', in K. Guidroz and M. T. Berger (eds) *The Intersectional Approach: Transforming the Academy Through Race, Class & Gender,* Chapel Hill: University of North Carolina Press.

Gupta, S. (2007) 'Autonomy, dependence or display? The relationship between married women's earnings and housework', *Journal of Marriage and Family* 69, 399–417.

Hafner-Burton, E. and Pollack, M. (2000) 'Mainstreaming gender in the European Union', *Journal of European Public Policy* 7(3): 432–56.

—— (2009) 'Mainstreaming gender in the European Union: getting the incentives right', *Comparative European Politics* 7: 114–38.

Hakim, C. (2000) *Work–lifestyle Choices in the 21st Century*, Oxford University Press: Oxford.

Halberstam, J. (1998) *Female Masculinity*, Durham and London: Duke University Press.

Hall, K. Q. (2011) *Feminist Disability Studies*, Bloomington: Indiana University Press.

Hall, S. (1980) 'Encoding/decoding', in Hall, Hobson Lowe and Willis (eds) *Culture, Media, Language*, London: Hutchinson, 128–38.

—— (1996a) 'Cultural identity and cinematic representation', in Baker et al. (eds) *Black British Cultural Studies a Reader,* Chicago: University of Chicago Press.

—— (1996b) 'Introduction: who needs "identity"', in S. Hall and P. du Gay (eds) *Questions of Cultural Identity*, London: Sage, 1–18.

—— (1996c) 'When was the postcolonial?', in I. Chambers, and L. Curti (eds) *The Post Colonial Question: Common Skies Divided Horizons*, London and New York: Routledge.

—— (2007) *Representation, Cultural Representations and Signifying Practices,* London: Open University Press and Sage.

Hankivsky, O. (2004) *Social Policy and the Ethic Of Care*, Vancouver: UBC Press.

Hanmer, J. (1990) 'Men, power and the exploitation of women', in Jeff Hearn and David Morgan (eds) *Men, Masculinities and Social Theory*, London: Unwin Hyman, 21–42.

Haraway, D. J. (1985) 'A manifesto for cyborgs: science, technology and socialist feminism in the 1980s', *Socialist Review* 80: 65–107.

—— (1988) 'Situated knowledges; the science question in feminism and the privilege of partial perspective', *Feminist Studies* 14(3): 581–607.

—— (1990) *Simians, Cyborgs, and Women: The Reinvention of Nature,* New York and London: Routledge.

—— (1991a) 'A cyborg manifesto: science, technology, and socialist-feminism in the late twentieth century', in D. J. Haraway (ed.) *Simians, Cyborgs and Women: The Reinvention of Nature,* New York: Routledge.

—— (1991b) *Simians, Cyborgs, and Women: The Reinvention of Nature,* London: Free Association Books.

—— (1991c) 'Situated knowledges: the science question in feminism and the privilege of partial perspective', in D. J. Haraway (ed.) *Simians, Cyborgs and Women: The Reinvention of Nature*, London: Free Association Books.

—— (1997) *Modest Witness@Second Millennium: FemaleMan Meets Oncomouse*, New York: Routledge.

Harcourt, W. (ed.) (1999) *Women@Internet: Creating New Cultures in Cyberspace*, London: Zed Books.

Harding, J. and Pribram, E. D. (eds) (2009) *Emotions: A Cultural Studies Reader*, London: Routledge.

Harding, S. (ed.) (2004) *The Feminist Standpoint Theory Reader: Intellectual and Political Controversies*, New York: Routledge.

Harding, S. and Norberg, K. (2005) 'New feminist approaches to social science methodologies: an introduction', *Signs* 30(4): 2009–15.

Harding, S. G. (1986) *The Science Question in Feminism*, Ithaca; London: Cornell University Press.

Hardt, M. (2007) 'Foreword: what affects are good for', in P. T. Clough (ed.) *The Affective Turn: Theorising the Social*, Durham: Duke University Press, ix–xiii.

Hark, S. (2007) 'Magical sign: on the politics of inter- and trans-disciplinarity', *Graduate Journal of Social Science* 4(2): 11–33.

Hartmann, B. (1995) *Reproductive Rights and Wrongs: The Global Politics of Population Control* (updated and revd edn), Boston: South End Publishers.

Hartmann, H. (1979) 'The unhappy marriage of Marxism and feminism: towards a more progressive union', *Capital and Class* 3(2): 1–33.

Hartsock, N. (2003) 'The feminist standpoint: developing the ground for a specifically feminist historical materialism', in S. G. Harding and M. B. Hintikka (eds) *Discovering Reality*, Dordrecht: Reidel, 283–310.

Hawkesworth, M. (1989) 'Knowers, knowing, known: feminist theory and the claims of truth', *Signs: Journal of Women in Culture and Society* 14(3): 533–57.

—— (1994) 'Policy studies within a feminist frame', *Policy Sciences* 27: 97–118.

—— (2004) 'The semiotics of premature burial: feminism in a postfeminist age', *Signs: Journal of Women in Culture and Society* 29(4): 961–85.

—— (2006) *Globalization and Feminist Activism*, Lanham, Maryland: Rowman & Littlefield.

Hayles, N. K. (1999) *How We Became Posthuman: Virtual Bodies in Cybernetics, Literature, and Informatics*, Chicago: University of Chicago Press.

Hearn, J. (1996) '"Is masculinity dead?" A critical account of the concepts of masculinity and masculinities', in M. Mac an Ghaill (ed.) *Understanding Masculinities: Social Relations and Cultural Arenas*, Milton Keynes: Open University Press, 202–17.

—— (2004) 'From hegemonic masculinity to the hegemony of men', *Feminist Theory* 5(1): 97–120.

Hearn, J. and Pringle, K. with members of Critical Research on Men in Europe (2006) *European Perspectives on Men and Masculinities: National and Transnational Approaches*, Basingstoke: Palgrave Macmillan.

Heath, A. F. and Britten, N. (1984) 'Women's jobs do make a difference: a reply to Goldthorpe', *Sociology* 18(4): 475–90.

Held, V. (2006) *The Ethics of Care: Personal, Political, and Global*, Oxford and New York: Oxford University Press.

Hemmings, C. (2005a) 'Invoking affect: cultural theory and the ontological turn', *Cultural Studies* 19(5): 548–67.

—— (2005b) 'Telling feminist stories', *Feminist Theory* 6(2): 115–39.

—— (2006) 'The life and times of academic feminism', in Kathy Davis, Mary Evans, et al. (eds) *Handbook of Gender and Women's Studies*, London: Sage.

—— (2011) *Why Stories Matter: The Political Grammar of Feminist Theory*, Durham: Duke University Press.

Henry, A. (2004) *Not My Mother's Sister: Generational Conflict and Third-Wave Feminism*, Bloomington: Indiana University Press.

Highmore, B. (2010) 'Bitter after taste: affect, food and social aesthetics', in M. Gregg and G. J. Seigworth (eds) *The Affect Theory Reader*, Durham: Durham University Press, 118–37.

Hill Collins, P. (2000) *Black Feminist Thought: Knowledge, Consciousness and the Politics of Empowerment*, New York: Routledge.

Hill, J. (1999) '"Race" and the politics of form, the black workshops and films of Isaac Julien', in *British Cinema in the 1980s,* Oxford: Oxford University Press, 219–40.

Hills, M. (2002) *Fan Cultures*, London: Routledge.

—— (2010) *Triumph of a Time Lord: Regenerating Dr Who in the Twenty-First Century*, London: I. B. Tauris.

Hinds, H., Phoenix, A. and Stacey, J. (eds) (1992) *Working Out: New Directions for Women's Studies*, London: Falmer Press.

Hird, M. J. and Roberts, C. (2011) 'Feminism theorises the nonhuman', *Feminist Theory* 12(2): 109–17.

Hochschild, Arlie R. (2003) [1983] *The Managed Heart: Commercialization of Human Feeling*, Berkeley: University of California Press.

hooks, bell (1989) *Talking Back: Thinking Feminist, Thinking Black*, London: Sheba Feminist Publishers.

—— (1992) 'The oppositional gaze: black female spectators', *Black Looks: Race and Representation*, Boston: South End Press, 115–31.

—— (1996) 'The oppositional gaze, black feminist spectators', *Reel to Real, Race, Sex and Class at the Movies*, New York: Routledge.

Horney, K. (1967) *Feminine Psychology*, London: Routledge and Kegan Paul.

Hoskyns, C. (1996) *Integrating Gender: Women, Law and Politics in the European Union*, London and New York: Verso.

Howson, R. (2006) *Challenging Hegemonic Masculinity*, London: Routledge.

Hubbard, R. (1990) 'Who should and should not inhabit the world?' in *The Politics of Women's Biology*, New Brunswick, NJ: Rutgers University Press, 179–98.

Hull, G. T., Scott, P. B. and Smith, B. (eds) (1982) *All the Women Are White, All the Blacks Are Men But Some of Us Are Brave*, The City University of New York, New York: The Feminist Press.

Humphries, J. (1977) 'Class struggle and the persistence of the working class family', *Cambridge Journal of Economics* 1(3): 241–58.

INCITE! Women of Color Against Violence (ed.) (2006) *Color of Violence: The INCITE! Anthology*, Cambridge, MA: South End Press.

Inhorn, M. (1994) *Quest for Conception: Gender, Infertility, and Egyptian Medical Traditions*, Philadelphia, PA: University of Pennsylvania Press.

Irigaray, L. (1974) *Speculum of the Other Woman*, trans. Catherine Porter, Ithaca, NY: Cornell University Press, 1985.

Jackson, C. and Pearson, R. (eds) (1998) *Feminist Visions of Development: Gender Analysis and Policy*, London: Routledge.

Jackson, S. (2004) 'Crossing boundaries', *Journal of International Women's Studies* 5(2): 1–5.

Jahan, R. (1995) *The Elusive Agenda: Mainstreaming Women in Development*, London: Zed Books.

Jamal, A. (2011) 'Just between us: identity and representation among Muslim women', *Inter-Asia Cultural Studies* 12(2): 202–12.

Jayawardena, K. (1986) *Feminism and Nationalism in the Third World*, London: Zed Books.

Jegger, A. M. (1989) 'Love and Knowledge: Emotion in Feminist Epistemology' in A. Jegger and S. Bordo (eds) *Gender/Body/Knowledge: Feminist Reconstructions of Being and Knowing*, New Brunswick: Rutgers University Press.

Jenkins, R. (1992) *Pierre Bourdieu*, London and New York: Routledge.

Jennings, A. (1993) 'Public or private? institutional economics and feminism', in M. A. Ferber and J. A. Nelson (eds) *Beyond Economic Man: Feminist Theory and Economics*, Chicago and London: University of Chicago Press, 111–29.

Jones, E. (1927) [1948] 'The early development of female sexuality', in *Papers on Psychoanalysis*, Baltimore, MD: Williams and Wilkins.

Jordan, B. (1980) *Birth in Four Cultures: A Cross-Cultural Investigation of Childbirth in Yucatan, Holland, Sweden and the United States*, Montreal and St Albans, VT: Eden Press Women's Publications.

Jouve, N. W. (1991) *White Woman Speaks with Forked Tongue*, London: Routledge.

Kabeer, N. (1994) *Reversed Realities: Gender Hierarchies in Development Thought*, London: Verso.

Kahn, S. M. (2000) *Reproducing Jews: A Cultural Account of Assisted Conception in Israel*, Durham: Duke University Press.

Kan, M. Y. (2008) 'Does gender trump money? Housework hours of husbands and wives in Britain', *Work, Employment and Society* 22: 45–66.

Kan, M. Y., Sullivan, O. and Gershuny, J. I. (2011) 'Gender convergence in domestic work: discerning the effects of interactional and institutional barriers from large-scale data', *Sociology* 45(2): 234–51.

Kandiyoti, D. (1988) 'Bargaining with patriarchy', *Gender and Society* 2(3): 274–90.

Kaplan, C., Alarcon, N. and Moallem, M. (eds) (1999) *Between Woman and Nation: Nationalisms, Transnational Feminisms, and the State*. Durham–London: Duke University Press.

Kaplan, E. A. (1983) 'Is the gaze male?' *Women and Film: Both Sides of the Camera,* New York: Methuen.

Kapoor, I. (2008) 'Hyper-reflexive development? Spivak on representing "Third-World Other"', in *The Postcolonial Politics of Development*, New York: Routledge.

Kappas, A. and Krämer, N. C. (eds) (2011) *Face-to-face Communication Over the Internet: Emotions in a Web of Culture*, Cambridge: Cambridge University Press.

Karlqvist, A. (1999) 'Going beyond disciplines: the meanings of interdisciplinarity', *Policy Sciences* 32: 379–83.

Katz, J. (2006) *The Macho Paradox: Why Some Men Hurt Women and How All Men can Help*, Naperville, IL: Sourcebooks.

Kavka, M. (2008) *Reality Television, Affect and Intimacy: Reality Matters*, Basingstoke: Palgrave Macmillan.

Kelly, L. (1988) *Surviving Sexual Violence*, Cambridge: Polity Press.

Khanna, R. (2003) *Dark Continents: Psychoanalysis and Colonialism*, Durham: Duke University Press.

Kimmel, M. S. (2002) '"Gender symmetry" in domestic violence: a substantive and methodological review', *Violence Against Women* 8: 1332–63.

Kimmel, M., Hearn, J. and Connell, R. (eds) (2005) *Handbook of Studies on Men and Masculinities*, Thousand Oaks, CA: Sage.

Kittay, E. F. (1998) *Love's Labor: Essays on Women, Equality, and Dependency*, New York and London: Routledge.

Kittay, E. F. (2001) 'A feminist public ethic of care meets the new communitarian family policy', *Ethics* 111(3): 523–47.

Klasen, S. (1994) 'Missing women reconsidered', *World Development* 22: 1061–71.

Klein, M. (1928) [1988] *Love, Guilt, and Reparation and Other Works 1921–45*, London: Virago.

Korek, J. (2009) 'Central and Eastern Europe from a postcolonial perspective', in *Postcolonial Europe* available online at http://www.postcolonial-europe.eu/index.php/en/essays/60nbsp;-central-and-eastern-europe-from-a-postcolonial-perspective, accessed 17 December 2010.

Kothari, U. (2006) 'An agenda for thinking about "race" in development'. *Progress in Development Studies* 6(1): 9–23.

Kristeva, J. (1984) *Revolution in Poetic Language*, trans. Margaret Waller, New York: Columbia University Press.

Kristol, W. (1998) 'A conservative perspective on public policy and the family', in C. Wolfe (ed.) *The Family, Civil Society, and the State*, Oxford: Rowman and Littlefield.

Kulick, D. and Wilson, M. (eds) (1995) *Taboo: Sex, Identity and Erotic Subjectivity in Anthropological Fieldwork*, London: Routledge.

Kulpa, R., and Mizielińska, J. (eds) (2011) *De-Centring Western Sexualities: Central and Eastern European Perspectives*, Farnham and Burlington, VT: Ashgate.

Kuntsman, A. (2007) 'Belong through violence: flaming, erasure, and performativity in queer migrant community', in K. O'Riordan and D. J. Phillips (eds) *Queer Online: Media, Technology & Sexuality*, New York, Oxford: Peter Lang, 101–22.

Kuppers, P. (2003) *Disability and Contemporary Performance: Bodies on Edge*, New York and London: Routledge.

Lacan, J. (1958) [1982] 'The Meaning of the Phallus', trans. J. Rose in J. Mitchell and J. Rose (eds) *Feminine Sexuality*, New York: W. W. Norton.

—— (1963) [1997] 'On the gaze as *objet a*', *Four Fundamental Concepts of Psychoanalysis,* trans. A. Sheridan, Harmondsworth: Penguin Books, 67–122.

—— (1975) *Le Seminaire,* Livre XX, *Encore, 1972–1973,* Paris: Editions de Seuil, trans. B. Fink (1998) *On Feminine Sexuality: The Limits of Love and Knowledge*, New York: Norton.

Lather, P. (1993) 'Fertile obsession: validity after poststructuralism', *The Sociological Quarterly* 34(4): 673–94.
Levine, P. (2003) *Prostitution, Race and Politics*, London and New York: Routledge.
Lewis, R. and Mills, S. (eds) (2003) *Feminist Postcolonial Theory: A Reader*, Edinburgh: Edinburgh University Press.
Lewis, S. and Giullari, S. (2005) 'The adult worker model family, gender equality and care: the search for new policy principles and the possibilities and problems of a capabilities approach', *Economy and Society* 34(1): 76–104.
Li, C. (1994) 'The Confucian concept of Jen and the feminist ethics of care: a comparative study', *Hypatia* 9(1): 70–89.
Lind, A. (2010) *Development, Sexual Rights and Global Governance*, London and New York: Routledge.
Lister, R. (1997) [2003] *Citizenship: Feminist Perspectives*, Basingstoke and New York: Palgrave Macmillan, also for the notion of 'differentiated universalism'.
—— (2007) 'Inclusive ctizenship: realizing the potential', *Citizenship Studies* 11(1): 49–61.
Lloyd, G. (1984) *The Man of Reason: 'Male' and 'Female' in Western Philosophy*, Minneapolis: University of Minnesota Press.
—— (1996) *Routledge Philosophy Guidebook to Spinoza and the Ethics*, London: Routledge.
Lombardo, E. (2005) 'Integrating or setting the agenda? Gender mainstreaming in the European Constitution-making process', *Social Politics* 12(3): 412–32.
Lombardo, E. and Verloo, M. (2009) 'Contentious citizenship', *Feminist Review* 92: 118.
Lombardo, E. and Meier, P. (2006) 'Gender mainstreaming in the EU: incorporating a feminist reading?' *European Journal of Women's Studies* 13(2): 151–66.
Loomba, A. (1998) *Colonialism/Postcolonialism*, London and New York: Routledge.
Loomba, A., et al. (2005) *Postcolonial Studies and Beyond*, Durham: Duke University Press.
Lorber, J. (1994) *Paradoxes of Gender*, New Haven and London: Yale University Press.
Lorde, A. (1979) 'Breast cancer: power vs. prosthesis', *The Audre Lorde Compendium: Essays, Speeches and Journals*, London: Pandora, 43–62.
—— (1984) *Sister Outsider: Essays and Speeches*, Trumansburg, NY: The Crossing.
Lovenduski, J. (2005) *Feminising Politics*, Cambridge: Polity Press.
Luibhéid, E. (2004): 'Heteronormativity and immigration scholarship: a call for change', *GLQ* 10(2): S. 227–35.
Lutz, C. (1988) *Unnatural Emotions: Everyday Sentiments on a Micronesian Atoll and Their Challenge to Western Theory*, Chicago: University of Chicago Press.
Lutz, H., Vivar, M. T. H. and Supik, L. (eds) (2011) *Framing Intersectionality: Debates on a Multi-Faceted Concept in Gender Studies*, Farnham, UK and Burlington, USA: Ashgate.

Lycklama à Nijeholt, G. et al. (eds) (1998) *Women's Movements and Public Policy in Europe, Latin America and the Caribbean*, New York: Garland.

Lykke, N. (2010) *Feminist Studies: A Guide to Intersectional Theory, Methodology and Writing*, New York: Routledge.

MacKinnon, C. (1987) *Feminism Unmodified: Discourses on Life and Law*, Cambridge, MA: Harvard University Press.

Mahmood, S. (2005) *Politics of Piety: The Islamic Revival and the Feminist Subject*, Oxford: Princeton University Press.

Manalansan IV, M. F. (2006) 'Queer intersections: sexuality and gender in migration studies', *International Migration Review* 40(1): 224–49.

Mann, P. S. (1994) Micro-politics: *Agency in a Postfeminist Era*, Minneapolis and London: University of Minnesota Press.

Mansfield, N. (2000) *Subjectivity: Theories of the Self from Freud to Haraway*, New York: New York University Press.

Marks, L. U. (1999) *The Skin of the Film: Intercultural Cinema, Embodiment, and the Senses*, Durham: Duke University Press.

Martin, E. (1987) *The Woman in the Body: A Cultural Analysis of Reproduction*, Boston, MA: Beacon Press.

Marx, K. and Engels, F. (2010) *The Communist Manifesto*, London: Vintage Books.

Massumi, B. (2002) *Parables for the Virtual*, Durham: Duke University Press.

Maynard, M. (1994) 'Race, gender and the concept of difference', in Haleh Afshar and Mary Maynard (eds) *The Dynamics of 'Race' and Gender: Some Feminist Interventions*, London: Taylor and Francis, 9–26.

Mazey, S. (2002) 'Gender mainstreaming in the EU: delivering on an agenda?' *Feminist Legal Studies* 10(3–4): 227–40.

Mazey, S. (ed.) (2000) 'Introduction: integrating gender. Intellectual and "real world" mainstreaming'. Special Issue: Women, Power and Public Policy in Europe, *Journal of European Public Policy* 7(3): 333–45.

Mazzarella, S. R. (2010) *Girl Wide Web 2.0: Revisiting Girls, the Internet, and the Negotiation of Identity*, New York and Oxford: Peter Lang.

McCall, L. (2005) 'The complexity of intersectionality', *Signs: Journal of Women in Culture and Society* 30(3): 1771–1800.

McClintock, A. (1993) 'The angel of progress: pitfalls of the term "post-colonialism"', in Patrick Williams and Laura Chrisman (eds) *Colonial Discourse and Post-colonial Theory. A Reader*, New York: Harvester Wheatsheaf.

—— (1995) *Imperial Leather: Race, Gender, and Sexuality in the Colonial Contest*, London and New York: Routledge.

McClintock, A., Mufti, A. and Shohat, A. (eds) (1997) *Dangerous Liaisons: Gender, Nation and Postcolonial Perspectives*, London and New York: Routledge.

McCorkel, J. A. and Myers, K. (2003) 'What difference does difference make? Position and privilege in the field', *Qualitative Sociology* 26(2).

McLaren, M. (2002) *Feminism, Foucault, and Embodied Subjectivity*, New York: State University of New York Press.

McNay, L. (1993) *Foucault and Feminism: Power, Gender and the Self*, Boston, MA: Northeastern University Press.

McNeil, M. (2007) *Feminist Cultural Studies of Science and Technology*, London: Routledge.
McRobbie, A. (2004) 'Notes on postfeminism and popular culture: Bridget Jones and the new gender regime', in A. Harris (ed.) *All about the Girl: Culture, Power, and Identity*, London: Routledge.
—— (2009) *The Aftermath of Feminism, Gender, Culture and Social Change*, London: Sage.
McRuer, R. (2006) *Crip Theory: Cultural Signs of Queerness and Disability*, New York: New York University Press.
Meer, N., Dwyer, C. and Modood, T. (2010) 'Embodying nationhood? conceptions of British national identity, citizenship, and gender in the "Veil Affair"', *The Sociological Review* 58: 1.
Mendonza, B. (2002) 'Transnational feminisms in question', *Feminist Theory* 3(3): 295–314.
Mercer, K. (1994) *Welcome to the Jungle. New Positions in Black Cultural Studies*, New York: Routledge.
Merleau-Ponty, M. (1962) *The Phenomenology of Perception*, London: Routledge.
Merry, S. E. (2009) *Gender Violence: A Cultural Perspective*, London: Blackwell.
Metz, C. (1977) *Cinema and Psychoanalysis: The Imaginary Signifier*, Basingstoke: Macmillan.
Mies, M. and Shiva, V. (1993) *Ecofeminism*, London: Zed Books.
Millett, K. (1970) *Sexual Politics*, London: Virago Press.
Mitchell, J. (1974) *Psychoanalysis and Feminism*, London: Allen Lane.
Mitchell, L. M. and Georgies, E. (1997) 'Cross-cultural cyborgs: Greek and Canadian women's discourses on fetal ultrasound', *Feminist Studies* 23(2): 373–401.
Mitchison, N. (1985) [1962] *Memoirs of a Spacewoman*, London: Women's Press.
Moallem, M. (1999) 'Transnationalism, feminism and fundamentalism', in C. Kaplan, N. Alarcon and M. Moallem (eds) *Between Woman and Nation: Nationalisms, Transnational Feminisms and the State*, Durham and London: Duke University Press.
Moghadam, V. (2005) *Globalizing Women: Transnational Feminist Networks*, Baltimore: Johns Hopkins University Press.
Mohanty, C. T. (1984) [1992] 'Under Western Eyes: feminist scholarship and colonial discourses', *Boundary 2* 12(3): 333–58; reprinted in C. T. Mohanty (2003) *Feminism without Borders: Decolonizing Theory, Practicing Solidarity*, Durham and London: Duke University Press.
—— (1992) 'Feminist encounters: locating the politics of experience', in M. Barrett and A. Phillips (eds) *Destabilising Theory: Contemporary Feminist Debates*, Cambridge: Polity Press, 74–93.
—— (2003) '"Under Western Eyes" revisited: feminist solidarity through anticapitalist struggles', in C. T. Mohanty, *Feminism without Borders: Decolonizing Theory, Practicing Solidarity*, Durham and London: Duke University Press, 221–51.
—— (2003a) *Feminism Without Borders: Decolonizing Theory, Practicing Solidarity*, Durham: Duke University Press.

—— (2003b) 'Under Western Eyes revisited: feminist solidarity through anticapitalist struggles', *Signs: Journal of Women in Culture and Society* 28(2) 499–535.

Molyneux, M. (1985) 'Mobilisation without emancipation? Women's interests, the state and revolution in Nicaragua', *Feminist Studies* 11: 227–54.

—— (2008) 'The "neoliberal turn" and the new social policy in Latin America: how neoliberal, how new?' *Development and Change* 39(5): 775–97.

Montecino, S. and Obach, A. (1999) 'De La Descripción Al Cambio En Las Relaciones De Género: Breve Análisis De Los Currículos De Mujer Y Género En Las Universidades Chilenas', in S. Montecino and A. Obach (eds) *Género Y Epistemología: Mujeres Y Disciplinas*, Santiago de Chile: LOM Ediciones.

Moore, H. L. (1994) *A Passion for Difference: Essays in Anthropology and Gender*, Cambridge: Polity Press.

—— (2007) *The Subject of Anthropology: Gender, Symbolism and Psychoanalysis*, Cambridge: Polity Press.

—— (2011) *Still Life: Hopes, Desires and Satisfactions*, Cambridge: Polity Press.

Moran, J. (2002) *Interdisciplinarity*, London: Routledge.

Moraña, M., Dussel, E. and Jáuregui, C. J. (eds) (2008) *Coloniality at Large: Latin America and the Postcolonial Debate*, Durham: Duke University Press,.

Morgan, D. (2002) 'The body in pain', in M. Evans and E. Lee (eds) *Real Bodies: A Sociological Introduction*, Basingstoke: Palgrave.

Morgan, R. (1984) *Sisterhood is Global: The International Women's Movement Anthology*, New York: the Feminist Press at the City University of New York.

Morgensen, S. (2011) *The Space Between Us: Queer Settler Colonialism and Indigenous Decolonization*, Minneapolis: Minnesota University Press.

Morley, L. (1998) *Organising Feminisms: The Micropolitics of the Academy*, New York: St Martin's Press.

Morley, L. and Walsh, V. (eds) (1995) *Feminist Academics: Creative Agents for Change*, London: Taylor and Francis.

Moser, C. (1993) *Gender Planning and Development: Theory, Practice and Training*, New York and London: Routledge.

Mukhopadhyay, M. (2004) 'Mainstreaming gender or "streaming" gender away: feminists marooned in the development business', *IDS* 35(4): 95–103.

Mulvey, L. (1974) 'Visual pleasure and narrative cinema', *Screen* 17(4): 6–18.

—— (1988) 'Afterthoughts on "visual pleasure and narrative cinema"', in L. Mulvey, *Visual and Other Pleasures*, Basingstoke: Macmillan, 29–38.

—— (2006) *Death 24x a Second: Stillness and the Moving Image*, London: Reaktion Books.

Muñoz, J. E. (1999) *Disidentifications: Queers of Color and the Performance of Politics*, Minneapolis: Minnesota University Press.

Nagar, R. and Geiger, S. (2007) 'Reflexivity and positionality in feminist fieldwork revisited', in A. Tickell, et al. (eds) *Politics and Practice in Economic Geography*, London: Sage, 267–78.

Nahman, M. (2008) 'Nodes of desire: Romanian egg sellers, "dignity" and feminist alliances in transnational ova exchanges', *European Journal of Women's Studies* 15(2): 65–82.

Narayan, U. (1997) *Dislocating Cultures: Identities, Traditions and Third-World Feminism*, New York and London: Routledge.

—— (2002) 'Minds of their own: choices, autonomy, cultural practices and other women', in L. M. Antony and C. Witt (eds) *A Mind of One's Own: Feminist Essays in Reason and Objectivity*, Colorado: Westview Press.

Nash, J. (2008) 'Re-thinking intersectionality', *Feminist Review* 89: 1–15.

Nayak, A. and Kehily, M. J. (2008) *Gender, Youth and Culture: Young Masculinities and Femininities*, Basingstoke: Palgrave Macmillan.

Newman, L. (2000) 'Transgender issues', in J. M. Ussher (ed.) *Women's Health: Contemporary International Perspectives*, Leicester: BPS.

Ngai, P. (2004) 'Women workers and precarious employment in Shenzhen Special Economic Zone, China', *Gender and Development* 12(2): 29–36.

Ngai, S. (2005) *Ugly Feelings*, Cambridge, MA: Harvard University Press.

Nicholson, L. (1999) *The Play of Reason: From the Modern to the Postmodern*, Buckingham: Open University Press.

Noddings, N. (2003) *Caring, a Feminine Approach to Ethics and Moral Education*, 2nd edn, Berkeley: University of California Press.

Nussbaum, M. (2000) *Women and Human Development: The Capabilities Approach*, Cambridge: Cambridge University Press.

—— (2002) 'Women's capabilities and social justice', in M. Molyneux and S. Razavi (eds) *Gender Justice, Development, and Rights*, Oxford: Oxford University Press, 45–77.

O'Riordan, K. and Phillips, D. J. (2007) 'Introduction' in K. O'Riordan and D. J. Phillips (eds) *Queer Online: Media, Technology and Sexuality*, New York and Oxford: Peter Lang, 1–9.

O'Toole, L. L., Schiffman, J. R. and Edwards, M. L. K. (eds) (2007) *Gender Violence: Interdisciplinary Perspectives*, New York: New York University Press.

Oakley, A. (1972) *Sex, Gender and Society*, London: Maurice Temple Smith.

Office for National Statistics (2011) *The National Statistics Socio-Economic Classification*. http://www.ons.gov.uk/about-statistics/classifications/current/ns-sec/index.html, accessed June 2011.

Okin, S. M. (1999) 'Is multiculturalism bad for women?', in Joshua Cohen, Matthew Howard and Martha C. Nussbaum (eds) *Is Multiculturalism Bad for Women?*, Princeton: Princeton University Press.

—— (1990) *Justice, Gender and the Family*, New York: Basic Books.

Oleksy, E. H. (ed.) (2009) *Intimate Citizenships: Gender, Sexualities, Politics*, New York and London: Routledge.

Ong, A. (1999) *Flexible Citizenship: The Cultural Logics of Transnationality*, Durham: Duke University Press.

Outshoorn, J. and Kantola, J. (eds) (2007) *Changing State Feminism*, Basingstoke: Palgrave Macmillan.

Ouzgane, L. (ed.) (2006) *Islamic Masculinities*, London: Zed Books.

Ouzgane, L. and Coleman, D. (1998) 'Postcolonial masculinities: introduction', *Jouvert: A Journal of Postcolonial Studies* 2(1).

Oxfam (KIT) (2007) *Revisiting Studies and Training in Gender and Development – The Making and Re-Making of Gender Knowledge*. http://www.kit.nl/net/KITPublicatiesoutput/ShowFile2.aspx?e=1031.

Parisi, L. (2004) *Abstract Sex: Philosophy, Bio-Technology, and the Mutations of Desire*, London: Continuum.

Parker, A. and Sedgwick, E. K. (eds) (1995) *Performativity and Performance*, London, Routledge.

Parpart, J. L. and Zalewski, M. (eds) (2008) *Rethinking the Man Question: Sex, Gender and Violence in International Relations*, London: Zed Books.

Pateman, C. (1988) *The Sexual Contract*, Cambridge: Polity Press.

—— (1989) *The Disorder of Women*, Cambridge: Polity Press.

Patton, C. and Sánchez-Eppler, B. (eds) (2000) *Queer Diasporas*, Durham: Duke University Press.

Pearce, D. (1978) 'The feminization of poverty: women, work and welfare', *The Urban and Social Change Review* 11: 23–36.

Pedwell, C. (2010) *Feminism, Culture and Embodied Practice: The Rhetorics of Comparison*, London: Routledge.

Pereira, M.dM. (2012) '"Feminist theory is proper knowledge, but.": the epistemic status of feminist scholarship', *Feminist Theory* 13(3).

Perrons, D. (2009) 'Spatial and gender inequalities in the global economy: a transformative perspective', in O. Cramme and P. Diamond (eds) *Social Justice in the Global Age,* Cambridge: Polity Press, 195–218.

Petchesky, R. P. (2009) 'The language of "sexual minorities" and the politics of identity: a position paper', *Reproductive Health Matters* 17(33): 105–110.

—— (1984) *Abortion and Women's Choice*, Boston: Northeastern University Press.

—— (2003) *Global Prescriptions: Gendering Health and Human Rights*, New York: Zed Books.

Phillips, A. (1992) 'Universal pretensions in political thought', in M. Barrett and A. Phillips (eds) *Destabilizing Theory: Contemporary Feminist Debates* (reprinted in Phillips, A. (1993) *Democracy and Difference,* Pennsylvania: Pennsylvania State University Press, 55–74).

—— (1995) *The Politics of Presence*, Oxford: Oxford University Press,.

—— (1998) (ed.) *Feminism and Politics*, Oxford: Oxford University Press.

—— (2010) *Gender and Culture*, Cambridge and Malden, MA: Polity Press.

Piercy, M. (1976) *Woman on the Edge of Time*, New York: Random House.

Pines, J. (1996) 'The cultural context of Black British cinema', in Baker, et al. *Black British Cultural Studies a Reader, Chicago: University of Chicago Press.*

Plant, S. (1998) *Zeros and Ones: Digital Women and the New Technoculture*, London: Fourth Estate.

Plummer, K. (1995) *Telling Sexual Stories: Power, Change and Social Worlds*, London and New York: Routledge.

—— (1998) 'Homosexual categories: some research problems in the labelling perspective of homosexuality', in P. M. Nardi and B. E. Schneider (eds) *Social Perspectives in Lesbian and Gay Studies. A Reader*, London: Routledge.

Pollock, G. (1988) [2003] *Vision and Difference: Feminism, Femininity and the Histories of Art*, London: Routledge.

Power, N. (2009) *One Dimensional Woman*, London: Zero Books.

Pratt, M. L. (1992) *Imperial Eyes: Studies in Travel Writing and Transculturation*, London and New York: Routledge.

Price, J. and Shildrick, M. (eds) (1999) *Feminist Theory and the Body: A Reader*, Edinburgh: University of Edinburgh Press.

Probyn, E. (2005) *Blush: Faces of Shame*, Minneapolis: University of Minnesota Press.

Projansky, S. (2007) 'Mass magazine cover girls: some reflections on postfeminist girls and postfeminism's daughters', in Y. Tasker and D. Negra (eds) *Interrogating Postfeminism: Gender and The Politics of Popular Culture*, Durham and London: Duke University Press.

Prosser, J. (1998) *Second Skins: The Body Narratives of Transsexuality*, New York: Columbia University Press.

Puar, J. (2007) *Terrorist Assemblages: Homonationalism in Queer Times*, Durham and London: Duke University Press.

Pujol, M. (1992) *Feminism and Anti-Feminism in Early Economic Thought*, Cheltenham: Edward Elgar.

Puwar, N. (2004) *Space Invaders: Race, Gender and Bodies out of Place*, Oxford: Berg.

Radford, J., Friedberg, M. and Harne, L. (eds) (2000) *Women, Violence and Strategies for Action: Feminist Research, Policy and Practice*, Buckingham and Philadelphia: Open University Press.

Raghuram, P. (2009) 'Caring about "brain drain" migration in a post-colonial world', *Geoforum* 40: 25–33.

Ragland-Sullivan, E. (2004) *The Logic of Sexuation: From Aristotle to Lacan*, State University of New York Press.

Rai, Shirin M. (ed.) (2003) *Mainstreaming Gender, Democratising the State? Institutional Mechanisms for the Advancement of Women*, Manchester: Manchester University Press.

Rankin, K. N. (2010) Reflexivity and post-colonial critique: toward an ethics of accountability in planning praxis, *Planning Theory* 9(3): 181–99.

Rapp, R. (1999) *Testing Women, Testing the Fetus: The Social Impact of Amniocentesis in America*, New York: Routledge.

Rattansi, A. (1997) 'Postcolonialism and its discontents', *Economy and Society* 26(4): 480–500.

Razavi, S. and Miller, C. (1995) 'From WID to GAD: conceptual shifts in the women and development discourse', *Occasional Paper 1, United Nations Research Institute for Social Development*, United Nations Development Programme, February.

Reay, D. (1996) 'Insider perspectives, or, stealing the words out of women's mouths', *Feminist Review* 53: 57–73.

Reay, D., David, M. E. and Ball, S. J. (2005) *Degrees of Choice. Social Class, Race and Gender in Higher Education*, Stoke on Trent: Trentham Books.

Rees, T. (1998) *Mainstreaming Equality in the European Union: Education, Training and Labour Market Policies*, London: Routledge.

Reeser, T. W. (2010) *Masculinities in Theory: An Introduction*, Malden, MA: Wiley-Blackwell.

Rich, A. (1980) 'Compulsory heterosexuality and lesbian existence', *Signs* 5(4): 631–60.

—— (1986) 'Notes towards a politics of location', in A. Rich, *Blood, Bread, and Poetry: Selected Prose, 1979–85*, New York: Norton, 210–31.

Richardson, D. (2005) 'Claiming citizenship? Sexuality, citizenship and lesbian feminist theory', in C. Ingraham (ed.) *Thinking Straight*, New York: Routledge.

—— (2008) 'Conceptualizing gender' in D. Richardson and V. Robinson (eds) *Everyday Masculinities and Extreme Sport: Male Identity and Rock Climbing*, Oxford: Berg.

Riley, D. (2005) *Impersonal Passion: Language as Affect*, Durham: Duke University Press.

Rivière, J. (1929) 'Womanliness as masquerade', *International Journal of Psychoanalysis* 10: 303–13.

Robinson, F. (1999) *Globalizing Care: Ethics, Feminist Theory, and International Relations*, Boulder, CO: Westview Press.

—— (2011) *The Ethics of Care: A Feminist Approach to Human Security*, Philadelphia: Temple University Press.

Rodenberg, B. (2004) 'Gender and poverty reduction: new conceptual approaches in international development cooperation', *Reports and Working Papers 4/2004*, Bonn: German Development Institute.

Rose, G. (1997) 'Situating knowledges: positionality, reflexivities and other tactics', *Progress in Human Geography* 21(3): 305–20.

Rose, H. (1994) *Love, Power and Knowledge: Towards a Feminist Transformation of the Sciences, Race, Gender, and Science*, Cambridge: Polity Press.

Rose, J. (1986) *Sexuality in the Field of Vision*, London: Verso.

Rose, N. (2006) *The Politics of Life Itself: Biomedicine, Power, and Subjectivity in the Twenty-First Century*, Princeton: University of Princeton Press.

Roseneil, S. (1995) *Disarming Patriarchy: Feminism and Political Action at Greenham*, Buckingham and Philadelphia: Open University Press.

—— (2000) *Common Women, Uncommon Practices: The Queer Feminisms of Greenham*, London and New York: Cassell.

Rothman, B. K. (1986) *The Tentative Pregnancy: How Amniocentesis Changes the Experience of Motherhood*, New York: Norton.

Rubin, G. (1975) 'The traffic in women: notes on the political economy of sex', in R. R. Reiter (ed.) *Toward an Anthropology of Women*, New York: Monthly Review Press.

—— (1991) [1984] 'Thinking sex: notes towards a radical theory of the politics of sexuality', in C. Vance (ed.) *Pleasure and Danger*, Boston: Routledge & Kegan Paul.

—— (1992) 'Of catamites and kings: reflections on butch, gender, and boundaries', in Joan Nestle *The Persistent Desire: A Femme-Butch Reader*, Boston, MA: Alyson Publications.

Rubin, M. and Bartle, J. (2005) 'Integrating gender into government budgets: a new perspective', *Public Administration Review* 65(3): 259–72.

Ruddick, S. (1995) *Maternal Thinking: Toward a Politics of Peace*; with a new Preface, Boston: Beacon Press.
Ruspini, E., Hearn, J., Pease, B. and Pringle, K. (eds) (2011) *Men and Masculinities around the World: Transforming Men's Practices*, New York: Palgrave Macmillan.
Russ, J. (1975) *The Female Man*, New York: Bantam.
Russo, M. (1994) *The Female Grotesque: Risk, Excess, and Modernity*, New York: Routledge.
Ruwanpura, K. N. (2008) 'Multiple identities, multiple discrimination: a critical review', *Feminist Economics* 14(3): 77–105.
Said, E. (1983) *The World, the Text and the Critic*, Cambridge, MA: Harvard University Press.
—— (1985) [1978] *Orientalism*, Harmondsworth: Penguin.
Salamon, G. (2010) *Assuming a Body: Transgender and Rhetorics of Materiality*, New York: Columbia University Press.
Salecl, R. (ed.) (2000) *Sexuation*, Durham: Duke University Press.
Sandelowski, M. (1991) 'Compelled to try: the never-enough quality of reproductive technology', *Medical Anthropology Quarterly* 5(1): 29–47.
—— (1993) *With Child In Mind: Studies of the Personal Encounter With Infertility*, Philadephia, PA: University of Pennsylvania Press.
Saunders, K (ed.) (2002) *Feminist Post-Development Thought: Rethinking Modernity, Post-Colonialism and Representation*, London: Zed Books.
Saunders, L. and Darity, W. Jr (2003) 'Feminist theory and racial economic inequality', in M. Ferber and J. A. Nelson (eds) *Feminist Economics Today: Beyond Economic Man*, Chicago and London: University of Chicago Press, 157–74.
Saxton, M. (1998). 'Disability rights and selective abortion', in Ricky Solinger (ed.) *Abortion Wars: A Half Century of Struggle (1950–2000)*, Berkeley: University of California Press, 374–93.
Scharnhorst, G. (2000) 'Historicizing Gilman: a bibliographer's view', in C. Golden and J. S. Zangrando (eds) *The Mixed Legacy of Charlotte Perkins Gilman*, London: Associated Press.
Schiebinger, L. (2004) *Nature's Body: Gender in the Making of Modern Science*, New Brunswick, NJ: Rutgers University Press.
Schor, N. and We, E. (eds) (1997) *Queer Theory Meets Feminism*, Bloomington: Indiana University Press.
Schutz, A. (1932) [1970] *On Phenomenology and Social Relations*, Chicago: University of Chicago Press.
Schwarz, H. (2005) *A Companion to Postcolonial Studies*, Malden, MA and Oxford: Blackwell.
Scott, J. W. (1986) 'Gender: a useful category of historical analysis', *The American Historical Review* 91(5): 1053–75.
—— (1992) 'Experience', in J. Butler and J. Scott (eds) *Feminists Theorize the Political,* New York and London: Routledge, 22–40.
Scott, J., Crompton, R. and Lyonette, C. (eds) (2010) *Gender Inequalities in the 21st Century*, Cheltenham, UK and Northampton, MA: Edward Elgar.
Sedgwick, E. K. (1991) *Epistemology of the Closet*, Berkeley: University of California Press.

—— (1994) *Tendencies*, London: Routledge.
—— (2003) *Touching Feeling: Affect, Pedagogy, Performativity*, Durham: Duke University Press.
Sedgwick, E. K. and Frank, A. (eds) (1995) *Shame and its Sisters: A Silvan Tomkins Reader*, Durham: Duke University Press.
Segal, L., Rowbotham, S. and Wainwright, H. (1979) *Beyond the Fragments: Feminism and the Making of Socialism*, London: The Merlin Press.
Seigworth, G. J. and Gregg, M. (2010) 'An inventory of shimmers', in Melissa Gregg and Gregory J. Seigworth (eds) *The Affect Theory Reader*, Durham: Duke University Press, 1–28.
Sen, A. (1990) 'Gender and cooperative conflicts', in Irene Tinker (ed.) *Persistent Inequalities: Women and World Development*, New York and Oxford: Oxford University Press.
—— (1999) 'Women's agency and social change', in A. Sen, *Development as Freedom*, Oxford: Oxford University Press, 189–203.
Sen, G. and Grown, C. (1987) *Development Crisis and Alternative Visions: Third World Women's Perspectives*, New York: Monthly Review Press.
Sevenhuijsen, S. (1998) *Citizenship and the Ethics of Care: Feminist Considerations on Justice, Morality, and Politics*, London and New York: Routledge.
Shalev, M. (2008) 'Class divisions among women', *Politics and Society* 36(3): 421–44.
Sharpe, P. (2001) *Women, Gender and Labour Migration*, London: Taylor and Francis.
Sheldon, S. (2002) 'The masculine body', in M. Evans and E. Lee (eds) *Real Bodies*, London: Palgrave.
Shilling, C. (1993) *The Body and Social Theory*, London: Sage.
—— (2007) 'Sociology and the body: classical traditions and new agendas', *The Sociological Review* 55(s1): 1–18.
Shohat, E. (1998) *Talking Visions: Multicultural Feminism in a Transnational Age*, New York: MIT Press.
Shot, E. and Stam, R. (1994) 'Stereotype, realism and the struggle over representation', in *Unthinking Eurocentrism, Multiculturism and the Media*, London: Routledge, 178–219.
Siebers, T. (2008) *Disability Theory*, Ann Arbor: University of Michigan Press.
—— (2010) *Disability Aesthetics*, Ann Arbor: University of Michigan Press.
Sigle-Rushton, W. and Perrons, D. (2007) 'Essentially quantified? Towards a more feminist modelling strategy'. Paper presented at the *Annual Meeting of the Population Association of America*, 29–31 March 2007, New York.
Sinha, M. (1999) 'Giving masculinity a history: some contributions from the historiography of colonial India', *Gender and History* 11(3): 445–60.
Skeggs, B. (1997) *Formations of Class and Gender: Becoming Respectable*, London: Sage.
—— (2004) *Class, Self, Culture*, London and New York: Routledge.
—— (2005) 'The re-branding of class: propertising culture', in F. Devine, M. Savage, J. Scott and R. Crompton (eds) *Rethinking Class: Culture, Identities and Lifestyles*, Basingstoke: Palgrave Macmillan.

Sokoloff, N. J. and Dupont, I. (2005) 'Domestic violence at the intersections of race, class, and gender: challenges and contributions to understanding violence against marginalized women in diverse communities', *Violence Against Women* 11: 38–64.

Soper, K. (1990) 'Feminism, humanism and postmodernism', *Radical Philosophy* 55: 11–17.

Spade, D. (2008) 'Documenting gender', *Hastings Law Journal* 59(1): 731–842.

Spar, D. (2006) *The Baby Business: How Money, Science, and Politics Drive the Commerce of Conception*, Cambridge, MA: Harvard Business School Press.

Spelman, E. V. (1988) *Inessential Woman: Problems of Exclusion in Feminist Thought*, London: The Women's Press.

Spillers, H. (1987) 'Mama's baby, papa's maybe: an American grammar book', *Diacritics* 17(2), Culture and Countermemory: The 'American' Connection: 64–81.

Spinoza, B. (1986) *Ethics and On the Correction of the Understanding*, trans. Andrew Boyle, London: Everyman Classics.

Spivak, G. C. (1988) 'Can the subaltern speak?', in C. Nelson, and L. Grossberg (eds) *Marxism and the Interpretation of Culture*, Basingstoke: Macmillan, 271–313.

—— (1993) 'Echo', *New Literary History* 24(1), *Culture and Everyday Life*: 17–43.

Spivak, G. C. and Rooney, E. (1994) 'In a word (Interview)', in N. Schor and E. Weed (eds) *The Essential Difference*, Bloomington: Indiana University Press, 151–84.

Squires, J. (1999) *Gender in Political Theory*, Cambridge: Polity Press.

—— (2005) 'Is mainstreaming transformative? Theorising mainstreaming in the context of diversity and deliberation', *Social Politics* 12(3): 366–88.

—— (2007) *The New Politics of Gender Equality*, Basingstoke: Palgrave Macmillan.

Stacey, J. (1987) 'Sexism by a subtler name? Postindustrial conditions and postfeminist consciousness in the Silicon Valley', *Socialist Review* 96: 7–28.

—— (1994) *Star Gazing: Hollywood Cinema and Female Spectatorship*, London: Routledge.

Stanley, L. (ed.) (1997) *Knowing Feminisms: On Academic Borders, Territories and Tribes*, London: Sage.

Steedman, C. (2009) *Labours Lost. Domestic Service and the Making of Modern England*, Cambridge: Cambridge University Press.

Steinbugler, A. C., Press, J. E. and Dias, J. J. (2006) 'Gender, race, and affirmative action: operationalizing intersectionality in survey research', *Gender and Society* 20: 805–25.

Stewart, K. (2007) *Ordinary Affects*, Durham: Duke University Press.

Stone, A. R. (1995) *The War of Desire and Technology at the Close of the Mechanical Age*, Cambridge, MA: MIT Press.

Strathern, M. (1992a) *After Nature: English Kinship in the Late-Twentieth Century*, Cambridge: Cambridge University Press.

—— (1992b) *Reproducing the Future: Anthropology, Kinship and the New Reproductive Technologies*, New York: Routledge.

Strathern, S. (1988) *The Gender of the Gift: Problems with Women and Problems with Society in Melanesia*, Berkeley: University of California Press.

Stratigaki, M. (2005) 'Gender mainstreaming vs. positive action: an on-going conflict in EU gender equality policy', *European Journal of Women's Studies* 12(2): 165–86.

Straus, Murray A. (2007) 'Conflict tactics scales', in N. A. Jackson (ed.) *Encyclopedia of Domestic Violence*, New York: Routledge.

Stryker, S. and Aizura, A. (forthcoming, 2012) *The Transgender Studies Reader, Vol. 2*, London: Routledge.

Stryker, S. and Whittle, S. (eds) (2006) *The Transgender Studies Reader*, London: Routledge.

Stuart, O. (2005) 'Fear and loathing in front of a mirror', in C. Alexander and C. Knowles (eds) *Making Race Matter: Bodies, Space & Identity*, Basingstoke: Palgrave Macmillan.

Subrahmanian, R. (2004) 'Making sense of gender in shifting institutional contexts: some reflections on gender mainstreaming', *IDS* 35(4): 89–94.

Sullivan, O. (2011) 'An end to gender display through the performance of housework? A review and reassessment of the quantitative literature using insights from the qualitative literature', *Journal of Family Theory and Review* 3: 1–13.

Sycamore, Matt Bernstein, A. K. A. Mattilda (ed.) (2006) *Nobody Passes: Rejecting the Rules of Gender and Conformity*, Emeryville: Seal Press.

Tait, J. and Lyall, C. (2001) *Final Report: Investigation into ESRC Funded Interdisciplinary Research*, SUPRA.

Tanesini, A. (1999) *An Introduction to Feminist Epistemologies*, Oxford: Blackwell.

Tangi, S. S. (1976) 'A feminist perspective on some ethical issues in population programs', *Signs* 1: 895–904.

Tasker, Y. and Negra, D. (eds) (2007) *Interrogating Postfeminism: Gender and The Politics of Popular Culture*, Durham and London: Duke University Press.

Taylor, Y. (2007) *Working-Class Lesbian Life: Classed Outsiders*, Basingstoke: Palgrave Macmillan.

Taylor, Y., Hines, S. and Casey, M. (eds) (2010) *Theorizing Intersectionality and Sexuality*, London: Palgrave.

Terry, G. with J. Hoare (eds) (2007) *Gender-based Violence*, Oxford: Oxfam.

Terry, J. and Calvert, M. (eds) (1997) *Processed Lives: Gender and Technology in Everyday Life*, London and New York: Routledge, 1–19.

Thapar–Björkert, S. and Henry, M. (2004) 'Reassessing the research relationship: location, position and power in fieldwork accounts', *International Journal of Social Research Methodology: Theory and Practice* 7(4): 363–81.

Thomas, C. (2007) 'The disabled body', in M. Evans and E. Lee (eds) *Real Bodies: A Sociological Introduction,* Basingstoke: Palgrave Macmillan.

Thompson, C. (2005) *Making Parents: the Ontological Choreography: Reproductive Technologies*, Cambridge, MA: MIT Press.

Thomson, R. G. (1997) *Extraordinary Bodies: Figuring Disability in American Literature and Culture*, New York: Columbia University Press.

—— (2002) 'Integrating disability, transforming feminist theory', *NWSA Journal* 14(3).

—— (2009) *Staring: How We Look*, New York: Oxford University Press.

Throsby, K. (2004) *When IVF Fails: Feminism, Infertility and the Negotiation of Normality*, Houndmills: Palgrave.

Todorova, Z. (2009) *Money and Households in a Capitalist Economy: A Gendered Post-Keynesian–Institutional Analysis*, Oxford: Edward Elgar.

Tölölyan, K. (2007) 'The contemporary discourse of diaspora studies', in *Comparative Studies of South Asia, Africa and the Middle East* 27(3): 247–55.

Tompkins, S. (1995) *Exploring Affect: The Selected Writings of Silvan S. Tompkins*, Virginia E. Demos (ed.), New York: Cambridge University Press.

Tremain, S. (2005) *Foucault and the Government of Disability*, Ann Arbor: University of Michigan Press.

Tremblay, M., Paternotte, D. and Johnson, C. (eds) (2011) *The Lesbian and Gay Movement and the State: Comparative Insights into a Transformed Relationship*, Farnham and Burlington, VT: Ashgate.

Tronto, J. C. (1987) 'Beyond gender difference to a theory of care', *Signs* 12(4): 644–63.

—— (1993) *Moral Boundaries: A Political Argument for an Ethic of Care*, New York: Routledge.

Tsikata, D. (2004) 'The rights-based approach to development: potential for change or more of the same?' *IDS, Bulletin* 35(4): 130–33.

Tyler, I. (2008) 'Chav Mum chav scum', *Feminist Media Studies* 8(1): 17–34.

UNDP (1995) *Human Development Report*, New York and Oxford: Oxford University Press for the United Nations Development Programme.

United Nations (1993) *Declaration on the Elimination of Violence against Women*. United Nations, General Assembly. A/RES/48/104 Retrieved 23 June, 2011, from http://www.un.org/documents/ga/res/48/a48r104.htm.

—— (1995) *Platform for Action, Violence Against Women Diagnosis*. United Nations Fourth World Conference on Women. Beijing, China. September 1995. Retrieved 23 June, 2011, from http://www.un.org/womenwatch/daw/beijing/platform/violence.htm.

—— (1997) *Report on the Economic and Social Council for 1997*, A/52/3.

—— (2006) *United National Convention on the Rights of Persons with Disabilities* http://www.un.org/disabilities/convention/conventionfull.shtml.

van Eerdewijk, A. and Davids, T. (2010) 'Escaping the mythical beast: gender mainstreaming revisited', *Equal is Not Enough,* edited volume from Antwerp Conference December 2010.

van Eerdewijk, A. and van der Vleuten, A. (2010) 'From velvet triangles to velvet pentangles? First steps in a methodological framework for multilevel dynamics of norm diffusion'. Paper presented at the conference *Equal is Not Enough*, Antwerp, 1–3 December 2010.

Verloo, M. (2001) 'Another velvet revolution? Gender mainstreaming and the politics of implementation', *IWM Working Paper No. 5/2001*, Vienna: IWM.

—— (2005) 'Reflections on the concept and practice of the Council of Europe approach to gender mainstreaming', *Social Politics* 12(3): 344–65.

Verloo, M. and Roggeband, C. (1996) 'Gender impact assessment: the development of a new instrument in the Netherlands', *Impact Assessment* 14(1): 3–21.

Villagómez, E. (2004) 'Gender responsive budgets: issues, good practices and policy options'. Paper presented at the *Regional Symposium on Mainstreaming Gender into Economic Policies*, Geneva, 28–30 January.

Visvanathan, N., Duggan, L., Wiegersma, N. and Nisonoff, L. (eds) (2011) *The Women, Gender and Development Reader*, 2nd edn, London: Zed Books.

Viveros, V. M. (2012) 'Sexuality and desire in racialised contexts', in P. Agggleton, P. Boyce, H. L. Moore and R. Parker (eds) *Understanding Global Sexualities*, London: Routledge.

Vogel, U. and Moran, M. (1991) *Frontiers of Citizenship*, Basingstoke: Macmillan, p. xvi.

Wakeford, N. (1997a) 'Cyberqueer', in S. R. Munt and A. Medhurst (eds) *The Lesbian and Gay Studies Reader: A Critical Introduction*, London: Cassell, 20–38. Reprinted in David Bell, and M. Kennedy (eds) *The Cyberculture Reader*, London: Routledge, 416–31.

—— (1997b) 'Networking women and grrrls with information/communication technology: surfing tales of the world wide web', in J. Terry and M. Calvert (eds) *Processed Lives: Gender and Technology in Everyday Lives*, London and New York: Routledge, pp. 51–66.

Walby, S. (1990) *Theorizing Patriarchy*, Oxford: Basil Blackwell.

—— (2005) 'Gender mainstreaming: productive tensions in theory and practice', *Social Politics*, Special Issue on Gender Mainstreaming 12(3): 321–43.

—— (2007) 'Complexity theory, systems theory, and multiple intersecting social inequalities', *Philosophy of the Social Sciences* (4): 449–70.

—— (2009) *Globalization and Inequalities: Complexity and Contested Modernities*, London: Sage Publications.

—— (2011) *The Future of Feminism*, Cambridge: Polity Press.

Walkerdine, V. (2003) 'Reclassifying upward mobility: femininity and the neoliberal subject', *Gender and Education* 15(3): 217–48.

Waller, W. and Jennings, A. (1990) 'On the possibility of a feminist economics: the convergence of institutional and feminist methodology', *Journal of Economic Issues* 24: 613–22.

Warner, M. (1991) 'Fear of a queer planet,' *Social Text* 29: 3–17.

Watkins, L. (2009) 'Colour and fluids: the (in)visibility of *The Portrait of a Lady* (Jane Campion, 1996)', in C. Columpar and S. Mayer (eds) *There She Goes, Feminist Filmmaking and Beyond*, Detroit, Michigan: Wayne State University Press, 195–206.

Weeks, J. (1995) *Invented Moralities: Sexual Values in an Age of Uncertainty*, Cambridge: Polity Press.

—— (2007) *The World We Have Won: The Remaking of Erotic and Intimate Life*, Abingdon and New York: Routledge.

—— (2011) *The Languages of Sexuality*, Abingdon and New York: Routledge.

Weinbaum, A. (2004) *Wayward Reproductions: Genealogies of Race and Nation in Transatlantic Modern Thought*, Durham: Duke University Press.

Wennerholm, C. J. (2002) *The 'Feminization of Poverty': The Use of a Concept*, Stockholm: Swedish International Development Cooperation Agency.

Werbner, P. (2002) 'The place which is diaspora: citizenship, religion and gender in the making of chaordic transnationalism', *Journal of Ethnic and Migration Studies* 28(1): 119–33.

West, C. and Zimmerman, D. H. (1987) 'Doing gender', *Gender and Society* 1(2): 125–51.

Wetherell, M. and Edley, N. (1999) 'Negotiating hegemonic masculinity: imaginary positions and psycho-discursive practices', *Feminism and Psychology* 9(3): 335–56.

Whelehan, I. (2000) *Overloaded: Popular Culture and the Future of Feminism*, London: The Women's Press.

—— (2010) 'Remaking feminism: or why is postfeminism so boring?', *Nordic Journal of English Studies* 9(3): 155–72.

Whitehead, S. M. (2002) *Men and Masculinities: Key Themes and New Directions*, Cambridge: Polity Press.

Whittier, N. (1995) *Feminist Generations: The Persistence of the Radical Women's Movement*, Philadelphia: Temple University Press.

Williams, C. H. (2012) 'The limits of "lesbian": nomenclature and normativity in feminist approaches to sexuality, gender and development', in P. Aggleton, P. Boyce, H. L. Moore and R. G. Parker (eds) *Understanding Global Sexualities: New Frontiers*, London: Routledge.

Williams, J. (2000) *Unbending Gender: Why Family and Work Conflict and What To Do About It*, Oxford and New York: Oxford University Press.

Williams, R. (1988) [1968, 1983] *Keywords*, London: Fontana Press, 266–69.

Willis, P. (1977) *Learning to Labour: How Working Class Kids Get Working Class Jobs*, Farnborough, Hants: Saxon House.

Wittig, M. (1992) [1980] *The Straight Mind*, Boston: Beacon Press.

Wollstonecraft, M. (1982) [1792] *Vindication of the Rights of Woman*, Harmondsworth: Penguin.

Wolmark, J. (1999) 'Introduction', in Jenny Wolmark (ed.) *Cybersexualities: A Reader on Feminist Theory, Cyborgs and Cyberspace*, Edinburgh: Edinburgh University Press.

Woodward, A. (2003) 'European gender mainstreaming: promises and pitfalls of transformative policy making', *Review of Policy Research* 1(20): 65–88.

—— (2004) 'Building velvet triangles: gender and informal governance', in T. Christiansen and S. Piattoni (eds) *Informal Governance in the European Union*, Cheltenham: Edward Elgar, 76–93.

Woodward, K. (2008) 'Gendered bodies, gendered lives', in D. Richardson and V. Robinson (eds) *Everyday Masculinities and Extreme Sport: Male Identity and Rock Climbing,* Oxford: Berg.

Woodward, K., et al. (1996) 'Global cooling and academic warming: long-term shifts in emotional weather', *American Literary History* 8(4): 759–79.

Wright, E. O. (1989) 'Women in the class structure', *Politics and Society* 17(1): 35–66.

Wylie, A. (2003) 'Why standpoint matters', in Robert Figueroa and Sandra G. Harding (eds) *Science and Other Cultures: Issues in Philosophies of Science and Technology*, New York and London: Routledge, 26–48.

Young, I. M. (1990) *Justice and the Politics of Difference*, Princeton: Princeton University Press.

—— (1994) 'Gender as seriality: thinking about women as a social collective', *Signs* 19(3): 713–38.

—— (2005) *On Female Body Experience: 'Throwing Like A Girl' and Other Essays*, New York: Oxford University Press.

Young, L. (1996) *Fear of the Dark, 'Race', Gender and Sexuality in the Cinema*, London: Routledge.

Young, R. (2001) *Postcolonialism: An Historical Introduction*, Oxford: Blackwell.

Yuval–Davis, N. (1997) *Gender and Nation*, London: Sage.

—— (2008) 'Intersectionality, citizenship and contemporary politics of belonging', in B. Siim and J. Squires (eds) *Contesting Citizenship,* London and New York: Routledge, 159–72.

Zack, N. (2002) *Philosophy of Science and Race*, New York and London: Routledge.

INDEX

Note: bold page numbers indicate main concept entries